THE POLITICS OF PEFORMANCE IN EARLY RENAISSANCE DRAMA

Greg Walker provides a new account of the relationship between politics and drama in the turbulent period from the accession of Henry VIII to the reign of Elizabeth I. Building upon ideas first developed in *Plays of Persuasion* (1991), he focuses on political drama in both England and Scotland, exploring the complex relationships between politics, court culture and dramatic composition, performance and publication.

Through a detailed analysis of one central dramatic form, the interlude or great hall play, and close study of key texts, Walker examines drama produced and adapted for varying conditions of performance: indoor and outdoor, private and public. He examines what happened when the play script was printed and sold commercially as a literary commodity.

The subjects of study range from the interludes of the Henrician catholic John Heywood to the Elizabethan tragedy *Gorboduc*. There are also chapters on the conditions of household performance and the early history of dramatic printing.

Greg Walker is Reader in English and Director of the Medieval Research Centre at the University of Leicester. He is also the author of *John Skelton and the Politics of the 1520s* (1988), *Plays of Persuasion: Drama and Politics at the Court of Henry VIII* (1991), and *Persuasive Fictions* (1996). He has edited *John Skelton* (1997).

THE POLITICS OF PERFORMANCE IN EARLY RENAISSANCE DRAMA

GREG WALKER

CAMBRIDGE
UNIVERSITY PRESS

PUBLISHED BY THE PRESS SYNDICATE OF THE UNIVERSITY OF CAMBRIDGE
The Pitt Building, Trumpington Street, Cambridge CB2 IRP, United Kingdom

CAMBRIDGE UNIVERSITY PRESS
The Edinburgh Building, Cambridge CB2 2RU, United Kingdom
40 West 20th Street, New York, NY 10011–4211, USA
10 Stamford Road, Oakleigh, Melbourne 3166, Australia

© Greg Walker 1998

First published 1998

Printed in Great Britain at the University Press, Cambridge

Typeset in Baskerville 11/12.5 pt [VN]

A catalogue record for this book is available from the British Library

Library of Congress cataloguing in publication data

The politics of performance in early Renaissance drama / Greg Walker
p. cm.
Includes index.
ISBN 0 521 56331 3 (hardback)
1. English drama – Early modern and Elizabethan, 1500–1600 – History and criticsm.
2. Theatre – Political aspects – Great Britain – History – 16th century.
3. Politics and literature – Great Britain – History – 16th century.
4. Great Britain – Politics and government – 1485–1603.
5. Political plays, English – History and criticism.
6. Lindsay, David, Sir, fl. 1490–1555. Satyre of the Thrie Estaitis.
7. Heywood, John, 1497?–1580? – Political and social views.
8. Udall, Nicholas, 1505–1556. Respublica.
9. Norton, Thomas, 1532–1584. Gorboduc.
10. Renaissance – Scotland.
11. Renaissance – England. I. Title.
PR649.P6W36 – 1998
822'.209358 – dc21 97–43342 CIP

ISBN 0 521 56331 3 hardback

For Matthew and David

Contents

Acknowledgements

This book has been developing over the years since the completion of my *Plays of Persuasion* (Cambridge, 1991), to which it acts as something of a companion piece. I owe many debts of gratitude to those who have helped me with invaluable information, support, and advice during its writing. The specific debts I have acknowledged in the headnotes to the relevant chapters, but the more general ones I would like to mark here, along with a recognition that the book would never have been completed without the generous help of a number of individuals and institutions.

My chief material debts are to the President and Fellows of the British Academy, who have funded a number of trips to libraries through the award of Small Grants in the Humanities, and to Dr Elizabeth Moores and the Awards Committee at the University of Queensland, whose grant of a George Watson Visiting Research Fellowship enabled me to spend time in the University Library in Brisbane during January 1996. Dr Chris Woolgar, the Director of the University of Southampton's Hartley Institute, was the source of invaluable support and advice later in 1996, when I spent a term's study leave as a Hartley Fellow, working with the *RSTC* microfilms and writing the first chapter of this book. The opportunities which the fellowship provided for sustained research in the Hartley Library, and for discussion with members of the departments of English and History, prompted me to rethink the direction and substance of the project at an important moment in its development, and have, I hope, had a beneficial effect on the end product.

More generally, I could not have finished this work without the supportive environment provided by colleagues in the English Department at Leicester, especially the Head of Department, Vincent Newey, Gordon Campbell, Elaine Treharne, Julie Coleman, Mark Rawlinson, Roger Warren, John Gough, David Salter, Michael Davies, Kathy Taylor, and Andrew and Michael Hagiioannu. Peter J. Smith of

Nottingham Trent University has also been a source of much good advice, as have Tony Kushner, John J. McGavin, Kate McLuskie, Peter Happé, and Kevin Sharpe of Southampton University, and Marie and Richard Axton of the University of Cambridge. As ever, George Bernard has been the readiest source of information, stimulating argument, and sound guidance. I remain indebted to him for his enthusiastic commitment to the belief that – to mangle the RSPCA slogan – a postgraduate student is for life, not just for three years. Sadly, legal advice suggests that I cannot blame any of the above for the, no doubt numerous, weaknesses which this book retains. I can, however, pass on my genuine gratitude for their diligence in pointing out the errors and inadequacies which they spotted in the various drafts I inflicted upon them. Those weaknesses which remain, I must accept as wholly my own.

Parts of three of the chapters which follow have appeared in other forms elsewhere. An earlier version of chapter 2 appeared in *Théta*, 4, edited by André Lascombes. A section of chapter 4 was published in the *Scottish Literary Journal* in 1989, and a shorter version of chapter 6 appeared as an article co-authored by myself and Henry James of Hereford Cathedral School, in the *English Historical Review* for 1995. I am grateful to the editors of all three publications, and to Addison Wesley Longman and the Association for Scottish Literary Studies, for permission to reprint material from those articles here. My thanks are due especially to Henry James, for allowing the fruits of our shared labours on 'The Politics of *Gorboduc*' to be plundered for this study.

This book is dedicated to my sons, Matthew and David, in the hope that they will forgive me for hogging the computer for word-processing when it should have been free for Championship Manager.

Abbreviations

BL   British Library

CSPSp   G. A. Bergenroth, *et al.*, eds., *Calendar of State Papers Spanish* (13 vols., London, 1862–1954)

CSPF   J. Stevenson, ed., *Calendar of State Papers Foreign, 1561–62* (London, 1866)

EETS   Early English Text Society

Hall   Edward Hall, *The Union of the Two Noble and Illustrious Houses of Lancaster and York*, ed. H. Ellis (London, 1809)

LP   J. S. Brewer, *et al.*, eds., *Letters and Papers, Foreign and Domestic, of The Reign of Henry VIII* (21 vols. in 36; London, 1862–1932)

METh   *Medieval English Theatre*

PRO   Public Record Office

REED   Records of Early English Drama

RSTC   A. W. Pollard and G. R. Redgrave, eds., *The Short Title Catalogue of Books Printed in England, Scotland, and Ireland, 1475–1640*, 2nd edition, revised and enlarged by W. A. Jackson, F. S. Ferguson, and K. F. Pantzer (London, 1976)

Introduction

In writing this book I have been intensely conscious of following in the footsteps of those scholars who have been this way before, chiefly David Bevington, T. W. Craik, Glynne Wickham, Peter Happé, and the chief pioneers of early drama studies, E. K. Chambers and W. W. Greg.[1] Most of what I will have to say has only been possible thanks to their ground-breaking work, and much of it will only add to, or seek to qualify points that they have already made. In a field in which the evidence remains frustratingly patchy, new analysis is often reliant upon – and deeply grateful for – the interpretative frameworks established by previous scholars, even where it seeks to amend or contradict them.

I have also been acutely aware of the problems of terminology which inevitably beset the theatre historian of the age before the playhouses. The word which I have most wanted to use in this book is, unsurprisingly, 'theatre' itself, with all its derivatives, closely followed by 'stage'. But, as one of my central assertions rests upon the fact that the interlude drama was precisely not 'theatrical' (in the sense of taking place in a building designed for drama), I have had to resist the temptation. The workplace of playwrights such as Heywood, Udall, and Lindsay, was a *theatrum mundi* indeed, coterminous with the world they inhabited in their extra-dramatic lives as courtiers, scholars, and politicians. Their drama lived in the spaces in which the real events which they allegorised also took place, and it drew rhetorical and symbolic strength from that fact. So words like 'theatrical' have precisely the wrong connotations. Similarly, to describe actors as being 'on-stage' (although I have fallen

---

[1] See, for example, E. K. Chambers, *The Medieval Stage* (2 vols., Oxford, 1903), and *The Elizabethan Stage* (4 vols., Oxford, 1923); W. W. Greg, *A Bibliography of the English Printed Drama to the Restoration* (4 vols., London, 1951–62); G. Wickham, *Early English Stages* (3 vols. in 4, London, 1959–63); T. W. Craik, *The Tudor Interlude* (Leicester, 1958); Peter Happé, ed., *Four Morality Plays* (Harmondsworth, 1979), and Richard Axton and Peter Happé, eds., *The Plays of John Heywood* (Woodbridge, 1991); David Bevington, *Tudor Drama and Politics: A Critical Approach to Topical Meaning* (Cambridge, MA, 1968).

into doing so at least once in what follows) is misleading if it implies that, where the interludes were concerned, there was a set area for acting in and another for watching it from. As chapter 2 will argue, the fact that the 'place' for acting was also the domestic space of its audience also had great significance for the creation and reception of these plays.

If I have felt disadvantaged by a terminological self-denying ordinance, however, I have been lucky in beginning this book when I did. After a fallow period following the heroic age of Chambers and Greg, the study of early drama in Britain has made great advances in recent years, perhaps most noticeably through the work of the Toronto based Records of Early English Drama project, which is making available the documentary evidence of dramatic and ceremonial activity in printed form. Other developments in English scholarship have refocused the study of Renaissance literature towards history once more and consequently much greater effort is now being directed towards uncovering the material conditions for the production of all forms of literary text in the period. Much work remains to be done, however, if these general developments are to produce a coherent account of the role of drama in early Renaissance culture which can satisfy the criteria of both literary and historical analysis. I hope that this study will contribute something to that account through an analysis of one aspect of early drama: the court interlude, in the years before the creation of the commercial theatres.

My aim in what follows is, through both a general analysis of interlude drama and a detailed study of specific key texts, to provide a new account of the relationship between political culture and drama in the period from the accession of Henry VIII to the reign of Elizabeth I. Building upon and developing the ideas first explored in *Plays of Persuasion*,[2] this study will focus upon the political drama of the early Renaissance period in both England and Scotland, and explore the often complex relationships between politics, court culture, and dramatic composition, performance, and publication. It will seek to answer a number of central historical questions. What role(s) was drama perceived to play within the culture(s) which produced and received it? How far did changing political circumstances affect the nature of the politicised drama created and performed in the period? Were the plays produced for the court during a royal minority, for example, fundamentally different from those designed for the court of an adult sovereign?

---

[2] Greg Walker, *Plays of Persuasion: Drama and Politics at the Court of Henry VIII* (Cambridge, 1991).

And how far do plays of the Marian and early Elizabethan periods support the notion that the gender of the monarch influenced the dramatic culture of the reign? Alternatively, how significant were the effects of the physical and cultural conditions under which a play was performed in shaping its exploration of political themes? Were outdoor, 'public' plays governed by different unstated rules and assumptions to the indoor, essentially 'private' drama of the court, the Inns of Court, or the noble household (although, as what follows will suggest, the terms 'public' and 'private' are not particularly helpful where interlude drama is concerned)? Finally, what happened when the play script was printed and sold commercially as a literary commodity? Were a new set of political and cultural factors brought into play by the shift from physical to textual performance and reception?

The following chapters will attempt to answer such questions by examining a number of carefully selected plays which explored political issues in a range of physical and cultural environments, from the interludes of the Henrician catholic 'dissenter' John Heywood, to *Gorboduc*, the first Senecan tragedy in English performed at the Elizabethan court. These plays provide valuable case studies of drama produced and adapted for various kinds of performance. Analysis of this material prompts a number of broad general conclusions concerning the nature of political drama in early Renaissance England and Scotland, in addition to suggesting specific interpretations of the individual texts and issues concerned.

This book offers a sustained argument concerning the nature of early Renaissance court drama, supported by the individual case studies contained in chapters 3 to 6. But each chapter can also stand alone as an exploration of a particular problem or text. Readers are consequently free to read either sequentially or selectively in the coming pages. The following brief description of the contents of each chapter may be used as a guide for those readers taking the latter course.

The opening chapter introduces the volume by addressing the central paradox that a study of Renaissance drama in performance must inevitably rely for its chief evidence upon the printed or manuscript text, a document whose relationship to the play as it was initially performed may not be a self-evident or simple one. The chapter attempts to clarify the relationship between performed and written texts through a close examination of the production of playbooks in the period. It begins with the most basic of questions: what first prompted publishers to produce printed playbooks, and how did they go about marketing them? How much did a playbook cost, and how many were printed? Who seems to have bought these texts? And what does this in turn suggest about the perception of dramatic literature in the period? Such questions have not been addressed in a sustained way before. In attempting to answer them the chapter charts the development of dramatic printing from the early experiments of the 1510s to the more sophisticated texts of the Elizabethan period. In conclusion, it offers some suggestions concerning the long-term implications of the decisions made by the early printers for the perception and reception of drama in the later playhouse period and beyond.

The second chapter builds upon the conclusions reached in the first, and focuses on the interlude, the form which provided the bulk of the texts printed in the pre-playhouse period. It examines the nature and significance of the form and explores its relationship to the physical and cultural context in which it was produced and performed. In particular it focuses on the often harsh moral and political comment to be found in early Tudor household drama. How did such criticism fit into the political culture of the royal or noble household? The model of household drama offered here will be tested against the different texts and contexts examined in subsequent chapters.

The third chapter offers a detailed exemplification of the household drama of the Henrician period in the work of John Heywood, whose interlude *The Play of The Weather* was the subject of detailed examination in *Plays of Persuasion*.[3] Here a wider analysis of Heywood's courtly drama is undertaken, revealing how the author was able to present an effective dramatic defence of catholic orthodoxy at court during the early years of the Henrician Reformation. In the course of this discussion, a number of new insights into Heywood's work are suggested, including a fresh and critical account of his apparent sympathy for Sir Thomas More's polemical defence of orthodoxy in the 1530s.

In chapter 4 the focus is widened, both geographically (as attention shifts to the drama and politics of early Renaissance Scotland) and generically (as we examine a play which was produced first as a courtly interlude in the household of James V, and subsequently as a much expanded outdoor production before the regency council during the

---

[3] Ibid., pp. 133–68. While working on Heywood, I have been grateful for the advice and insights offered by Peter Happé, whose research into the playwright's life and work has often followed parallel tracks to my own. See, for example, Happé, 'Staging Folly in the Early Sixteenth Century: Heywood, Lindsay, and Others', in C. Davidson, ed., *Fools and Folly* (Kalamazoo, 1996), pp. 73–111.

minority of his daughter Mary). Lindsay's *Ane Satyre of The Thrie Estaitis* provides an intriguing case study of the differing dynamics governing the two forms of drama, allowing us to trace the often fundamental changes made to the household play to prepare it for production before a wider audience. Lindsay's use of drama here also provides valuable evidence of the importance of the medium for the political process in the early years of the Reformation in Scotland. That the author, a prominent courtier and herald, highly active in the political arena, chose to express some of his most contentious political and religious views in dramatic form is itself telling. That he did so in the ways which this chapter will explore illuminates important aspects of both Scottish political culture in this period and the author's role within it.

Chapter 5 examines Nicholas Udall's courtly interlude *Respublica*, performed at the English court in the early months of the reign of Mary Tudor. It argues that the play is not, as critics have argued, an unexceptionable moral drama celebrating the return of catholicism in generalised terms, but a play born out of the religious, political, and economic crises of the mid-Tudor period, in which Udall advanced a carefully articulated strategy for the defence of crucial aspects of the Reformation.

Norton and Sackville's tragedy *Gorboduc*, the subject of chapter 6, is a play more often cited as a seminal event in the history of drama than it is subjected to extended analysis. Drawing upon recently discovered evidence of its original performance, this chapter provides a detailed analysis of the play, its auspices and political themes. It sets the tragedy firmly in the context of contemporary debates about the queen's marriage and the royal succession.

Taken together, these chapters will, I hope, contribute to the ongoing exploration of early drama mentioned above. Their aim is to suggest not only that the interlude drama was a sophisticated, flexible, and immensely powerful dramatic form worthy of study in its own right, but that in its original contexts in the courts and great households of Renaissance Britain, it was also an intensely and inevitably politicised form whose study has considerable implications for our understanding of Renaissance culture in general.

CHAPTER I

Playing by the book: early Tudor drama and the printed text

The following chapters will analyse a number of early plays chiefly as moments of performance.[1] What did it mean, politically and culturally, to perform particular plays under particular conditions at particular times and places? The evidence used to answer these questions will, however, be almost wholly textual. As is the case with all history-writing, I will be trying to recreate three-dimensional events from the two-dimensional evidence of written records. This is always to some degree a speculative venture. But there is a special awkwardness in attempting to perform this alchemy with the evidence of early drama, an art form which is realised only in performance, when actors take the written words from off the page and begin to play with them.

This is not the only problem we will encounter, however. Even the most basic questions relating to the production of plays and playbooks prove on closer inspection to be problematic. The evidence of the interlude drama, which forms the basis of this study, is relatively abundant. Many of the texts were produced in printed editions during the sixteenth century, and so survived where many manuscript playbooks have not. But the very fact of printed publication raises difficulties of its own. What are we looking at when we read a play in printed form? What is the relationship between the text in our hands and the performance which it seeks in one way or another to represent? And what kind of performances do they reflect? Are the playbooks which have survived from the early sixteenth century primarily records of performance, or notes towards it, or (in some or all cases) inevitably both? Did playwrights always write for immediate performance, or, once there was a

---

[1] I am grateful to Drs G. W. Bernard, John J. McGavin, and Chris Woolgar of Southampton University, and my colleague at Leicester Roger Warren, who kindly read early drafts of this chapter and offered invaluable help and advice.

market for printed playbooks, was it possible for some authors at least to write directly for the printing press? And in more general terms what does this evidence suggest about the cultural significance of the printed text? What are the implications of the move from publication through performance to publication in print – from dramatic performance to textual performance? Indeed, whom should we see as effecting that move? Whose text, ultimately, are we reading: the author's, the printer's, the actors', or some combination of these?[2]

It is, however, with the more mundane and pragmatic questions of textual production that this chapter must begin. For without the most basic information about the nature of the relationship between play-writing and play-printing, it will be impossible to answer either the more specific or the more wide-ranging questions which analysis of the texts themselves provokes.

THE PRINTER'S ROLE

The role of the printer in the production of playbooks is a relatively visible one. We know from colophons and title pages who printed a play in most cases, even when we cannot be sure who originally wrote it. But what that role entailed, and how it was played, is less clear. How did printers get hold of play texts, and what prompted them to print some plays and not others? Was there a direct and profitable arrangement between writer and printer, or were most plays printed largely without their author's knowledge, in various forms of what would later become recognised as piracy? And, once the text was in the printer's hands, how was it transformed and commodified into a printed book for sale alongside other wares in the bookseller's or stationer's shop? Is it possible to talk about its being designed for particular readerships or markets at this early stage? How profitable, indeed, was the market for printed playbooks? How large were print runs, and how quickly, if at all, did they sell out? How much did playbooks sell for? Who bought them, and for what purpose? In the murky and under-researched world of early drama publishing there are few ready answers to even basic questions such as these. What follows will, however, attempt to ask such questions of what limited evidence is available and tease out some

[2] For a consideration of related themes see D. F. McKenzie, *Bibliography and the Sociology of Texts* (London, 1986), pp. 18ff.

tentative suggestions about the relationship between stage and page in this period.[3]

The printing of playbooks in the pre-playhouse period

What prompted a printer to turn a dramatic script in English into a printed book for the first time? [4] The printing of play scripts is something that modern readers and theatre-goers take for granted. One expects to be able to buy the script of a successful play (and, increasingly, of a successful film) to read at home, and a theatre manager would be falling down on the job if he or she did not have a pile of 'books of the play' available for purchase by audiences as they left the auditorium. Yet the link between stage and printed page is not, and was not, *prima facie*, a natural one, and might indeed have appeared counter-intuitive, especially during the early sixteenth century when playbooks first appeared in printers' shops. As Richard Beadle has argued,

> more than in any subsequent era, the plays composed in that time were intended to be seen and heard, not read. As 'quick [living] books', they were designed for a general audience which was more accustomed to hearing its literature than to reading it silently, and it is essential to grasp that both the conceptual substance and the imaginative qualities of such plays are inseparable from their theatricality.[5]

Indeed, the idea that early English plays were for playing rather than reading is the founding assumption of much of the recent revival of academic interest in the field, as a glance at any recent textbook or issue of *Medieval English Theatre* will confirm.[6]

---

[3] In 1989 Derek Pearsall concluded that 'In the present state of scholarship, any book on publishing and book-production in the century before the introduction of printing is bound to be limited in its ambitions, tentative in its statements, and, to some extent or in some ways, premature.' D. Pearsall, 'Introduction', in J. Griffiths and D. Pearsall, eds., *Book Production and Publishing in Britain, 1375–1475* (Cambridge, 1989), pp. 1–10, p. 1. These conclusions seem doubly pertinent to the study of the publishing of plays in the century after the introduction of printing, the limited and tentative suggestions offered here being both long overdue and very premature.

[4] Between *c.* 1512 and *c.* 1516 John Rastell printed an edition of Henry Medwall's *Fulgens and Lucrece* (*RSTC* 17778). In late 1515 or early 1516 Wynkyn de Worde published an edition of the anonymous *Hick Scorner* (*RSTC* 14039). These two texts would seem to be the likeliest contenders for the distinction of earliest surviving printed playbook in England, although Richard Pynson's edition of *Everyman* (*c.* 1510–19, but probably towards the latter end of that period) might be an outside candidate. No earlier dramatic texts printed in English have as yet been discovered.

[5] R. Beadle, 'Preface', in R. Beadle, ed., *The Cambridge Companion to Medieval English Theatre* (Cambridge, 1994), p. xiii.

[6] See, for example, W. Tydeman, 'An Introduction to Medieval English Theatre', in Beadle, ed., *Companion*, pp. 1–36, p. 1 ('Medieval plays were not designed as reading matter'), and Meg Twycross' 'The Theatricality of Medieval English Plays', ibid., pp. 37–84, p. 37 ('Plays are for playing').

Music, song, stage business, the vibrant physicality of performance seemingly called for everywhere in these plays – but perhaps most obviously in the parts of the vices – are all lost to the reader of the written text, rendering his or her experience of these plays a substantially impoverished one. Why, then, would anyone wish to pay good money for such an inadequate substitute for a performance? And, more importantly, why would a shrewdly profit-minded printer or bookseller try to sell one? The answer to this last question would seem self-evident. A printer will only go to the trouble of setting up and running off a text if he is confident that he can sell it at a profit, whether to a particular contracting customer or to a more general market.[7] But this conclusion only raises further questions. What prompted the first printers to conclude that they could sell dramatic texts as printed books, and to whom did they intend to sell them? Is it safe to assume that players formed the market for printed playbooks from the outset, and that printed playbooks were produced to convey scripts for performance from their authors to the widest possible range of actors? If so, what does this tell us about the connections between the acting and the printing professions? If not, where else might playbooks have found a market, and what effect did this have upon their production?

Printing history

It has been argued that the publication in 1616 of the first folio of Ben Jonson's *Works* marked the watershed in the fortunes and respectability of drama as a literary form. Before the appearance of the Jonson volume, 'play scripts had not . . . been regarded as serious literature . . . In retrospect we can see Jonson's decision as a brave and important moment in the history of literature, redefining the significance of drama, and paving the way for Shakespeare's first folio of 1623'.[8] There is no doubt something in this view, although the appearance of the *Works* might be better described as a milestone in the long and gradual process of the gentrification of drama rather than the revolutionary moment which this formulation suggests. For Jonson's decision to present his plays in a certain textual form, evoking the iconography and rhetoric of other, more prestigious genres, was in many ways simply a repetition of the decisions and practices of the early printers, who began to produce playbooks in a variety of forms almost exactly 100 years earlier.

[7] Graham Pollard, 'The English Market for Printed Books', *Publishing History*, 4 (1978), pp. 7–46, p. 9. [8] R. Dutton, *Ben Jonson: To the First Folio* (Cambridge, 1983), p. 4.

When at some point between 1512 and 1516 John Rastell printed the 'godely interlude' of *Fulgens and Lucrece*, he was probably breaking new ground. Prior to this it is likely that no printer had published a dramatic text in English. Caxton had certainly not done so, presumably as he did not perceive a market for them – or at least not a sufficiently wide market to repay the investment. As recent studies have shown, England's first printer was willing to innovate in a number of ways. He experimented with woodcut devices, colophons, and prefaces addressing his readers directly, fashioning a new role for himself as an informed mediator between author, text and reading public, a role clearly distinct from that of the scribal producers of manuscript texts. But he was far more reluctant to experiment in the choice of the material published, remaining satisfied to reproduce the sorts of works which were already selling well in manuscript form.[9]

By 1516, however, printers were seemingly ready to take the risk and add playbooks to their stocklists. Rastell had printed *Fulgens and Lucrece* by this time, de Worde had issued *Hick Scorner*, and even the normally cautious Richard Pynson had probably printed at least one of his two editions of the anonymous morality *Everyman*.[10] What had happened to convince these men that the time was right to produce playbooks? One significant factor was probably the popularity of the Latin drama published in both manuscript and printed form in the previous two decades. As humanist teaching methods found their way into the curricula of the English universities and schools, the plays of Plautus, Seneca, and particularly Terence began to find favour as set texts. Terence was taught at Cambridge from 1502, and at Oxford from some point after 1505.[11] As early as 1483 Magdalen School, Oxford, had appointed a grammar master, John Anwykyll, who published a textbook which drew heavily upon Terence's comedies for its material for translation.[12] By

---

[9] See, for example, H. S. Bennett, *English Books and Readers* (2nd edn, 3 vols., Cambridge, 1969), I, p. 17; A. S. G. Edwards and Carole M. Meale, 'The Marketing of Printed Books in Late Medieval England', *The Library*, 6.15 (1993), pp. 95–112, pp. 95–6; N. F. Blake, *Caxton and His World* (London, 1969), pp. 64–78; Elizabeth L. Eisenstein, *The Printing Press as an Agent of Change: Communications and Cultural Transformations in Early Modern Europe* (2 vols., Cambridge, 1979), I, p. 59.

[10] *Everyman* (pre-1519, *RSTC* 10604 and 10604.5). Pynson generally limited his output to texts either sponsored by individuals or institutions willing to share the financial burden of production, or religious, educational or legal texts certain of a ready market. Indulgences constituted nearly half of his output. See Bennett, *English Books*, I, p. 90; Edwards and Meale, 'Marketing', p. 114.

[11] I. Lancashire, *Dramatic Texts and Records of Britain: A Chronological Topography to 1558* (Cambridge, 1984), p. xxiv.

[12] John Anwykyll, *The Vulgaria quedam abs Terentio in Anglicum Linguam Traducta* (1483). See W. Nelson, ed., *A Fifteenth Century School Book from a Manuscript in The British Museum (MS Arundel 249)* (Oxford, 1956), p. x.

1531 Winchester College was apparently teaching the comedies to its fourth-formers six days a week.[13] Richard Pynson attempted to take early advantage of this new development, and in the late 1490s printed Latin editions of six of the comedies for the academic market.[14] What evidence there is suggests that the experiment was a success,[15] and this may well have encouraged Pynson and his rivals to consider appealing to a broader market with vernacular play texts.[16]

The motives of the early printers can, however, only be guessed at in the light of the limited available evidence. The most helpful evidence in this respect is provided by the texts themselves, the cost at which they were sold, and the quantities in which they were produced. Hence it is with such basic matters that any attempt to understand the early history of drama publishing must begin.

Print runs

Little can be said with any certainty about the print runs for early drama. There is only a little extant evidence which bears directly upon the problem, and what analogous evidence there is is largely unhelpful. Those texts for which information is available tend to be *sui generis*. We know, for example, that William Tyndale's New Testament, printed in Cologne in 1525, went into an initial run of 3,000 copies in octavo, and later editions also ran into thousands.[17] But religious texts – and Bibles in particular – are likely to have been produced in significantly greater numbers as a rule, as they were assured of a wide and steady readership.[18] And Tyndale's was a biblical text with a polemical, evangelical

---

[13] Nelson, ed., *Fifteenth Century School Book*, p. 284.

[14] Ibid. p. xxiv. The six plays were the *Andria, Eunuchus, Heauton Timorumenos, Adelphoe, Phormio,* and *Hecyra,* all printed *c.* 1495–7.

[15] The number of copies of the comedies, along with other Latin playbooks listed in the wills and inventories of Oxford scholars in the early sixteenth century provides an index of the market for texts in the universities (Lancashire, *Topography*, p. 245). See also Claire Cross, ed., *York Clergy Wills, 1200–1600,* I, *Minster Clergy,* Borthwick Texts and Calendars, Records of the Northern Province, 10 (York, 1984), pp. 18 and 44, for references to copies of Terence (1528) and Seneca (1539). John Dorne, the Oxford bookseller, was apparently doing a brisk trade in copies of Terence and other plays in Latin and Greek in 1520, as his surviving day-book records. F. Madan, 'The Day Book of John Dorne', Oxford Historical Society *Collectanea*, 1 (1885), pp. 71–178.

[16] Certainly Pynson's choice of *Everyman* for his first vernacular dramatic publication would suggest caution on his part. The play was adapted from the Dutch drama *Elkerlijc,* which had already been successfully published in the Low Countries.   [17] Bennett, *Books and Readers,* I, p. 225.

[18] The 'Matthew Bible' of 1537, for example, was initially printed in a run of 1,500 copies. Ibid., I, p. 225.

purpose, whose run was likely to be considerably in excess of normal levels.

Other print runs which have left documentary evidence tend to have done so because they were the subject of special contractual arrangements or disputes. When Richard Pynson agreed to print 800 copies of William Horman's *Vulgaria* in 1519, for example, he did so at the author's request and on the understanding that it would be at Horman's own expense. Horman, who was vice-provost of Eton, took all the copies himself to sell to what was no doubt a captive student market. Similarly, when Pynson printed 750 copies of Palsgrave's *Lesclarcissement de la Langue Francoyse* (?1525–9), or John Schott, the Strasbourg printer, produced 2,000 copies in different formats of William Roy's *Rede Me and Be Nott Wrothe*, they did so on the authors' instructions and took no serious financial risks themselves.[19] Such agreements cannot provide useful guidelines for the printing of playbooks for commercial sale.

More helpful is the evidence provided by lawsuits in which Pynson was involved, which give information on less contentious, secular texts. And from these it seems that Pynson had printed at least 600 copies each of five named texts, including the moral tract *Dives and Pauper*, Lydgate's *Fall of Princes*, and John Myrk's *Festial*.[20] Each of these was a popular work with a relatively wide appeal to the educated classes in the late medieval period, so would have made relatively safe choices for publication in print. But the figures involved are suggestive. Was this something close to the norm for secular, moral literature?[21] If so, it might provide a rule of thumb for Pynson's first playbooks, which, although they did not have the track record of these tried and trusted manuscript bestsellers, were much smaller texts which could be set up at significantly lower cost, thereby constituting a markedly lower financial risk[22]

The only evidence relating directly to playbook print runs, the inventory of John Rastell's stock drawn up two years after his death, in 1538, would tend to support such an assumption. The titles of four plays appear in the list, along with the number remaining in the printer's shop

---

[19] Ibid., I, p. 227.
[20] H. R. Plomer, 'Two Lawsuits of Richard Pynson', *The Library*, n.s. 10 (1909), pp. 115–33; Bennett, *Books and Readers*, I, p. 226.
[21] Perhaps significantly, *Lambard's Perambulations of Kent* (1576), one of the few titles from later in the century for which print figures are known, was also issued in an initial run of 600 copies. Bennett, *Books and Readers*, I, p. 227.
[22] In 1588 the Stationers' Company established a limit of '1250–1500' copies for any text other than the Bible. H. S. Bennett concludes that 'we shall not be far wrong in thinking that very special reasons were required to persuade a printer to print more than 600–700 copies of any ordinary work in the first 75 years of printing in England', Bennett, *Books and Readers*, I, p. 278.

at the time that the document was drawn up. The inventory records that there were 370 copies of 'the play of Melibea' (*Calisto and Melebea*), 284 copies of *Good Order*, 80 of *Gentleness and Nobility*, and 8 of the otherwise unknown 'second part of the Play of Epicure'.[23] This information is helpful but raises a number of problems. What are we to make of the relative abundance of some texts and the meagre stock of others? Do the larger figures for *Calisto* and *Good Order* suggest that these were more popular works, printed in greater quantities than the other plays, or rather (perhaps more plausibly) that they were unexpectedly poor sellers, leaving Rastell with a considerable surplus unsold? Similarly, what of the titles known to have been printed by Rastell which do not feature on the list, such as *The Nature of The Four Elements* (printed *c.* 1525–7), *Fulgens and Lucrece* (printed *c.* 1512–16) or Skelton's *Magnyfycence* (printed *c.* 1530)? Should we assume that these titles had already sold out their print runs completely by 1538, or, perhaps, that Rastell's son William had taken possession of the remaining copies of these plays for sale under his own auspices, as he may well have done with a number of other works originally owned by his father?[24] The evidence, here as elsewhere, is suggestive rather than truly informative. But overall the larger figures cited here would support the idea that print runs of up to 500–600 copies were possible, and perhaps standard, for dramatic texts.

Playbook prices

The prices at which playbooks were sold in the period is also a matter for informed speculation rather than confident assertion. The usual sources of information about book prices are not forthcoming where play texts are concerned. The latter tend not to appear in wills or inventories of possessions with any frequency because they were rarely bound individually and were usually of insufficient value to be worth recording as separate items.[25] They may also have been considered by many testators or their priestly scribes to be too frivolous an item to be recorded in so solemn and formal a document as a will.[26] Thus we are left to extrapolate possible prices from the costs of other texts recorded in those booklists and account-books which survive from the earlier sixteenth

---

[23] R. J. Roberts, 'John Rastell's Inventory of 1538', *The Library*, 6.1 (1979), pp. 34–42.

[24] Ibid., p. 40.

[25] Francis R. Johnson, 'Notes on English Retail Book-Prices, 1550–1640', *The Library*, 5.5 (1950), pp. 83–112, p. 91.

[26] P. J. P. Goldberg, 'Lay Book Ownership in Late Medieval York: The Evidence of Wills', *The Library*, 6.16 (1994), pp. 181–9, p. 184.

century and from the prices of playbooks recorded in library lists from later periods. What evidence there is for the 1550s and earlier is largely tangential. It helps us little, for example, to know that John Rastell's three-volume, 798–page *La Grande Abbregement de le Ley* (1516) sold at 40 shillings, or that Edward Hall's *Chronicle* could fetch a little over 12 shillings per copy in 1553–4.[27] For these were substantial publications, in many ways essential purchases for educated men of affairs, and so could be expected to sell at a premium. Play texts were far less substantial works and, when they appear in booklists at all, tend to be gathered together under the heading of 'pamphlets' or with ephemeral pieces such as ballads valued at 'a few pence'. It is salutary to note that Sir Thomas Bodley initially listed plays along with almanacs and proclamations among the 'idle books and riff-raffs' which he wished to exclude from the shelves of the library which he founded. 'Haply some plays may be worth the keeping', he conceded, 'but hardly one in forty'.[28]

By the end of the sixteenth century, playbooks seem to have been selling for, on average, between 6d and 8d per text. The library lists of an anonymous Cambridge physician, drawn up on 14 February 1595, listed his playbooks along with other ephemeral works, and priced a newly published edition of Marlowe's *Edward II* at 6d, and *The True Tragedy of Richard Duke of York* (the 'bad quarto' of Shakespeare's *Henry VI Part 3*) at 8d.[29] Similar prices were still being asked in the Jacobean period, for Sir Edward Dering of Surrenden, Kent (1598–1644) was able to buy over 225 playbooks for his collection between 1619 and 1624, paying most commonly either 6d or 8d per copy.[30]

Allowing for inflation and judging from a comparison of similar types of book, playbooks would seem likely to have sold for rather less earlier in the sixteenth century. In 1552, for example, it was possible to obtain copies of Sir Thomas More's *Utopia* and the 1520 edition of his Latin *Epigrams* for 2d each.[31] At this time, the same purchaser valued a (Latin?) copy of Plautus's *Comedies* at 8d. The day-book of the Oxford bookseller

[27] Bennett, *Books and Readers*, I, p. 229; Johnson, 'Notes', *passim*; John N. King, 'The Account Book of a Marian Bookseller, 1553–4', *British Library Journal*, 13 (1987), pp. 33–57, p. 43.

[28] Bennett, *Books and Readers*, I, p. 186; G. W. Wheeler, ed., *Letters of Sir Thomas Bodley to Thomas James, Keeper of the Bodleian Library* (Oxford, 1926), pp. 219–22. For the ballad literature and other 'cheap print', see Tessa Watt, *Cheap Print and Popular Piety, 1550–1640* (Cambridge, 1991), especially pp. 11–38 and 264–74.

[29] Bodleian Library MS Rawlinson D 213, cited in Johnson, 'Notes', p. 91.

[30] E. S. Leedham-Green and R. J. Fehrenbach, eds., *Private Libraries in Renaissance England: A Collection and Catalogue of Tudor and Early Stuart Book-Lists*, I (2 vols., Binghampton, NY, 1992), I, pp. 137ff.

[31] Ibid., II (Binghampton, NY, 1993), II, pp. 204–21; the will of the scholar Edward Beaumont.

John Dorne for 1520 contained a number of secular texts roughly analogous in size and content to playbooks. It priced a copy of *The Rhyme of Robin Hood* at 2d, the romances of *Sir Eglamour* and *Robert the Devil* at 3d or 3½d, various broadsheet ballads at ½d or 1d and single-leaf carols, saints' lives, and prognostications at 1d each.[32] Significantly, at some point around 1535 the bookshop initially owned by de Worde was selling an unspecified playbook for 2d.[33] It would seem, therefore, that one might realistically expect to pay somewhere between 2d and 6d for a playbook, depending upon its length and dimensions, in the early sixteenth century.[34]

THE ROLE OF THE MARKET: THE SALE OF PRINTED PLAYBOOKS

It seems, then, that playbooks were produced in relatively large numbers, perhaps up to 500 or 600 copies, and sold relatively cheaply, at a price analogous to that of such 'popular' literature as almanacs and ballads. But at whom were these books aimed and how were they marketed? The assumption has been that playbooks were sold primarily to actors, who bought the texts with the intention of performing them. But this is only part of the story.

Who bought playbooks? The internal evidence

The playbooks themselves in their prefaces, stage directions, and title pages, have much to tell us about the nature and development of early drama printing. Wynkyn de Worde's edition of *Hick Scorner* (1511–16) provides a valuable example of the experimental nature of the earliest texts.[35] The play itself was clearly written originally for performance (the

---

[32] Madan, 'Day-Book', pp. 71–178; Bennett, *Books and Readers*, 1, p. 231. In 1556 the library of Sir William More of Losely, Surrey, included a copy of Alexander Barclay's *Fifth Eclogue* (*RSTC* 1385), printed *c.* 1518, priced at 1d. H. S. Bennett, 'Notes on English Retail Book-Prices, 1480–1560', *The Library*, 5.5 (1950), pp. 172–8, p. 175.

[33] W. A. Jackson, 'A London Bookseller's Ledger of 1535', *The Colophon*, n.s.1 (1936), pp. 498–509, p. 502.

[34] Bennett suggests that if we take 1d for every 2–3 sheets of an unbound book as a norm, 'we may feel fairly assured that we have a reasonably accurate yardstick by which to establish the price of an early sixteenth-century book', Bennett, *Books and Readers*, 1, p. 233. By the end of the century, book prices generally tended to be based upon the number of sheets of paper used to make them, a system formalised on 19 January 1598 by a Stationers' Company ordinance stating that new books printed after that date should be sold at not more than 1d for every two sheets they contained if they were printed in pica or larger type, and 1d for every sheet and a half for smaller type. W. W. Greg and E. Boswell, eds., *Records of the Court of the Stationers' Company, 1576–1602* (London, 1931), p. 58.   [35] *RSTC* 14039.

concluding prayer addresses an audience, asking God to bring into the company of the saints 'your soules that here be present' (lines 1023–4)), and it may well have been constructed with a four-man troupe specifically in mind.[36] But the text as printed is nowhere described as a play, and contains no stage directions, suggesting an unfamiliarity on de Worde's part with the conventions and requirements of dramatic production.[37] Indeed, as Ian Lancashire has suggested, it may well have been that 'de Worde thought of *Hick Scorner* less as a play than as a verse satire'.[38] It was not until John Waley's edition, printed by William Copland in 1550, that it was specifically referred to as 'the enterlude of Hycke Scorner'.[39]

A similar uncertainty about the nature and appeal of a dramatic text is evident in the title page of Pynson's edition of *Everyman* (*c.* 1510–19), which describes the work as

a treatyse how the / hye fader of heven sendeth dethe / to Somon every creature to / come and gyve a counte / of theyr lyves in this worlde and is in ma- / ner of a morall / playe.[40]

Here the generic status of the work is not clarified until the end of the description, and then only in equivocal terms. It is 'a treatyse . . . in manner of a morall playe': the didactic content takes precedence over the dramatic form to the point where the latter seems almost an afterthought, and no effort appears to have been made to sell the text to actors.[41]

Ironically, given that he was himself an actor, playwright, and producer of plays, the early output of John Rastell shares something of the awkwardness with dramatic material evident in de Worde's earliest play text. But it also offers the first clear evidence of a conscious attempt to sell plays as scripts for performance. Rastell's edition of Medwall's

[36] I. Lancashire, ed., *Two Tudor Interludes* (Manchester, 1980), p. 32.

[37] Lancashire's suggestion (ibid., p. 31) that the directions are generally implicit in the dialogue is valid, but does not fully explain the curious lack of explicit directions in the text. Many other plays exist in which stage business, entrances, and exits are clearly signalled in the dialogue, but the vast majority of these also contain stage directions.

[38] Ibid., p. 12; N. F. Blake, 'Wynkyn de Worde: The Later Years', in Hans Widman, ed., *Gutenberg-Jahrbuch* (1972), pp. 135–6. De Worde's edition of *Mundus et Infans* (17 July 1522), *RSTC* 25982, shows a greater familiarity with at least the terminology of dramatic literature, describing its contents as 'a propre newe interlude of the worlde and the chylde', sig. Ai.

[39] *RSTC* 14040, sig. Ai.   [40] *RSTC* 10604.

[41] As Pamela King has observed, the text also makes none of the claims to offer 'diverting' entertainment frequently made elsewhere by printers on behalf of their dramatic offerings (see below, p. 21). *Everyman* was sold as resolutely moral matter. Pamela M. King, 'Morality Plays', in Beadle, ed., *Companion*, pp. 240–64, p. 256. See G. A. Lester, *Three Medieval Morality Plays* (London, 1981), p. xxv, for an account of *Everyman*'s 'awe-inspiring seriousness'.

Fulgens and Lucrece describes it simply as 'a godely interlude . . . devyded in two playes / to be played at / ii tymes'.[42] This suggests an evening performance between the courses of a meal, or after meals on successive nights – the conventional occasion for interlude drama, and probably the conditions under which the play was originally performed in the household of Archbishop Morton.[43] The appeal would, then, appear to be, not simply to players in general (it is, notably, a text 'to be played'), but to a particular section of the playing public: the producers of household plays, rather than to travelling companies who might perform under a variety of different conditions and auspices. As we shall see, this was to become a feature of Rastell's marketing of texts.

With his edition of Heywood's *Gentleness and Nobility* (*c.* 1529) – a play in which he may have had a substantial creative input[44] – Rastell seems to reflect something of Pynson's uncertainty with the dramatic genre. He describes the text as

A dyalogue betwen the Marchau[n]t the / Knyght and the plowman disputyng who is the verry Gen / tylman . . . Compilid in maner of an en- / terlude.[45]

Again the appeal is to another, better established form: the dialogue, claiming that the text is simply a variation of this more respectable genre cast ('compilid') 'in [the] maner of an enterlude'. The dramatic nature of the text is presented, not as a distinct selling point, but almost as an incidental feature, the very word 'enterlude' being divided over two lines of type and so rendered ineffectual within the iconographic economy of the page.[46]

Rastell's edition of his own *The Nature of The Four Elements* (pre-1530; probably 1525–7) is rather more confident about its generic status. It is described as

A new interlude and a mery . . . which interlude yf ye whole matter be played // Wyl conteyne the space of an hour and a halfe / but // yf ye lyst ye maye leve out muche of the sad [i.e. serious] mater // [such] as the messengers p[ar]te / and some of naturys parte // and some of experyens p[ar]te and yet the matter wyl de // pend convenyently/ and than it wyll not be paste // thre quarters of an hour of length.[47]

[42] *RSTC* 17778, sig. Ai.
[43] A. H. Nelson, ed., *The Plays of Henry Medwall* (Woodbridge, 1980), pp. 9–19.
[44] R. Axton and P. Happé, eds., *The Plays of John Heywood* (Cambridge, 1991), p. 5; R. Axton, ed., *Three Rastell Plays* (Cambridge, 1979), p. 1.   [45] *RSTC* 20723, sig. Ai.
[46] A similar apologetic attitude seems to mark Rastell's edition of *Calisto and Melebea* (*c.* 1525–30), *RSTC* 20721, although here the reference to the text's being made 'in manner of an interlude' has more pointed relevance, the text being a translation into dramatic verse of the original Spanish prose narrative.   [47] *RSTC* 20722, sig. Ai.

The placing of the generic marker first, suggesting greater confidence in the dramatic nature of the work, the specificity of the playing choices offered, the evident knowledge of their consequences for the length of performance, and the ready appreciation of the need for actors to have a script flexible enough for cutting down for shorter performances, all reflect Rastell's status as author as well as printer of the piece, someone who, presumably, had first-hand experience of the play in performance. But, for all its direct appeal to the needs of actors, the text also reveals a naiveté about the most effective way to sell a dramatic text. Compared to the terse functionality of later playbook title pages ('Foure may easely play this enterlude', etc.[48]), there is an obvious counterproductive verbosity to Rastell's prolegomena. In addition to the description of the possible cuts which can be made to the text, there is also an extensive list of 'dyvers matters whiche be in // this interlude conteynyd', ranging from 'The sytuacyon of the four elementis, that is to sey, the yerth, the water, the ayre, and fyre, and theyr qualytese and propertese' to 'the cause of the lyghtnynge of blasyng sterrys and flamys fleynge in the ayre', and a list of the *dramatis personae* concluding with the observation 'Also yf ye lyst ye // may brynge in a dysgysynge' (sig. Ai). The overall effect is of a cluttered page in which no one piece of information stands out, or is readily conveyed to the eye, a product perhaps of over-enthusiasm on Rastell's part that every virtue of his play should be appreciated, and of the didactic – even evangelical – attitude to its scientific material which the text displays. The vagueness of the declaration that a disguising might be brought in, without a statement of how it might be organised, is also revealing. It suggests still more clearly that Rastell envisaged an evening performance by household players (or possibly by school or college companies) for the plays which he printed. Only such groups would have the resources to stage this type of event, which was well beyond the capabilities of the typical itinerant company. Moreover, there is an assumption here that any would-be purchasers will know what Rastell is describing. They will be familiar with disguisings and be able to introduce their own at the desired moment in the production. The playbook does not contain all the information necessary for its full potential to be realised, and needs to be fleshed out in the context of an evening's performance. These are notes towards a production rather than an 'off-the-peg' blueprint for one.

[48] See below, pp. 22–4.

With Rastell's son William's editions of the interludes of John Heywood, the presentation of playbooks as practical guides to performance is taken a stage further. But it is hard to determine whether this reflects a greater appreciation of dramatic literature on the part of the printer, or simply Heywood's own sense of the needs of acting companies. Each of Heywood's texts shows signs of having been written for performance, with detailed, functional stage directions, cues for songs, and indications of stage business. But the overall packaging of the texts, in terms of prolegomena and layout is, at least for those plays printed in 1533, rudimentary, offering little evidence of their being advertised as 'player-friendly'. Only gradually did the presentation of the printed volumes match the sophistication of the plays themselves and develop something akin to a strategy and vocabulary for selling them as scripts.

Johan Johan (12 February 1533),[49] for example, has the sort of directions necessary if the action is to be realised effectively ('Than he bryngeth the payle empty' (sig. Bii); 'Here they fyght by the erys a whyle and than / the preest and the wyfe go out of the place' (sig. Biv (v)). But the edition as a whole is a rather rudimentary production, with no separate title page and no mention of the author's name anywhere in the text. Indeed, the fact that Rastell describes it as 'A mery play // *betwene* John John the // husband / Tyb the // Wyfe and syr Johan // the preest' (sig. Ai, my italics) suggests that he may have thought of it as an animated dialogue, similar in nature to those which he was printing for Sir Thomas More at this time, rather than as a play with distinct conventions and desiderata of its own. *The Pardoner and The Friar*, printed two months later on 5 April 1533,[50] displays a similar equivocation. Again there are detailed directions as to how the desired effects are to be created ('Now shall the frere begyn his sermon / and evyn at // the same tyme the pardoner begynneth also to shew and // speke of his bullys / and auctorytes from Rome' (sig. Aiii); and, at sig. Biv(v), as the final fight begins, a succinct direction pairs off the combatants with few concessions to a reader, in precisely the way actors would require: 'Prat with the pardoner / and the parson with the frere'). Yet the text is again described as a play 'between' the characters involved, there is no title page setting out the nature of the interlude, and no reference is made to its author.

The Play of The Weather (1533) and *A Play of Love* (1534),[51] suggest greater confidence with the material on Rastell's part. Each has a title page – in

---

[49] *RSTC* 13298.   [50] *RSTC* 13299.   [51] *RSTC* 13305 and *RSTC* 13303 respectively.

the case of *Love* a substantially illustrated one – and each shows signs of being tailored more specifically for acting. The list of *dramatis personae* for *Weather* declares that the actor playing the boy should be 'the le[a]st that can play', and the text contains cues for songs ('At thende of this / staf the god hath a / song play in his / trone or [i.e. 'ere'] Merye re / port come in' (sig. Aiv). *Love* similarly offers detailed directions for staging ('here they go both out and the lover be / lovyd entreth with a songe' (Bi); 'here the vyse cometh in ronnyng sodenly aboute // the place among the audyens with a hye co- // pyn tank on his hedfull of squybs fyred // cryeng water / fyre fyre / fyre wa // ter / water/ fyre / tyll the fyre in the squybs be spent' (sig. Div(v)). But again it is hard to apportion responsibility for this appreciation of the needs of performers to Rastell rather than to Heywood himself.

Further problems arise concerning the origin and purpose of these stage directions. Were they added to the printed text as a conscious marketing ploy, an attempt to make the intentions of the dramatist accessible to companies with whom he would have no personal contact? Or were they manuscript notes from the author to the original actors, carried over into the printed text without conscious design? Again the evidence provides no clear answers.

Subsequent printers began to build upon the innovations developed by Rastell and Heywood, and added touches of their own designed to enhance the appeal of their playbooks. Many texts were advertised on the strength of their moral function. Like all literature, and indeed all works of art in the medieval and early modern periods, plays were ideally intended to carry a didactic, improving function. But this general desideratum took on added potency in the wake of the Act for the Advancement of True Religion of 1543, which declared it lawful to 'sette forth songes, plaies and enterludes' only if they were 'for the rebuking and reproaching of vices and setting foorth of vertue'.[52] Thereafter printers had an added incentive to declare the moral value of their wares. Thus John Allde described his edition of Ulpian Fulwell's *Like Will to Like* (*c.* 1568) as a text

very godly and ful of pleesant mirth. Wherin is declared not onely what punishment followeth those that wil rather followe licentious living, then to esteem and followe good councel: and what great benefits and commodities they receive that apply unto vertuous living and good exercises.[53]

[52] A. Luders, *et al.*, eds., *Statutes of the Realm* (11 vols., London, 1810–28), III, p. 894.
[53] *RSTC* 11473.

Similarly William Wager's *The Longer Thou Livest the More Fool Thou Art* (*c.* 1569) was described by its printer, Richard Jones, as 'A myrrour very necessarie for youth, and / specialy for such as are like to come to dignite and promotion',[54] while John King advertised the improving nature of his edition of *Nice Wanton* (*c.* 1560) as its chief attraction, turning the title page itself into a moral lesson in miniature: 'A Preaty Interlude, called Nice Wanton, Wherein ye may se, / Three braunces of an yll tree, / The mother and her chyldren three / Twoo naught, and one godlye, / Early sharpe, that wyll be thorne, / Soone yll, that wyll be naughte: To be naught, better unborne, / Better unfed, than naughtely taught.'[55] The earliest, and perhaps the most fulsome example of this strategy is provided, however, by John Rastell's folio edition of *Calisto and Melebea* published well before the 1543 act, whose title page advertises it as

A new commodye in englysh in maner / of an enterlude ryght elygant and full of craft of rethoryk / wherein is shewd and dyscryvyd as well the bewte and good propertyes of women / as theyr vycys and evyll condicions / with a morall conclusion and exhortacyon to vertew.[56]

Other texts were presented in more hedonistic terms. Thus Rastell described *Gentleness and Nobility* (*c.* 1529), somewhat mendaciously, as 'compilid in maner of an enterlude with divers toys and gestis addyd therto / to make mery pastyme and disport',[57] Skelton's *Magnyfycence* (printed *c.* 1530) was described as 'a goodly interlude and a mery',[58] while the later *Albion Knight* (*c.* 1565), whose printer Thomas Colwell clearly believed in losing no opportunity to advertise his products, was described even in the Stationers' Register as 'a mery playe, both pythy and pleasaunt'.[59] Other printers attempted to hedge their bets. John Allde offered William Wager's *Enough is as Good as a Feast* (1565–70) as 'A Comedy or Enterlude . . . very fruteful, godly and ful of pleasant mirth'.[60]

But, beyond these general recommendations of the content of their

---

[54] *RSTC* 24935, sig. Ai.   [55] *RSTC* 25016.   [56] *RSTC* 20721, sig. Ai.

[57] *RSTC* 20723. The only 'toys and gestis' evident would seem to be the moment of slapstick violence when the Plowman beats the Knight.   [58] *RSTC* 22607.

[59] *RSTC* 275 (a fragment). Colwell was to use a similar combination of epithets ('A Pretie new Enterlude both pithie and pleasaunt') to describe his edition of the biblical play *King Darius* (1565), *RSTC* 6277. Other 'merry' plays included Heywood's *Johan Johan* (1533), *RSTC* 13298; *The Pardoner and The Friar* (1533), *RSTC* 13299, and *The Play of The Weather* (1533), *RSTC* 13305; William Copland's edition of *Wealth and Health* (*c.* 1557), *RSTC* 14110 ('very mery and full of pastyme'); *Jack Juggler* (*c.* 1562), *RSTC* 14837 ('both / wytte, very playsant and merye'); *Cambises* (?1569), *RSTC* 20287; and *New Custom* (1573) *RSTC* 6150 ('A new Enterlude / No lesse wittie than pleasaunt').

[60] *RSTC* 24933, sig. Ai.

plays, printers also increasingly made strong and specific claims for the structural suitability of their texts as scripts for performance. In particular we find increasing stress placed upon two key points: the novelty of their products and the small size of the cast needed to play them. *Wealth and Health* (*c.* 1557) describes itself as 'An enterlude . . . newly at this tyme / imprinted' and claims 'foure may easely play this playe'.[61] *Impatient Poverty* (*c.* 1560), printed by John King, is 'A new in / terlude . . . newly Imprinted', and declares on the title-page 'Foure men may well and eas / ilye playe thys interlude', including a doubling plan to make good the claim.[62] Given the small size and limited resources of most touring companies, the fact that a play could be performed by a small cast would make it an attractive option for them. The majority of touring companies in the period before 1576 were probably made up of six or fewer predominantly adult males.[63] On the strength of a survey of some sixty troupes from the reign of Henry VIII for which membership details survive, Ian Lancashire concludes that over half of them consisted of only four players. Only 'a little over 10 per cent had five players' (i.e. the 'four men and a boy' frequently assumed to be the standard composition of Renaissance companies).[64] This figure is reflected in the average size of companies visiting Selby Abbey between 1431 and 1532, and in a number of royal household records for the period before 1540.[65] This sample may not, however, tell the full story. By 1577, the average composition of companies visiting Southampton for which numbers were recorded was eight.[66] And logic alone prompts scepticism. If one accepts the smaller figure as the norm, one is faced with the unlikely prospect that a large number of the playbooks produced in the period made a point of advertising themselves as unplayable (as they required more than four actors) by the majority of their prospective buyers.[67]

[61] *RSTC* 14110, sig. Ai.   [62] *RSTC* 14112.5, sig. Ai.

[63] T. W. Craik, 'The Companies and the Repertory', in Norman Sanders, *et al.*, eds., *The Revels History of Drama in English*, II (London, 1980), pp. 102–13, pp. 135–6; D. Bevington, *From 'Mankind' to Marlowe* (Cambridge, MA, 1962), pp. 79ff.   [64] Lancashire, *Topography*, p. xxv.

[65] S. Westfall, *Patrons and Performance: Early Tudor Household Revels* (Oxford, 1990), appendix A, pp. 210–12.

[66] David Bradley, *From Text to Performance in the Elizabethan Theatre: Preparing the Play for the Stage* (Cambridge, 1992), p. 61.

[67] Plays advertised as for four players include *The Trial of Treasure* (*c.* 1566), *RSTC* 14112; Lewis Wager's *The Life and Repentance of Mary Magdalene* (*c.* 1566), *RSTC* 24932; William Wager's *The Longer Thou Livest The More Fool Thou Art* (*c.* 1569), *RSTC* 24935; and *New Custom* (1573), *RSTC* 6150. Ulpian Fulwell's *Like Will to Like* (*c.* 1568), *RSTC* 11473, was advertised as for five players. John Pickering's *Horestes* (1567), *RSTC* 19917 and the anonymous *King Darius* were doubled for six players. William Wager's *Enough is as Good as a Feast* was doubled for seven, and John Phillip's *Patient and Meeke Grissil* (?1569), *RSTC* 19865 and Thomas Garter's *The Most Virtuous and Godly Susanna* (*c.* 1578), *RSTC* 11632.5 were doubled (in the case of the former somewhat misleadingly) for eight.

Similarly, while the fact that a work was being printed for the first time is likely to have been attractive to all kinds of purchasers, readers, and players alike, actors considering adding it to their repertoire for touring might well need particular reassurance that the work they were investing in was not stale material. Hence from de Worde's edition of *Mundus et Infans* (1522) onwards, printers frequently referred to the novelty of their playbooks in title pages and prefaces, in what looks like a conscious attempt to advertise them to acting companies.[68] So important did the need to advertise plays as both new and economical in casting become, indeed, that printers can be found making such claims even when they are patently untrue. Second and even third editions of old plays continued to be advertised as 'a new interlude'.[69] John Tisdale and Anthony Kitson were, for example, still describing Heywood's *Play of The Weather* as a new work in *c.* 1554–60, despite the fact that it was by this time into its third edition.[70] William Pickering and Thomas Hackett printed the text of *Godly Queen Hester* in 1561 as 'a newe enterlude . . . very necessary / newly made and imprinted in this present year', even though the play was at least thirty years old.[71]

Claims about the size of the cast needed to play a script were also occasionally no more than token assertions of their playability, and sometimes not even that. Hence Abraham Vale's edition of R. Wever's *Lusty Juventus* gestured vaguely in the direction of a doubling plan without actually committing itself to any details ('foure may play it

---

[68] See, for example, Copland's 'newe play [of Robin Hood] for to be played / in Maye games' (Nov. 1560), *RSTC* 13691; *Jack Juggler* (Nov. 1562?), *RSTC* 14837 ('A new Enterlued for / chyldren to playe . . . Never before Imprinted'); *Thersites* (1561–3), *RSTC* 23949 ('A new Enterlude'); *King Darius* (1565?), *RSTC* 6277 ('A Pretie new En / terlude . . . Never before Imprynted'); *Jacob and Essau* (1568), *RSTC* 14327 ('A newe mery and wittie / Comedie or Enterlude, newly / imprinted'); *The Disobedient Child* (1569?), *RSTC* 14085 ('A pretie / and mery new En- / terlude'); *New Custom* (1573), *RSTC* 6150 ('A new Enterlude / No lesse wittie; than pleasant . . . devysed of late and for diverse / causes nowe sette forthe, never before this time Imprinted'); *Appius and Virginia* (1575), *RSTC* 1059 ('A new Tragicall Comedie'). Greater specificity can be found in those plays – particularly those originally played at court – the date of whose first performance is cited on the title page. In this group would come *Sappho and Phao* (*RSTC* 17086), 'Played beefore the / Queenes Majestie on Shrove- / Tewsday' and printed *c.* April 1584, and *Campaspe* (*RSTC* 17048), 'Played before the Queenes Ma- / jestie on twelfe day at night'. Here the novelty of the text would seem to be a clear selling point. But, as these plays seem to appeal to readers as well as to players, they will be considered in detail below.

[69] William Copland's 1561 edition of *Impatient Poverty* (*RSTC* 14113) gave pride of place on the title page to the claim that it was 'A newe enterlude' (sig. Ai). His second edition of *Jack Juggler* made the same claim, describing the text as 'Newly Imprinted' (*RSTC* 14837a), as did John Allde's third edition of the same play (*RSTC* 14837a.5). Henry Bynneman's 1568 edition of *Jacob and Esau* (*RSTC* 14327) is described as 'A newe mery and wittie / Comedie or Enterlude, newly / Imprinted', despite the play having been entered in the Stationers' Register eleven years earlier.

[70] *RSTC* 13306.

[71] *RSTC* 13251. For the dating of *Hester*, see Greg Walker, *Plays of Persuasion* (Cambridge, 1991), pp. 102–5.

easely, takyng such par / tes as they thinke it best: so that any one tak / of those partes that be not in the place at once').[72] The fact that even entirely fraudulent claims could be made – such as Copland's assertion that *Wealth and Health* could be played by only four actors, when it in fact requires at least five – suggests that by the mid-1560s there existed a competitive market for playbooks, and printers had to try all the tricks that they knew to increase the attractiveness of their products.[73]

A readier appreciation of both the needs and the capabilities of dramatic companies also seems increasingly apparent in playbooks printed from the mid-1560s onwards. Henry Bynneman's edition of *Jacob and Esau* (1568) gives clear, if rather perfunctory guidance on the costuming and staging of the interlude.[74] The title page makes clear that the company will have to make some effort to present a plausible Old Testament ambience for the play, identifying

The partes and names of the Players / who are to be consydered to be Hebrews / and so should be apparailed with attire. (sig. Ai)

This strategy is continued in the marginal directions, such as when Esau and his servant Ragau enter and it is stated:

Ragau entreth / with his horn / at his back and / his huntyng / staffe in hys / hande, and lea / deth iij grey- / houndes or one / as may be got / ten.' (sig. A ii)

The final qualification would seem evidence of a sober acceptance of the limitations upon touring companies – or companies of any sort – putting on plays in less than ideal circumstances. Similar familiarity with the nature of troupes and the realities of playing would seem evident in the direction later on the same page, where the actor playing Ragau is given room to improvise mannerisms and other business within the confines of a piece of dialogue.

Here he count / erfaiteth how / his maister cal / leth hym up in / the mornings / and of his an / sweres. (sig. Aii, line 9)

Other texts show a similar familiarity with the improvisational methods and playing styles of contemporary actors – especially those playing the

[72] *RSTC* 25148, sig. Ai.
[73] *RSTC* 14110. As T. W. Craik has argued, *Wealth and Health* requires at least five players to run smoothly, and six if a production is to avoid 'awkward pauses'. T. W. Craik, 'Companies', in Sanders, *et al.*, eds., *Revels History*, p. 110. At sig. Ci and again at Civ(v), Liberty, Wealth and Health return to the place, while Shrewd Wit and Ill Will are still there. John Phillip's *Patient and Meeke Grissell* and Lewis Wager's *The Repentance of Mary Magdalene*, contain similarly misleading statements, the former supporting it with a flawed doubling plan. See T. W. Craik, *The Tudor Interlude* (Leicester, 1958), pp. 29–30.   [74] *RSTC* 14327.

roles of clowns or vices. William Wager's *The Longer Thou Livest the More Fool Thou Art* (*c.* 1569), contains the direction that the actor playing Moros, the comic hero, is to read aloud from his book 'as fondely as you can devise', but no further clues are given as to the ensuing business.[75] Similarly, the vice Ill Will in *Wealth and Health* (1557–65) is directed to enter 'with some jest',[76] while, Sin, the vice in Thomas Lupton's *All For Money* (1578) is given even greater freedom, as a royal decree is read out to 'turne the proclamation to some contrarie sence at everie time All For Money hath read it'.[77] All this suggests that playwrights – and perhaps even printers – were by this stage becoming familiar with the improvisational techniques of comic actors of the sort which Richard Tarlton and Will Kemp would later turn into a high art, and were making allowances in their scripts for them.[78] Hamlet's injunction to the players to 'let those that play your clowns speak no more than is set down for them' was thus a reaction to a long dramatic tradition rather than a recent innovation.[79]

The playing companies and the market for printed texts

So, following one strand of evidence, the early history of drama publishing in England might be written as an evolutionary process in which printers gradually gained confidence in the nature and function of the dramatic material which they were producing, and in their own ability to sell it, learning how to package the texts which came into their hands, not as the poor cousins of other, more prestigious genres, but for sale in their own right to a target market of acting companies and the producers of household entertainments. But so simple a narrative conceals as much as it illuminates.

---

[75] *RSTC* 24935. William Wager, *The Longer Thou Livest and Enough Is As Good As A Feast*, ed. R. Mark Benbow (London, 1968), before l. 702.   [76] *RSTC* 14110, sig. Bii.

[77] *RSTC* 16949, sig. Di. See Lois Potter, 'The Plays and the Playwrights', in *Revels History*, II, pp. 141–257, p. 204. See also *The Prodigal Son* (*c.* 1525–34), *RSTC* 20765.5, after line 51: 'Here the servant cometh in spekyng some straunge language', printed in Malone Society, *Collections*, I (Oxford, 1907), p. i.

[78] See, for example, D. Wiles, *Shakespeare's Clown: Actor and Text in the Elizabethan Playhouse* (Cambridge, 1987). That it was not simply playwrights but printers too who were increasingly aware of and catering for the general needs of playing companies seems clear from Richard Jones' edition of Richard Edwards' *Damon and Pithias* (1571), which was evidently a script specially modified for printing with subsequent performance needs in mind. The play was, its title page declared, 'Newly Imprinted, as the same was shewed before the Queenes Majestie, by the Children of her Graces / Chapell, except the Prologue that is somewhat al- / tered for the proper use of them that hereafter / shall have occasion to plaie it, either in / private or open audience'. *RSTC* 7514, sig. Ai.   [79] *Hamlet* (Alexander text), 3.2.37–9.

Could acting companies and household players really have formed a large enough constituency to justify print runs of up to 600 copies? It seems unlikely. The total number of known groups of players in the early sixteenth century does not exceed the 600 or so required to sell out a single print run, albeit surviving figures may be simply the tip of an iceberg of itinerant and semi-itinerant activity.[80] Moreover, the chronological development of the acting profession does not seem to offer any plausible reason for the sudden decision of a number of printers to produce playbooks in the early to mid-1510s. If there was a period of marked increase in either the numbers or the activity of touring companies in the period before 1558, it can more plausibly be located in the 1520s than in the 1500s or 1510s, although the nature of the surviving evidence makes any such calculation perilous.[81] It is hard, then, to present a fully convincing account of the development of drama printing as strictly 'market led'.

Turning to the needs of the acting companies directly, it might be inferred from what is known about the economics of playing that printed playbooks would constitute a sound investment for touring companies. Lewis Wager's *Mary Magdalene* refers to the players having 'ridden and gone many sundry waies' (suggesting that touring companies were envisaged by the author as the major market for the text) and states that they will give the audience value for money 'whether you geve halfpence or pence'.[82] If this suggestion reflects the realities of

---

[80] Scholars differ over the buying potential of the itinerant companies and the extent to which printers may have attempted to court them. Their arguments have, however, been inevitably impressionistic. Whereas David Bevington assumes that the professional troupes formed the major market for those printed playbooks which contained a doubling plan (D. Bevington, *From 'Mankind' to Marlowe*, p. 5), David Bradley has suggested that 'it seems doubtful if publishers would have found much of a market in that [area]' (Bradley, *Text to Performance*, p. 17). P. W. White makes a similar point, suggesting that 'it is highly doubtful that printers could profit much from selling interludes at this time'. He argues that playbooks may have been printed from a desire to please the author's patron or from protestant zeal on the printer's part (P. W. White, *Theatre and Reformation: Protestantism, Patronage, and Playing in Tudor England* (Cambridge, 1993), p. 72). Sir Edmund Chambers goes further, claiming that the printed texts may well have been aimed largely at readers or 'schoolmasters in search of suitable pieces for performance by their pupils' (Chambers, *Elizabethan Stage*, III, pp. 178–80). The internal evidence cited to support this last suggestion is, however, somewhat tenuous. The provision of maximum cast sizes and doubling patterns would tend to suggest a market among small troupes of professionals. Neither readers nor schoolmasters with large numbers of potential players at their disposal would have needed such lures to buy the texts.

[81] Lancashire, *Topography*, pp. 349–408. A rough count of the first references to itinerant companies recorded by Lancashire would suggest a fairly stable growth rate in their number, with a very minor peak in the 1520s. Only with the publication of the complete run of Records of Early English Drama volumes, however, will it be possible to produce even rough estimates of touring activity with any confidence. [82] *RSTC* 24932, sig. Aiii.

playing experience even roughly, it suggests a healthy situation for playing companies *vis-à-vis* the raw materials of their trade. Even paying a halfpenny a head, one audience of sixty people would repay an initial investment in even a relatively expensive 5d playbook for each member of a six-man troupe, and in practice a company might well have managed with a single purchased copy to act as a prompt book, from which separate parts could be copied by hand. But not enough is known about the details of playing practice to enable us to be clear about the companies' precise needs for playbooks.[83] Did those touring troupes who used the printed playbooks conform to later playhouse practice and use plots (summaries of the action used by the property master and/or stage manager to ensure that everything and everyone was where they should be at any given moment in the performance) and parts (the lines and cues of individual roles prepared as texts for the actor concerned)? The survival of a small number of manuscript parts from the fifteenth century would suggest that the practice was not unknown.[84] The evidence is, however, inconclusive. In the case of both the fifteenth-century companies and the Elizabethan playhouses the original texts from which these documents were prepared would themselves have been manuscripts: in the first case because there were no printed texts available, in the second because the companies were working from the playwright's holograph text or a 'cleaned up' scribal copy. Thus producing handwritten copies of the relevant sections of text would have been the most practical and economical option. Whether the pre-playhouse companies would have gone to the same trouble when it was possible to buy full printed copies of the text for each member of the cast for just a few pence is less clear. Consequently it is hard to gauge the exact needs of the company for playbooks.

Surviving evidence also suggests that troupes might realistically expect rather more by way of financial return for a performance than 30d. Clearly the amount that a company might receive for a single performance would vary greatly according to individual circumstances: the prestige of their noble patron or the goodwill of their hosts towards their

[83] Donald C. Baker, 'When is a Text a Play?: Reflections Upon What Certain Late Medieval Dramatic Texts Can Tell Us', in M. G. Briscoe and John C. Coldewey, eds., *Contexts for Early English Drama* (Bloomington, 1989), pp. 20–40, p. 22; White, *Theatre and Reformation*, p. 72.

[84] See, for example, the player's part from a Cornish play produced *c.* 1400, with speeches offering advice on marriage, printed in R. H. Nance, 'New Light on Cornish', *Old Cornwall*, 4 (1943–51), pp. 214–16; the Duke's part from *Dux Moraud*; the speech for 'Delight' from a play possibly of East Anglian origins; and the part of 'Secundus Miles' in the 'Ashmole Fragment', all collected and edited in Norman Davis, ed., *Non-cycle Plays and Fragments*, EETS, ss 1 (1970), pp. 94, 121–2, and 120 respectively.

place of origin, the nature of the performance and the generosity of the local community or host. But the evidence of those performances wholly or partly sponsored by local landlords or civic authorities (which have consequently left a trace in household or civic account books) suggests a range of rewards beginning at 20d and rising to considerably more substantial sums. It was claimed, for example (albeit by a hostile witness), that four members of the King's Players were able to gross £30 touring England in 1527/8. Certainly the King's troupe gained 8s for a single performance before the London Drapers' Company in 1527, and this seems to have been the going rate for plays brought to the Drapers' hall in this period.[85] Even allowing for the costs of costumes and travelling, the limitations upon the playbook market might therefore be not so much the number of copies which a company could afford, as the number which they would wish to buy. Equally, actors would have been anxious to avoid the problems of duplication, and so may well not have purchased every new playbook which appeared on the market.

A further complication concerns the number of plays which a company might have 'in repertory' at any one time. It seems likely that some local, amateur, or semi-professional groups might have had only one play worked up for touring within their local region in any given year. But what about the fully professional troupes? Did they have a wider repertoire from which to choose? Later playhouse companies had an

[85] Lancashire, *Topography*, p. 62; J. Robertson and D. J. Gordon, eds., *A Calendar of Dramatic Records in the Books of the Livery Companies of London, 1485–1640*, Malone Society, *Collections*, III (Oxford, 1954), p. 137. It has been estimated that, whereas 3 or 4 shillings per performance may have been the normal yield for the King's Players on their visits to Kent in the fifteenth century, 10s had become 'almost a minimum' by 1550, and by 1580 the norm was nearer to £1 (Giles E. Dawson, ed., *Records of Plays and Players in Kent, 1450–1642*, Malone Society, *Collections*, VII (Oxford, 1962), p. xviii). The King's – or Queen's – Company was, of course, exceptional in both its prestige and its capacity to attract funds from loyal civic purses. More normal may have been the 3s 4d gained by 'the players that came from bullyngbrooke' when they visited Long Sutton in Lincolnshire in 1560/1, or the 5s they received on their return there in 1564/5 (S. J. Kahrl, ed., *Records of Plays and Players in Lincolnshire, 1300–1585*, Malone Society, *Collections*, VIII (Oxford, 1974), p. 71). The mixture of 'official' contribution and commercial 'collection money' which such 'gala' performances before civic officials involved probably made them more than usually lucrative for companies, as it clearly did for the 'Players of Ipswich' when they visited Long Sutton in 1564/5 and were given 5s from town coffers 'over and besyde yt was gathered' (ibid., p. 71). Similar payments seem also to have been the norm in Canterbury, where the Lord Chancellor's Players received 3s 4d '[over] and above vjs viijd gathered at the play' (Dawson, *Records*, p. 110). Companies might also expect to supplement their incomes by eating and drinking, and perhaps even sleeping at their hosts' expense, at least on the night of the performance before the town fathers or when they visited a noble household (see, for example, the hospitality afforded the King's Players in the L'Estrange household books from Hunstanton, in D. Galloway and John Wasson, eds., *Records of Plays and Players in Norfolk and Suffolk, 1330–1642*, Malone Society, *Collections*, XI (Oxford, 1980), pp. 21–2). See also Westfall, *Patrons and Performance*, pp. 132 and 149.

astonishingly demanding repertory schedule, involving the performance of up to thirty-eight separate plays in one season.[86] But what of the earlier itinerant companies? The archetypal fictional troupe that appears in *The Book of Sir Thomas More* had a 'divers' portfolio of seven separate interludes to offer to their hosts at each stop on their touring itinerary. Although none of them could have been performed by Cardinal Wolsey's players as the play claims – they all post-date his death, some by decades – the names of the interludes listed by the Player are, nonetheless, suggestive. The company could, he declared, perform any one of the following: *The Cradle of Security*; *Hit Nayle O'th' Head*; *Impatient Poverty*, Heywood's *The Four PP*; *Dives and Lazarus*; *Lusty Juventus*, and *The Marriage of Witt and Wysdome*. Of these, *The Cradle* is known to have been part of the touring repertory of at least one company, as an account survives of its having been played in Gloucester at some point in the 1560s and 1570s. *Dives and Pauper* and *Hit Nayle* have not survived, but versions of the former (such as that written for his students by the Hitchin schoolmaster Ralph Radcliffe in the 1550s) existed in the sixteenth century. *Poverty*, *Four PP*, *Juventus*, and *The Marriage* were all printed during the period. While it would be unwise to take this list as evidence of actual playing practice, it does suggest a plausible repertoire for a company in the second half of the century, and might reflect the authors of *The Book*'s generalised recollections of earlier touring practice.[87]

Given these limits upon the requirements of acting companies, printers would have been wise to attempt to sell their playbooks to a wider market than players alone. And there is evidence that they did so, targeting interludes at a variety of other prospective buyers. John Charlewood clearly envisaged a mixed market for his edition of Wager's *Mary Magdalene*, which he sold as a text playable by four actors, but also described as 'very delectable for those / which shall heare or reade the same'.[88] Other printers operated in similar ways.

By the 1570s at the latest it is clear that a number of plays were being printed primarily for readers. Prior to this, as we have seen, the academic 'closet' drama of Seneca had been produced in translation for a

[86] A. Gurr, *The Shakespearean Stage, 1574–1642* (3rd edn, Cambridge, 1992), pp. 103–14.

[87] C. F. Tucker, ed., *The Shakespeare Apocrypha* (Oxford, 1908). For *The Cradle*, see R. Willis, *Mount Tabor, or The Exercises of a Penitent Sinner* (1639), *RSTC* 25752, pp. 110–14. For Radcliffe, see Lancashire, *Topography*, pp. 154–5. See also Westfall, *Patrons and Performance*, pp. 111–12.

[88] *RSTC* 24932, sig. Ai. Baker, 'When is a Text?', p. 22.

readership of scholars and gentlemen.[89] But by the time of John Daye's edition of *The Tragidie of Ferrex and Porrex* (the *c.* 1570 edition of *Gorboduc*), it is clear that printers were aware of and seeking to exploit a market among private readers beyond the schools and universities. Daye prefaced his edition with a prologue 'The P[rinter] to the Reader',[90] as did Richard Jones in his edition of George Whetstone's *Promos and Cassandra*.[91] It is also clear that an increasing number of these plays were being sold as records of a particular prestigious performance, for consumption by people who had not been present but who could be offered a vicarious experience of the event through ownership of a copy of the playbook. Thus *Ferrex and Porrex* was described on its title page as a text 'set forth without addition or alte- / ration but altogether as the same was shewed on stage before the Queenes Majestie / about nine yeares past, vz the / xviij day of Januarie, 1561 / by the gentlemen of the Inner Temple'.[92] Likewise the edition of Lyly's *Sappho and Phao* (1584) was described as 'Played before the Queenes Majestie on Shrove- / Tewsday by her Majesties / Chyldren and the Boyes / of Paules' and contained copies of the variant prologues from the performances at court and the Blackfriars theatre.[93]

---

[89] See, for example, *Troas*, translated by Jasper Heywood (1559), *RSTC* 22221; *Thyestes*, trans. Heywood (1560), *RSTC* 22226; *Hercules Furens*, trans. Heywood (1561), *RSTC* 22223; *Agamemnon*, trans. John Studley (?1566), *RSTC* 22222; *Medea*, trans. Studley (?1566), *RSTC* 22224; and *Octavia*, trans. 'T. W.' or 'T. N.' (?1566), *RSTC* 22229. The educative, readerly functions of these editions is made clearest in the prologue to *Hercules Furens*, which describes the text as 'for the profit of young / schollars so faithfully translated into En- / glish metre, that ye may se verse for verse / tourned as farre as the phrase of the english permitteth'. See also *The Lamentable Tragedie of Oedipus*, translated by Alexander Nevyle (1563), *RSTC* 22225, which was similarly accompanied by an Epistle to scholarly readers, and the edition of Terence's *Andria*, translated by Maurice Kyffin (1588), *RSTC* 23895, which was sold as 'A furtherance for the attain / ment unto the right knowledge and true propriete, of the / Latin Tong. And also a commodious meane of help, / to such as have forgotten Latin, for their / speedy recovery of habilitie, to un- / derstand, write and speake, / the same'.

[90] *RSTC* 18685, sig. Aii. William Griffiths' earlier edition of the play, (*c.* 1565), *RSTC* 18684, carried similar prose glosses and explication of the Dumbshow action, implying a similar engagement with a reading public.

[91] *RSTC* 25347 (20 August 1578). See also John Lyly's *Endimion, the Man in the Moone*, published by I. Charlewood in 1591, *RSTC* 17050.

[92] *Ferrex and Porrex*, sig. Ai. In part the claim to absolute authenticity was a response to Griffiths' earlier (Daye claimed corrupt) edition, which its editor had described as 'sett forthe as the same was shewed before the / Quenes most excellent Majestie, in her highnes / Court of whitehall, the xviij day of January, / Anno Domini 1561 / By the Gentlemen / of Thynner Temple in London'.

[93] John Lyly, *Sappho and Phao* (1584), *RSTC* 17086. See also *Campaspe* (1584), *RSTC* 17048: 'A moste excellent Co- / medie . . . / Played beefore the Queenes Ma- / jestie on twelfe day at night, by / her Majesties Children and the / Children of Poules'; *Fedele and Fortunio* (1584–5), *RSTC* 19447: 'translated out of the Italian and set / downe according as it hath beene pre / sented before the queenes most / excellent Majestie'; and *Love and Fortune* (1589), *RSTC* 24286: 'Plaide before the

Some efforts were made to refashion the texts for differing conditions of performance or private reading. Thus the court prologue to Richard Edwards' *Damon and Pithias* was replaced with one more adaptable to the circumstances of commercial performance, while Richard Jones' edition of Marlowe's *Tamburlaine the Greate* (1590) removed a number of the comic scenes ('some fond and frivolous gestures') felt by the printer to be unsuitable for the more dignified circumstances and refined tastes of private readers.[94]

Thus playbooks might be printed as souvenirs of theatrical events for those who had witnessed them in performance, as with *Tamburlaine,* or as windows on to a courtly dramatic world that the majority of readers could not aspire to inhabit in person, as in the case of *Ferrex and Porrex, Endimion* or *Damon and Pithias.* By 1609, it was even possible to sell a text on the strength of its not yet having been played on the public stage at all. Thus the 1609 quarto edition of Shakespeare's *Troilus and Cresseid* was described as conferring an exclusive privilege upon its readers.

Queenes most excellent Majestie: wherin are / manye fine conceites / with great de- / light'. Richard Jones' edition of *The Princely Pleasures at the Courte of Kenelworth* (1576) makes the commercial strategy still clearer. In his prologue to the reader, the printer announced his motivation for printing the text.

Being advertised (gentle Reader) that in this last progresse, hir Majestie was (by the Ryght Noble Earle of Leycester) honorably and triumphantly receyved and entertained, at his Castle of Kenelworth: and that sundry pleasaunt and Poeticall inventions were there expressed, aswell in verse as in prose. All which have been sundrie tymes demaunded for, aswell at my handes, as also of other Printors, for that in deede, all studious and well disposed yong Gentlemen and others, were desyrous to be partakers of these pleasures by a profitable publication: I thought meete to trye by all meanes possible if I might recover the true Copies of the same, to gratifye all suche as had requyred them at my handes, or might here-after bee styrred with the lyke desire. (W. W. Greg, *A Bibliography of the English Printed Drama to the Restoration* (4 vols., London, 1939–62), IV, pp. 168–9).

The Misfortunes of Arthur, printed by Robert Robinson (1587), *RSTC* 13921, goes into even greater length to describe the authenticity of its contents and their precise relationship to the 'CERTAIN DE- / v[ic]es and shewes presented to / her MAJESTIES by the Gentlemen of / Grayes-Inne at her Highness Court in / Greenewich, the twenty eighth day of Februarie in the thirtieth yeare of her / MAJESTIES most happy / Raigne'. The text was, it claims, 'The Misfortunes of Arthur . . . reduced into Tragicall notes by THOMAS HUGHES, on of the societie of Grayes-Inne, And here set downe as it past from under his handes and as it was presented, excepting certaine wordes and lines, where some of the Actors either helped their memories by brief omission: or fitted their acting by some alteration, with a note in the ende of such speaches as were penned by others in lue of some of these hereafter following.'

94 For *Damon and Pithias,* see above, p. 25 note 78. Jones' Epistle 'To the Gentlemen Readers: and others that take pleasure in reading Histories', expressed a hope that the two parts of *Tamburlaine* wil be now no lesse acceptable unto you to read after your serious affaires and studies, than they have bene (lately) delightfull for many of you to see, when the same were shewed in London upon stages: I have (purposely) omitted and left out some fond and frivolous jestures, digressing (and in my poore opinion) far unmeet for the matter, which I thought, might seeme more tedious unto the wise, than any way els to be regarded, though (happly) they have bene of some vaine co[n]ceited fondlings greatly gaped at, what times they were shewed upon the stage in their graced deformities: nevertheless now, to be mixtured in print with such matter of worth, it wuld proove a great disgrace to so honorable and stately a history. *RSTC* 17425 (1590), sig. Aii.

A never writer, to an ever reader. Newes. / Eternal reader, you have here a new play, never stal'd with the stage, never clapper-clawd with the palmes of the vulger, and yet passing full of the palme comicall.[95]

But, on the evidence of the surviving texts, playing companies rather than readers were the intended market for the majority of playbooks. What, then, was the relationship between those companies and the printed texts? Where did the play texts originate, and by what process or processes did they end up in the hands, first of the printer and then of the acting troupes?

There has been a general assumption among scholars, based upon extrapolation from later playhouse practice, that the earlier professional touring companies produced their own scripts initially in manuscript, and then toured with them until either the material became stale or financial constraints upon the company prompted them to sell the texts to a printer for publication, at which point their usefulness to their original creators would cease. Sir Edmund Chambers made the point most succinctly:

It is generally supposed, and I think with justice, that the acting companies did not find it altogether to their advantage to have their plays printed . . . Presumably the danger was not so much that readers would not become spectators, as that [rival] companies might buy the plays and act them . . . the marked fluctuation in the output of [printed] plays in different years is capable of explanation on the theory that, so long as the companies were prospering, they kept a tight hold on their 'books' and only let them pass into the hands of the publishers when adversity broke them up, or when they had a special need to raise funds.[96]

Similarly G. E. Bentley argued that companies released texts for printing only once the period of their usefulness as performance scripts was over, or the company was otherwise constrained to realise its prime material assets.[97] But there is very little evidence that this was in fact the case in the pre-playhouse period. Those texts which were printed show little sign of an extensive playing history of the sort which later play-house playbooks suggest, nor do they show evidence of adaptation to the

[95] William Shakespeare, *The Historie of Troylus and Cresseid* (1609), *RSTC* 22331, printed by G. Eld for R. Bonion and H. Walley, sig. Aii. The point being made here may be that the play had never been played before a 'vulgar' audience (i.e. in the open-air playhouses), rather than that it had not been played at all. I am grateful to Professor Kate McLuskie for this suggestion.

[96] Chambers, *Elizabethan Stage*, III, pp. 183–4. See also Bradley, *Text to Performance*, p. 89.

[97] G. E. Bentley, *The Professions of Dramatist and Player in Shakespeare's Time, 1590–1642* (Princeton, 1986), pp. 264–6.

multiplicity of playing spaces and conditions likely to be encountered on tour. Rather, they read as records of single performances in a known location with familiar conditions for which the script has been especially tailored, records which found their way into the hands of the printer, sometimes soon after their initial production, sometimes only after a number of years had passed.[98] In most cases these texts were then printed still bearing the signs of that initial performance in their dialogue and stage directions, with only limited efforts (such as the occasional concessions to the limited resources of other companies noted earlier) having been made to prune away such idiosyncratic details in the interests of providing a functional touring text. The printed text of *Godly Queene Hester*, for example, still calls for the use of a 'chapel' to sing while the Queen prays; for 'manye maidens' to line up for the virtue-and-beauty parade from which Hester is chosen by King Assewerus; and for a large number of male attendants to accompany Aman. All of these would have been readily available in the courtly milieu of its original 1529 production, but would present distinct difficulties for the rather more limited resources of a touring company. *Damon and Pithias* similarly calls confidently for 'Regalles' to accompany Pithias' song, *The Marriage of Wit and Science* requires the services of a consort of viols, and *Cambises* directs actors to appear with lute and cittern, instruments familiar to a hall audience but rare and largely inaudible in an outdoor context.

Scholars have remarked upon the overwhelming preponderance of

---

[98] The delay involved in the appearance of some plays can be accounted for by a number of factors other than a lengthy intervening touring history. In some cases the text may only have been obtained by the printer on or after the author's death, as may have been the case with Skelton's *Magnyfycence*, published by Rastell probably within a year of the poet's death in 1529. In other cases the plays may have either remained with their author, or found their way into a variety of hands: amateur actors, the members of household companies, scholars, friends of the maker, the patron, or his household staff, any of whom might have held on to them for a period before deciding, or being persuaded, to pass them on to a printer for publication. For an account of the difficulties that might be involved in prising a playbook from the hands of its owner (and creator?), see the anonymous letter in MS Arundel 249, printed in Nelson, *School Book*, p. xxix. Having been asked to acquire 'interludes or comedies in English or the vulgar tongue', the correspondent writes that 'I have finally acquired them by the greatest exertion of effort. For, up to now, they are rare and the owners of them are so inconstant that to exert or strive with respect to such may justly be denominated or called almost a vain effort. For which reason, in order that I might satisfy your wishes, I have with assiduous exertion of effort and with flattering words, finally softened the soul of an owner. I have acquired it on condition that as soon as you transcribe the original you will then return it to me so that I may restore it to the owner'. As the letter suggests, however, it was not so much a fear of the loss of copyright that the owner feared as the possible loss or damage to the unique text.

moral plays and interludes among those plays printed in the pre-
playhouse period.[99] What has attracted less notice is the necessary
corollary that almost all of these plays were intended for a single physical
environment. Of the 81 playbooks printed before 1580 which survive in
whole or part, at least 47 show evidence of having been written for
performance in a great hall, whether at court, in the houses of the
nobility or higher clergy, or in the Inns of Court, university colleges, or
the merchants halls of the capital.[100] The printing of playbooks thus
represents part of a wider cultural trend of considerable significance,
whereby texts designed and produced for one, elite, reading or interpretative community, were refashioned, however rudimentarily, for circulation within a far wider, less elevated one.[101] After John Rastell's initial
attempts to produce playbooks for a self-selecting audience among
scholars and household servants (significantly in the prestigious folio
format rather than the cheaper quarto which became the norm for later
editions), printers began to aim more definitively at something ap-
proaching a mass market with cheaply produced large print-run texts.
The wider implications of this fact will be explored in more detail below.

Once the text came into the hands of a printer, did the playwright
maintain any control over its printing or the form in which it appeared?
Elizabeth Eisenstein helpfully draws attention to the greater possibilities
for involvement in the production process available to an author of the
Renaissance period. A scientific pioneer like Kepler, living close to the
printshop in which each part of the process was conducted, would have
found it far easier to follow his work from initial draft to printed and
bound text than would his modern academic successor, alienated from
the processes of publication by greater professional specialisation and
the economic and geographical exigencies of the international book
trade.[102] But it is not necessary to assume that, because some authors
chose for their own reasons to keep a close eye upon the preparation of
their work for publication, that all did. Indeed, those men responsible
for the creation of the majority of playbooks were also churchmen,
teachers, court or government servants: writing was only one part of
their professional duties, and may even have been only a spare-time
activity. Such men may not have had the time to follow their work's

---

[99] See, for example, Lancashire, *Topography*, p. xxv; Bradley, *Text to Performance*, p. 17; Chambers,
Elizabethan Stage, II, pp. 178–80; Tydeman, 'Introduction', pp. 1–36.
[100] See appendix II, below.
[101] See R. Chartier, *The Order of Books*, trans. Lydia G. Cochrane (Oxford, 1994), p. 8.
[102] Eisenstein, *The Printing Press as an Agent of Change* I, p. 18.

journey into print with any care, even if they had the inclination. N. Bohmberg of Cologne's edition of 'H. N.' [Hendrik Niclas's] *The Interlude of Minds* (?1574), declares that it was set forth by the author 'and by him newly perused and amended'.[103] But the fact that this point was felt worthy of advertisement on the title page suggests that it was not a common occurrence at this time.[104] Individual circumstances might permit a writer to develop a closer relationship with his printer or printers. The close familial ties between John Heywood and the Rastells clearly gave him privileged access to the presses which produced his interludes, and, as chapter 3 will argue, the result was a close collaboration between author and printer in what amounted to a publishing campaign designed to intervene directly in the religious and political controversies of the 1530s.[105]

Such co-operation seems, however, to have been the exception rather than the rule. Other texts suggest quite clearly that no authorial oversight was involved in the printing process. No author would, presumably, have allowed the mangled text of *St John The Evangelist* to emerge from the presses in the state that it did, with several sections of dialogue obviously missing. And no-one with experience of the play in production would have allowed the printer to produce a text of John Phillip's *Patient and Meeke Grissell* with a doubling plan requiring one actor to be in two places at once.[106] In all likelihood, play scripts took a variety of routes to the printshop, but, once they were there, their fate was determined largely by the printer himself (albeit, the evidence suggests that printers only rarely made major changes to the texts they received). In some cases authors may have sold manuscripts to a printer directly, although no contracts or records of such sales are extant. Alternatively actors or others into whose hands the books fell may have chosen to cash in on their good fortune independently. It was alleged that the first edition of *Gorboduc*, printed by William Griffiths in *c.* 1565, was produced from a text obtained 'at some yongmans hand that lacked a little money and much discretion'. This in turn, it was claimed, prompted the authors to make a cleaner text available to a second printer, John Daye,

---

[103] *RSTC* 18550, sig. Ai.
[104] What other evidence there is of authorial involvement concerns scholarly translations, whose creators would have had greater interest in ensuring that the finished work did not contain errors which could compromise their careers and reputations, and had greater freedom to indulge that interest. See Jasper Heywood's preface to his translation of Seneca's *Thyestes*, which describes Richard Tottel's alleged failure to implement corrections to the proofs of his earlier translation of the *Troas*, and the 'Letter to the Reader' preceding George Whetstone's *Promos and Cassandra* (1578). [105] See below, pp. 100–16.
[106] *St John The Evangelist*, see, for example, sigs. Aiii and Bi; *Patient and Meeke Grissell*, sig. Ai.

to rectify the damage done to the play, and to their reputations, by the 'corrupt' earlier edition.[107]

The degree to which a printed playbook presents itself as a script for performance: the extensiveness and clarity of the stage directions, the presence and utility of notes for entrances and exits, and the guidance or lack of it regarding stage business and the use of props, all of this probably owed far more to the condition of the manuscript as it left the hands of the playwright and passed to its original players, than to any work done subsequently in the printshop.

Did the printed text then find its way directly into the repertoires of touring companies? It is initially alarming to note that there is no direct evidence of professional companies touring with printed playbooks in this period. No printed texts survive with annotations demonstrably indicating their use by itinerant players, and no records of performances, where the title of the works performed are listed, mention a play which we know had been printed before that time. This is not, however surprising. Players' copies of a script would have been in frequent and heavy use, and so prone to loss or disintegration.[108] They may well also have been more readily disposed of as surplus to requirements once their contents had become stale or old-fashioned than copies in private libraries. Thus it would be wise not to conclude from the lack of surviving evidence that printed playbooks did not find their way into the hands of touring players. As so few texts survive from this period at all, whatever their provenance, such reasoning would leave us with the nonsensical conclusion that these texts were not purchased by anyone in the sixteenth century.

Who brought printed playbooks? The external evidence

If we turn from speculation about who might have purchased play texts to hard evidence about those who actually did so, the picture alters considerably. The majority of the surviving evidence of ownership of printed playbooks concerns copies in private libraries. But here again the evidence needs careful reading. By no means every gentleman with an interest in secular literature and catholic tastes owned playbooks. Sir

---

[107] Thomas Sackville and Thomas Norton, *Ferrex and Porrex*, printed by John Daye (1570–1), sig. A ii.
[108] Kate Harris, 'Patrons, Buyers, and Owners: The Evidence for Ownership and the Role of Book Owners in Book Production and the Book Trade', in Griffiths and Pearsall, eds., *Book Production*, pp. 163–99; A. I. Doyle, 'The Manuscripts', in D. Lawton, ed., *Middle English Alliterative Poetry and its Literary Background* (Cambridge, 1982), pp. 88–100, p. 88.

William More of Loseley, Surrey, for example, possessed no dramatic texts among the approximately 120 volumes which he kept in his closet in 1556.[109] An MP with a house in Blackfriars, who played host to Queen Elizabeth and her court on three occasions, More was presumably familiar with interludes and their role in court culture. Yet he did not purchase any scripts. Why not? Perhaps the low prestige of drama among literary forms was a factor. More, a polyglot scholar with a strong interest in the law, did have a marked preponderance of 'serious' literature in his collection.[110] But he also possessed a fair number of more popular texts, including Skelton's 'Works' (valued at 4d); John Heywood's prose satire *The Spider and The Fly*, hot from the press and selling at 20d; a manuscript book of proverbs, a book of songs and two prognostications (each of the latter valued at 4d).[111]

The limited availability of playbooks may also have been a curb upon widespread ownership. Not all booksellers, and especially those in the provinces, seem to have stocked them.[112] But again, this should not have been a problem for Sir William, who had ready access to the centre of the English book trade in London. Evidently more than just a healthy interest in entertaining and improving literature in the vernacular was necessary if a reader was to invest in playbooks.

One such motivating factor may well have been strong local antiquarian interest, or pride in the traditions and culture of one's regional community. The unique copy of Rastell's printing of Medwall's *Fulgens and Lucrece*, for example, was once in the collection of Myles Blomefylde (1525–1603), a physician and alchemist of Bury St Edmunds and Chelmsford. Also in his library were manuscript copies of three of the four Digby Plays: *The Conversion of St Paul*, *Mary Magdalene*, and *Wisdom* (this

---

[109] John Evans, 'Extracts from the Private Account Book of Sir William More of Loseley Surrey in the Time of Queen Mary and Queen Elizabeth', *Archaeologia*, 36 (1856), pp. 284–310.

[110] Alongside the works in Latin, Italian, and French, and the collections of statutes, he had a copy of the works of Chaucer, Lydgate's *Fall of Princes* and *Troy Book*, and John Gower's *Confessio Amantis* (ibid., p. 290).

[111] Ibid., p. 290. Interestingly, More also had a marked interest in works dealing with the duties, virtues, and vices of women. He possessed copies of Sir Thomas Elyot's *Defence of Good Women* (which he valued at 2d); 'The Instruction of Women' (1d); 'The Commentary of Ladies' (1d); 'For the Apparell of Women' (1d); 'A Boke of Women' (1d); and, perhaps slightly more fancifully, 'The Mayden's Dreame' (1d). Perhaps revealingly his wife possessed only five books in her closet, four books of prayers and 'a boke de *ptu* mulieris' (ibid., p. 293).

[112] A partial inventory of the stock of Neville Mores, a York stationer, drawn up during April or May 1538, lists 126 volumes valued at a total of £3 3s 10d, but a copy of the Latin text of Terence's *Sex Commoediarum Opus*, *RSTC* 23885, 23894, or 23899–901, is the only dramatic text mentioned. D. M. Palliser and D. G. Selwyn, 'The Stock of a York Stationer, 1538', *The Library*, 5.27 (1972), pp. 207–19.

last being only a partial text), all three of which were probably performed in Chelmsford in the 1560s.[113]

Plays with a clear political or religious agenda might also be purchased by readers with no obvious interest in acting or play-going. Thus John Dudley, Lord Lisle (the son of John Dudley, the Edwardian Duke of Northumberland), had in his library 'a tragidie in englishe of the unjust supremacie of the bisshope of rome', 'a play called Old Custom', and copies of Heywood's *A Play of Love*, *The Four PP*, and *The Play of The Weather*.[114] Similarly, Sir John Harrington possessed at least 135 playbooks in his library in 1610, including most of the overtly political dramas of the previous forty-five years, such as *Lusty Juventus* (*c.* 1565), *Ferrex and Porrex*, and *Cambises* (*c.* 1569).[115]

There were, of course, individuals with an enthusiasm for drama who collected plays to read, or to produce for private performance at home. But this type of collecting seems to have been a product of the later Elizabethan and Jacobean period, after theatre-going had become an established part of elite metropolitan culture. Sir Edward Dering of Surrenden, Kent (1594–1644) bought over 225 playbooks and visited the theatre on numerous occasions between 1619 and 1624. At least some of these plays were purchased with a view towards acting (or at least reading among friends?), as, for example, the '6 play bookes of Band, Ruff and Cuff' (*A Merie Dialogue Betweene Band, Cuffe, and Ruff* (1615)[116]) bought for a shilling on 4 December 1623, or the three copies of Beaumont and Fletcher's *The Woman Hater* (1607),[117] bought for two shillings on 16 March 1624.[118] This kind of private dramatic connoisseurship needs to be distinguished from involvement in amateur or semi-professional drama on a community level of the sort which was

[113]   Donald C. Baker and J. L. Murphy, 'The Books of Myles Blomefylde', *The Library* 5.31 (1976), pp. 377–85; J. Coldewey, 'Early Essex Drama', Ph.D. thesis, University of Colorado, 1972. The plays are so named because they were part of a collection once owned by Sir Kenelm Digby. Whether there was a local connection behind the ownership of *Fulgens* is unclear.

[114]   Greg, *Bibliography* IV, p. 1651. The inventory was compiled at various points between 1545 and 1550–1. Greg's assertion that the list could not refer to Northumberland's own collection does not fully exclude the possibility. The editions of Heywood's plays, listed as quartos, seem to have been Middleton's printings of 1544, rather than the Rastell 1533/4 editions, which were all in folio. Lisle's possession of these texts would seem to reflect Heywood's general reputation as a critic of clerical abuses, rather than the more subtle conservative agenda of these particular plays described below in chapter 3. A similar interest may well have motivated the unknown individual who, in 1553/4, visited a bookseller and purchased a 'boke of sarvis in 8to', 'i boke of sarvis in Latane in fornell', and 'i playe of love', for a total of 3s 4d (i.e. a Book of Common Prayer in English (*RSTC* 16279), one in Latin (*RSTC* 16423), and Rastell's 1534 printing of Heywood's *A Play of Love* (*RSTC* 13303)).

[115]   BL MS Add. 27632, f. 43, calendared in Greg, *Bibliography*, IV, pp. 1306ff.   [116]   *RSTC* 1355.

[117]   *RSTC* 1692.   [118]   Leedham-Green and Fehrenbach, eds., *Private Libraries*, I, pp. 255 and 257.

common throughout the period and probably relied exclusively upon manuscript texts. In the latter category one might list the activities of Bennett Kynge, a surgeon of Bungay, Suffolk, who was clearly involved in the production of plays in his locality. At his death in 1595 the inventory of his goods listed a box of 'playeboockes' in his chamber, along with one of 'dysgysings for players' and £1 worth of 'gam[e] players aparell' in a chest in his kitchen.[119] Similar bequests survive from the earlier period. The will of John Slade of Blunham, Bedfordshire, registered 13 December 1528, bequeathed 'all my play bookes and garmentes with all the properties and o[ther] thynges belongyng to the saim' to his parish church, while in 1538 Sir Robert Cooke, vicar of Haughley, Suffolk, left all his 'play boks' to his brother.[120]

SOME CONCLUSIONS AND FURTHER QUESTIONS

Books in (and out of) print

There are, then, certain practical assumptions which one can make on the basis of the available information. Playbooks were probably produced in print runs of about 500–600 copies, and sold at a few pence per copy, by printers whose chief aim was to make a commercial profit from their sale. Except in particular cases, such as that of the Rastells and John Heywood (where the playwright and printer(s) were well known to each other and probably collaborated closely), or that of Norton and Sackville (whose approach to John Daye concerning the printing of a second edition of *Gorboduc* was probably prompted, as the printer claimed, by a desire to issue a text over which they had some control, to counter the influence of an earlier, pirated edition), these printers probably had little direct contact with the original authors of the texts they published. And the latter probably had little influence over the nature of the published text, hence perhaps the frequent failure even to name an author in many printed playbooks.

By the mid-sixteenth century these playbooks were being produced in an increasingly sophisticated form, seemingly aimed primarily at a market among actors – principally those working in small companies,

---

[119] David Dymond, 'Three Entertainers from Tudor Suffolk', *Records of Early English Drama Newsletter*, 16 (1991), pp. 2–5. The churchwarden's accounts of Holy Trinity, Bungay record a number of payments to Kynge for 'serving' a local interlude and a parish 'game' in 1567 and 1568. For the economics of local playing generally, see Coldewey, 'Some Economic Aspects of the Late Medieval Drama', in Briscoe and Coldewey, *Contexts*, pp. 20–40.

[120] See Lancashire, *Topography*, p. 172.

for whom economy of casting was an important consideration. The early experiments of John Rastell and others with texts designed specifically for household production, calling for large casts, allowing for the incorporation of disguisings, or structured around the gaps in a meal, thus gave way to apparently more flexible texts adaptable to a wider range of playing conditions, and performable by a small number of versatile actors. Playbooks continued to be produced for other markets, chiefly for private readers who wished to buy 'hard copies' of performances that they had witnessed – or wished that they had witnessed. But the bulk of printed playbooks seems to have been aimed at buyers among the touring – or at least mobile – theatre companies.

This situation gives rise to an intriguing irony. For, although these texts designed for playing were increasingly advertised as flexible scripts for touring, the bulk of them actually originated, as we have seen, in the households of noblemen or churchmen, in schools, colleges, lawyers' or merchants' halls. Those printed playbooks which were taken on tour by the itinerant professional companies were thus, not examples of local acting practice and dramatic tradition, but records of performances in quite different social and cultural conditions, which had been crudely adapted as scripts for popular performance. And in most cases the traces of great hall performance remain evident in the printed texts. Those scholars who have searched among the printed playbooks for evidence of the living traditions of popular drama have, then, been looking in the wrong place. Almost by definition, the playbooks surviving in printed form are not the unmediated records of folk drama or community theatre, but posthumous descriptions of productions of high culture.

This may well account for the seeming indifference to printed drama shown by the authorities at this time (see appendix I, below). When actors performed plays from printed scripts they were already producing politically circumscribed material, not because the texts had been subject to rigorous censorship, but because the plays were created for very different cultural and political circumstances. They were politically sensitive only in the conditions for which they were produced, in performance in a known household, college, or Inn of Court, before a familiar, or at least predictable audience, for whom the playwright had tailored his didactic, moral, and political material. Heywood's dramatic appeals for political and religious accommodation, like Norton and Sackville's counsel that the queen should marry Robert Dudley rather than King Eric of Sweden, had their greatest political significance only in the context of the royal court and the Inner Temple, at the time when these were live issues. Their political strategies were subtle, oblique, and deliberately encoded in ways which would make full sense only to those particular audiences at those particular times. Allowing such plays to circulate beyond the court, whether as texts for reading or scripts for playing, carried little threat to the crown – or to anyone. Other audiences, other readers, did not possess the specific knowledge, or the specific cultural experience, to decode them.[121]

Thus far we have asked questions of those plays which were published in printed form. How and why were they printed, and to what effect? It is as illuminating to approach the issue from the opposite angle and ask why certain other plays were not printed at all in this period. Why, for example, were the great civic play cycles of Chester, York, Wakefield, and elsewhere not printed at any point during their long and hugely successful performance history? After the late 1530s, as their didactic content became increasingly out of step with the official doctrine of the Church of England, one can appreciate printers' lack of enthusiasm for them. But what of the pre-Reformation period, or the reign of Mary Tudor, when they were entirely acceptable doctrinally? What prevented printers from attempting to publish play texts which had a proven record of attracting crowds in their thousands year in and year out in the great cities of the north of England? The answers to this question are suggestive of wider issues concerning the printing of drama.

One factor militating against the printing of these plays was purely geographical. These were very much regional works, produced well away from the centre of the publishing industry and the book trade in London. From a printer's point of view they may well have appeared simply too parochial, and too bound to their original civic conditions of production, to attract purchasers in the capital and the south-east. Similarly the distances involved may well have prevented the owners of the texts and their potential printers becoming aware of each other's possible interest in a publishing venture. More plausibly, however, the owners of the working texts may well have had cogent and powerful reasons for not considering publication. The public nature of the texts was itself a powerful argument against the likelihood of printing. These were communally owned, public plays, and this was an intrinsic part of their resonance and significance. It is unlikely that the city fathers of York or Chester would have wanted their text printed for wider con-

---

[121] For studies of these plays, see below pp. 76–116 and 196–221. For a somewhat different discussion of the reception of household plays by aristocratic and more popular audiences, see Westfall, *Patrons and Performance*, p. 164.

sumption, out of both a possessive civic pride, and a sense that such works as their Corpus Christi play had no business – and no purpose – being printed, whether for private reading or playing elsewhere. They may well have thought that, if people wanted to become better acquainted with the York play, then the way to do so would be to witness it in its proper context: in performance in the streets of York. It is entirely likely, too, that such people would have thought print too vulgar a medium for plays with such a sacralising function as the Corpus Christi play.[122]

The very fluidity of the performance text, reflected in the emendations, alterations, additions, and excisions from a document like the York 'Register' or the 'Regynal' which lies behind the surviving Chester manuscripts also militates against a desire to establish a printed version. Printing, by its very nature fixes a text, and renders it incapable of the kind of spontaneous, organic growth which was inherent to the civic cycles. Where the process does allow for change, it is of a kind not directly associated with performance, exposing a work to mutation through printers' errors, the incorporation of variant readings, or 'cleaner' copy texts.[123] Those civic guardians of the play texts who had it in their power to make them available for publication would have known that any printed version could never definitively represent the play in any meaningful sense, as the form in which it was performed this year would not be identical to that in which it was performed last year, or in which it would be performed next year. Thus the cycle texts remained in manuscript.[124]

---

[122] A. S. G. Edwards and Carole M. Meale, 'The Marketing of Printed Books in Late Medieval England', *The Library*, 6.5 (1993), pp. 95–124, p. 95.

[123] For the dynamic and unstable nature of the York cycle, see R. Beadle, 'The York Cycle', in Beadle, ed., *Companion*, pp. 85–108, especially pp. 90–8, and R. Beadle, *The York Plays* (London, 1982), especially pp. 10–13.

[124] This question raises the more general issue of how we should read the transition of play texts from manuscript to printed book as a cultural process. Should it be interpreted as a movement from elite to popular auspices, or vice versa? Does a play, once it is printed move from the hands of the communities which produced it in the public arena of performance to the hands of a privileged class of educated, wealthy purchasers who thereafter enjoy it in the private realm of solitary reading? Or should the move be seen rather as an egalitarian process, in which texts which had hitherto been the private property of local communities were opened up to wider reading and spectating communities in the public sphere? In the case of the York cycle, it was probably both. The precise degree of civic control over the contents of the York cycle remains unclear, but the nature of the alterations to the Register suggest that the monitoring of the performance, by the servant of the Common Clerk, was an attempt to record the details of the production accurately rather than – as has often been assumed – an act of political censorship and regulation. Where the performance varied from the script in the Register, it seems to have been the latter that was amended, not the acted version. For the most recent rejection of the idea of political censorship at work, see Beadle, 'York Cycle', p. 92. The authorities' retention of

Harold Love has argued, for a later period, that we should think of manuscripts, by and large, as 'the outcome of a discontinuous series of acts of publication in editions of one'.[125] But in the case of the great cycle play manuscripts – and especially those intimately associated with performance, as opposed to those second generation texts produced, as at Chester, for antiquarian purposes – this idea of 'acts of publication' does not seem to apply. In this sense, the York cycle was never 'published' at all, except in performance, until the nineteenth century.[126]

It might appear rather too obvious to observe that manuscript playbooks had a more immediate and intimate association with their creators and users than did their printed counterparts. But the nature of that association is not entirely self-explanatory, and an understanding of the variety of purposes for which manuscript playbooks were created helps us to understand more clearly the roles and functions of dramatic texts in the period. Significantly, none of the extant dramatic manuscripts from the pre-playhouse period seem to have been created solely to be sold for commercial gain, whether as scripts for playing or as reading matter. They were neither presentation texts, de-deluxe manuscripts for private sale, nor products of the bookshop: they were working documents, either notes of or towards performance or antiquarian productions, created to record local playing traditions for posterity.

Here again the great civic play cycles provide valuable – although far from the only – examples. At York, the great Register of the pageants provided an omnibus of the constituent parts of the cycle, through which the city each year symbolically reasserted its collective cognisance and ownership of the drama produced under its auspices. Sitting at the first playing station, the servant of the Common Clerk vicariously performed an act of reassurance on behalf of the city he served, figurat-

---

the Register – as far as we know the only text of the complete cycle of pageants – in their own hands was clearly a gesture of control – an investing of the city government with the sole right to oversee and legislate for the play and its performance. But it had popularising consequences. The York cycle remained as a consequence realisable only in performance within the city, for which it needed the participation of the local population, both as performers and producers and as the audiences that validated and necessitated the performance. It thus remained an irreducibly 'popular' production.

[125] Harold Love, *Scribal Production in Seventeenth Century England* (Oxford, 1993), p. 44.

[126] As Ian Doyle has observed, fresh authorship (and we might add manuscript compilation) 'itself does not entail *publication*, which must comprise at least, communication (not necessarily by the author) of a piece to another person or persons, with leave (perhaps tacit) or motivation to pass it on to others; which *may* be preceded or followed by the growth of knowledge of its existence and interest, causing a desire for further copies, consequent reproduction and gradual dissemination to a greater or lesser extent'. A. I. Doyle, 'Publication by Members of the Religious Orders', Griffiths and Pearsall, eds., *Book Production*, pp. 109–23, p. 110.

ively accommodating the potentially fractious energies of the individual guilds within the corporate endeavour by ensuring that whatever was happening on or around each of the pageant wagons was faithfully absorbed into the textual record of the play as a whole. Through careful attention to detail and the occasional piece of creative accounting, the sum of the parts was always made to tally with the whole.

At Chester the impulse seems to have been rather different, a result, in part at least, of the later date of the surviving manuscripts, which come from after the cycle's performance history rather than, as at York, its creative peak.[127] Here the individual initiatives by which scholars copied the play texts into a single comprehensive document seem to have been part of a wider attempt to secure the plays in the regional cultural memory: a process which had national as well as merely local echoes. In London, John Stowe was to perform a similar feat in his prose *Survey*, remapping the lineaments of a past catholic culture on to the streets, buildings, and civic spaces of later Elizabethan London.[128] In Chester, Edward Gregory, of Bunbry, and George Bellin, scribe, antiquarian, and member of Chester's Ironmongers' Company, charted with equal care the contours of their city's cycle play, noting not only the doctrinally and politically correct forms and observations of the post-Reformation revisions, but also the earlier traces of 'superstitious' catholic practice – ensuring that no detail of Chester's dramatic topography was lost from record.

The N-Town and Townely plays seem to have been born out of a different impulse again, having been copied from disparate source texts to produce a composite didactic cycle suitable for playing or reading for doctrinal instruction.[129] In none of these cases were the texts produced for simple commercial gain. These were acts of individual spiritual and cultural negotiation in which print had no part to play. The profits which accrued to the York, Chester, and N-Town scribes were not primarily financial.

If we turn directly to the interlude drama, the questions become more pointed still. Why were some playbooks printed but other, superficially very similar ones, not? Why, for example, was *Everyman* printed, but

---

[127] The cycle was last performed in 1575, all the surviving manuscripts of the complete cycle date from 1591 or later. For the creation of the Chester text, see R. M. Lumiansky and David Mills, *The Chester Mystery Cycle: Essays and Documents* (Chapel Hill, 1983); and David Mills, 'The Chester Cycle', in Beadle, ed., *Companion*, pp. 109–33.

[128] John Stowe, *Survey of London*, ed. Valerie Pearl (London, 1987).

[129] Peter Meredith, 'The Towneley Cycle', and Alan J. Fletcher, 'The N-Town Plays' in Beadle, ed., *Companion*, pp. 134–62 and 163–88 respectively.

Mankind not? Why were Bale's *God's Promises*, *The Temptation of Our Lord*, and *The Three Laws* printed, but his *King Johan* not? Initially the choice seems merely capricious, but on closer examination a revealing tendency is suggested.

When considering the differing fates of *Everyman* and *Mankind*, it seems clear that the particularity of the latter may have been its downfall (or its saving grace, depending upon one's viewpoint). Far from being the archetypal touring play which some scholars have suggested, a flexible script which might be played anywhere (calling for a small number of players and still fewer props), the text is in fact remarkably specific in its requirements and in identifying its intended audience.[130] Unlike the universalising *Everyman*, *Mankind* addresses a relatively small constituency in East Anglia, reflecting and playing upon their local concerns and prejudices. Particularity is, as I will argue in what follows, a feature of all the interludes, owing to the nature of their initial audiences and the playwrights' relationship with them. But the particularity of *Mankind*, like that of the York and Chester cycles and the interlude *Wisdom* only to a more marked degree, is of a special kind.[131] It names local individuals and places directly, and much of its humour and moral potency relies on the precise significance of those names in the culture which its audience inhabits. Outside that local community many sections of the play (unlike the printed interludes) would not only have had less efficacy, they would have made little sense. Hence it is no surprise that its producers were not interested in making it available to a wider audience.

A rather different dynamic determined the fortunes of Bale's dramatic texts. His religious cycle, of which *God's Promises*, *The Temptation*, and *The Three Laws* are a part, was an evangelical project, an attempt to take what he saw as protestant religious truth to a popular audience. Print therefore offered a prime medium for the circulation of the text – indeed the only one immediately available to an author exiled abroad

---

[130] For comments on the play's flexibility, see John C. Coldewey, 'The Non-Cycle Plays and the East Anglian Tradition', in Beadle, ed., *Companion*, pp. 189–210, p. 195, and Pamela M. King, 'Morality Plays', ibid., pp. 240–64, p. 247. For an attempt to reconstruct the play's staging in an inn-yard, see William Tydemann, *English Medieval Theatre, 1400–1500* (London, 1986), pp. 31–54. For the suggestion that it might have originated in a chapel setting, see Westfall, *Patrons and Performance*, pp. 54–5.

[131] For *Wisdom*, see M. Eccles, *The Macro Plays*, EETS, os 262 (Oxford, 1969), pp. 113–52. For the motives which may have prompted the monk Thomas Hyngham to copy out the texts of *Mankind* and *Wisdom* for his own use, see R. Beadle, 'Monk Thomas Hyngham's Hand in the Macro Manuscript', in Richard Beadle and A. J. Piper, eds., *New Science Out of Old Books* (Aldershot, 1995), pp. 315–41.

during the Marian period. When the opportunity arose, Bale supplemented textual circulation with individual performances to seek the widest possible audiences, such as the infamously unsuccessful staging in Kilkenny on Mary's Coronation Day. *King Johan*, on the other hand, was a work of far more pointed and particular concern. As I have argued elsewhere, it was an intervention in the debate conducted at court and in its environs concerning the direction of Henry VIII's religious policy, and relied, not upon the broad brush of anti-catholic polemic, but upon nuances.[132] It reflected and commended the general flow of royal policy, but sought to fine tune the detail in a more radical direction. As such it had a very specific intended audience: the circle of clerics and ministers influential in the debates over policy, and ultimately Henry VIII himself. Beyond this audience, the play could not do what its author wished it to. Hence Bale did not release the play to the printers, but kept it about him, ready for revival when the circumstances dictated, as seems to have happened at the accession of Elizabeth I, when the text was revised and updated in the author's own hand for a further courtly performance, where it set its sights once more upon pushing a royal audience in the direction of further radical reformation.

The dramatic consequences of printing

Much critical attention (the majority of it operating in the field defined by D. F. McKenzie as 'the Sociology of Texts') has been focused upon the cultural impact of printed books upon the societies within which they circulated. The same questions can profitably be asked of the 'interpretative communities' formed by the reception of drama – but the answers one might offer to them differ profoundly depending upon whether one takes the short- or the long-term view. In the short term, during the first 100 years of the print trade in England, the circulation of printed playbooks probably affected such things hardly at all. For the vast majority of the rural population or the citizens of towns such as York or Chester, with their own indigenous playing traditions, the experience of drama in this period probably remained predominately aural and visual, and in most cases based ultimately upon manuscript rather than printed texts. The printing of plays in London, on a relatively small scale at least until the 1560s, and their very limited availability in provincial bookshops, probably made no difference at all in many localities to all but a tiny minority of literate individuals.

---

[132] See Walker, *Plays of Persuasion*, pp. 169–221.

The surviving evidence is not specific enough to allow clear and exclusive divisions to be drawn, but it is possible to sketch out two distinct forms of dramatic activity. One was largely orally transmitted or manuscript based and localised, confined to a single town, village, or rural area in which local people produced 'their' plays (which may have remained the same or similar for many years or even generations) for performance, chiefly in their own communities or on a limited tour of the region to raise funds for a parochial project or celebrate a festive occasion. The other form was predominantly professional, chiefly textual, and increasingly employed printed playbooks. Its practitioners were more wide-ranging in their ambit, as itinerant companies took a changing repertoire of plays (the majority of which were probably not written within the company) on a tour of urban centres, manor houses, and other lay and religious households. These two forms intersected at certain points, most obviously when the amateur companies took their plays to local houses or a nearby town which might also be stops on the itineraries of the professional players, but any resulting cross-fertilisation between amateur practice and the professional repertoire seems to have been limited.

In terms of many of the most vital and powerful traditions of early English drama, then, the printing of playbooks was, in the short term at least, only a marginal phenomenon. Metropolitan printers published the play texts which found their way to the capital, chiefly through performance, whether at court, in the Inns of Court, the guild-halls, schools, or the London residences of magnates or the higher clergy, or, less frequently through texts being brought to the capital by scholars from the universities. The dramatic texts of the great northern urban centres, like those of the rural touring routes of East Anglia and elsewhere, seem, for the reasons suggested above, never to have entered their ambit.

The longer term significance of the printing of playbooks was considerably more important. Evolutionary theories of drama are generally unhelpful if they seek to trace and celebrate only those forms of playing which were to survive and develop into something regarded as a superior form – invariably in this context, the drama of Shakespeare and his contemporaries.[133] Drama in sixteenth-century England was a diverse and pluralistic field, giving rise to many forms of activity. This book is about only one of them: the interlude drama played at court and in the households of nobles and the social elite. As one among many

---

[133] For criticism of the evolutionary approach, seen as 'heavily biased in favour of moral interludes', see Lancashire, *Topography*, p. xxvi.

forms of drama, the interludes have no automatic claim upon scholarly interest over and above the other forms prevalent at the time. Yet neither should they be shunned in some form of inverted snobbery simply because they were a privileged form with significant implications for later drama. Rather there is merit in tracing the influence of the form upon its successors, and charting the role of print in the development of that influence, for through the capricious, commercially inspired activities of the early printers, the forms and nature of dramatic activity in Britain and beyond were influenced profoundly.

Like its impact upon the history of the English language as a whole, the introduction of print into the field of drama production resulted in the dominance of one regional form and its establishment as Standard English Drama thereafter. Print formalised and valorised the traditions of great hall drama, and created from them the standard form of 'theatre', which was in turn taken up and magnified by the commercial playhouses, made definitive in the work of Shakespeare and his contemporaries, and passed on thereafter as the mainstream mode of dramatic presentation down to the modern period.

The fact that the vast majority of plays printed in the sixteenth century were the product of the great hall tradition established as natural the notion that the default environment for play production was a walled space, bounded on three or four sides by an audience, with a wall at one end providing the single plane through which entrances and exits would occur. The precise relationship between the screens of the great hall and the rear wall and the tiring house of the commercial London theatres is a much debated subject. But the general debt of the playhouse architecture to the lineaments of the Tudor hall is undoubted. When they looked to existing models for their inspiration, the first Tudor playhouses naturally drew from the hall environment for which the bulk of the existing dramatic repertoire was created, and from the booth stage which reproduced its chief features in their most portable form. Whether consciously or unconsciously, they rejected alternative models like the Cornish or East Anglian 'rounds', with their opportunities for multiple points of entry and exit, and multiple foci of action in place and scaffold productions (structures which otherwise, with their own more direct echoes of the classical amphitheatre, might well have commended themselves to the Renaissance entrepreneur in search of inspiration).[134] In the Tudor playhouse, entrances would be from the

---

[134] For the Cornish drama, see, for example, E. Norris, *The Ancient Cornish Drama* (2 vols., London, 1859), and Brian O. Murdoch, 'The Cornish Medieval Drama', in Beadle, ed., *Companion*, pp.

rear of the stage, through a series of two, or possibly three doors, over which a structure echoing the configuration and function of the great hall musicians' gallery was constructed.[135] The action would take place in a single space, towards which the attention of the audience would be continually directed. It was for this space that Renaissance playwrights wrote the plays which would define the physical forms of English theatres thereafter. From the playhouse stage it was only a modest development which brought about the shift to the proscenium arch, and the classic alignment of stage and audience which has only been tinkered with in subsequent centuries.[136]

As David Bradley has noted, the basic configuration of the playhouse stage was a flexible and suggestive one, amenable to a variety of illusionistic presentational techniques and certainly not hostile to the procedures of classical drama, based upon the unities of time, place, and action. Yet, other than in such conscious neoclassical experiments as Jonson's comedies or oddities like Thomas Nabbes' *Covent Garden* (1633), such techniques were never developed by the playhouse companies, who instead relied upon a non-illusionistic, diverse form of performance, in which the unities were treated with cavalier disregard, and 'time and place flowed with imaginative freedom at the bidding of the spoken word'.[137] Bradley concludes that this failure to exploit the full potential of the playing space they inhabited was a consequence of the conservative organisation and structure of the playhouse companies. But it might more plausibly be seen as a legacy of great hall playing practice, carried through the medium of the printed texts into the methodology of the later professional playwrights. The acting space of the great hall – the 'place' (or *platea*) referred to in numerous stage directions and pieces of dialogue – was, as the following chapter will demonstrate, in physical terms at least, an undifferentiated space. Its

---

211–39. For an alternative reading of playhouse development, stressing the innovative and 'highly integrated design' of the first professional theatre, the Red Lion, Stepney, see John Orrell, *The Human Stage: English Theatre Design, 1567–1640* (Cambridge, 1988), especially pp. 21–9. See also, Gurr, *Shakespearean Stage*, pp. 115–73.

[135] For the powerful influence of the playhouse stage doors upon the shape and structure of Renaissance drama, see Bradley, *Text to Performance*, pp. 25–8.

[136] The distinctiveness of the 'thrust stage' of the early playhouses is now having to be rethought in the light of the evidence of the Globe excavations, which suggest that a rather more lozenge shaped, less intrusive stage was the norm. Consequently the alignment of stage to audience in the playhouses may well have had more in common with the later proscenium arch stages than was once thought. For the contrary view, that the introduction of the proscenium arch was 'an event as revolutionary in the history of drama as the invention of printing has been in the history of literature', see Wickham, *Early English Stages* (3 vols. in 4, London, 1959–63) I, pp. xxix–xxx, and Lancashire, 'History', p. 282.   [137] Bradley, *Text to Performance*, p. 21.

'stage' was created solely through the actions of the players, sometimes quite literally as they cleared the way and marked out a space for themselves and their colleagues as they entered the hall.[138] It was transformed, incompletely and temporarily, from the domestic space of the presiding noble patron, college, or merchant company, into the imaginary world of ancient Rome or the virtual realms of abstract morality, purely by the words of the players.[139] At other times it remained simply 'here', the great hall itself, into which the actors walked and brought their play, for the entertainment and edification of the diners.[140] In such an environment there was no need, and literally no room, for the unities: no scenic or temporal fixed points beyond the here and now upon which they could seek a purchase. The legacy of this practice, as Sir Philip Sidney was to lament, was a dramaturgy in which even the most classically educated of playwrights felt free to play fast and loose with the unities, having Asia on one half of the stage and Africa on the other, 'and so many other under-kingdoms, that the player, when he cometh in, must ever begin with telling where he is, or else the tale will not be conceived'.[141]

Similarly the dramatic forms which the later Elizabethan and Jacobean playwrights borrowed and adapted were those which had been produced in that great hall context and naturalised in the medium of print. The old canard of whether or not Shakespeare had witnessed the drama of the Corpus Christi cycle at Coventry in his youth is thus largely irrelevant for the great bulk of his work as a dramatist.[142] It was not from the drama of the regional, civic, or rural communities that he drew his models. The plays which Shakespeare read, and witnessed on the London stages as he learned and developed his craft, were the printed texts produced by the third and fourth generations of London printers, texts taken directly from the elite drama of the nation's great households. It is to those texts and to those households which one needs to look if one is to understand the nature and development of the most obviously political form of English drama, and the roles it performed in early Renaissance culture.

---

[138] See below, p. 58–9.   [139] See, for example, 'To the orchard let us go!' (*Susanna*, sig. Civ).

[140] See, for example, *King Darius*, sig. Aii(v), where the vice, Iniquity, tells the audience, 'I come gladly to talk with you here', Ignorance's question 'Is there anyone here in this place[?]' in Wager's *The Longer Thou Livest*, line 245; or *Patient and Meeke Grissel* (Aii(v)), where Gautier, although notionally in his own palace, welcomes the Messenger 'hartely . . . to this place'.

[141] Sir Philip Sidney, *An Apology For Poetry*, ed. Geoffrey Shepherd (Manchester, 1973), p. 134.

[142] For an invaluable analysis of Shakespeare's influences, see E. Jones, *The Origins of Shakespeare* (Oxford, 1977), *passim*.

CHAPTER 2

Household drama and the art of good counsel

AUTHORITY AND NEGOTIATION IN THE TUDOR INTERLUDE

The scholarly consensus on Renaissance drama would seem to be that dramatic texts, if they engaged with political issues at all, could do so only in highly circumscribed ways.[1] New Historicists and Cultural Materialists alike seem to concur that such plays might only either confront political authority directly or else connive in its operation. The only differences of opinion have been over whether a given text can be rescued for a 'progressive' tradition of subversive oppositional writing, or must be consigned among those plays which tacitly or overtly endorsed the status quo, representing power in ways which reinforced the spectacle of royal or aristocratic hegemony.[2] What a study of the interludes considered in this volume suggests is that this is far too limited a model to employ. Contrary to the thrust of recent writing, one of the most striking features of the interlude drama was its curiously ambivalent attitude towards royal and noble authority: its frequently cavalier attitude to the sensibilities of its patrons.

The great hall plays of the early Tudor period do not fit neatly into this subversive-or-supportive antithesis. They appear both to have en-

[1] A version of this chapter was delivered at the Literature and History conference at the University of Reading in July 1992. I am very grateful for the helpful comments offered on that occasion by Professor James Shapiro of Columbia University and Professor Sheila Lindenbaum of Indiana University, and by Professor Kevin Sharpe of the University of Southampton and Dr Elaine M. Treharne of the University of Leicester, who kindly read the typescript in draft form.

[2] See, for example, S. Greenblatt, 'Invisible Bullets: Renaissance Authority and its Subversion', in J. Dollimore and A. Sinfield, eds., *Political Shakespeare* (Manchester, 1985), pp. 18–47; and J. Dollimore, 'Shakespeare, Cultural Materialism and New Historicism', ibid., pp. 2–17; M. Bristol, *Theater and Carnival: Plebeian Culture and the Structure of Authority in Renaissance England* (London, 1985); R. Dutton, 'Shakespeare's Roman Carnival', *English Literary History*, 54 (1987), pp. 31–44; L. Tennenhouse, *Power on Display: The Politics of Shakespeare's Genres* (London, 1986); S. Mullaney, *The Place of the Stage* (Chicago, 1988). For a valuable corrective view, see Kevin Sharpe, *Criticism and Compliment: The Politics of Literature in the England of Charles I* (Cambridge, 1987). These issues will be dealt with in greater detail in what follows.

dorsed established political authority by praising and applauding their patrons *and* to have engaged with it in complex and genuine negotiations over the use of that authority (and the power it wielded) for concrete political ends. They could also confront their royal and noble audiences with often quite brutal criticisms, seemingly with impunity. How might such apparent ambivalence be understood? And how was such criticism possible in an elite culture in which, we are told, deference was the keystone of public conduct, and the system of patronage upon which every writer relied was overseen by Tudor monarchs and noble patrons whose mercurial temperaments and capacity to take offence were legendary? To take specific examples, how could John Skelton present in *Magnyfycence* a king, clearly modelled in part upon Henry VIII, yet fallen into every manner of self-indulgent vice, and still have hoped for preferment from his sovereign? How could the author of *Godly Queene Hester*, writing for a courtly audience, have portrayed a king blinded by flattery into persecuting his own subjects, or the author of *Hick Scorner* have criticised the financially motivated marital adventures of his patron, the Duke of Suffolk, yet have expected their plays to be favourably received by those very people?[3] An attempt to answer these disarmingly simple questions can in fact illuminate much of the politics of Henrician dramatic literature and of early Tudor culture more generally. But what is essential to note is that, in each case, the play was the product of very particular circumstances and conditions of production, performance, and reception: circumstances which any model of dramatic politics needs to take into account if it is to have validity.

The simple answer to the questions advanced above, that one was allowed to say things in works of literature which were taboo in other forms of communication, merely postpones answering the question: *why* was this so? As we shall see in the chapters which follow, part of the answer may be related to the specific personalities and situations of those involved. But there was also a wider cultural principle at work, a product of the way drama was perceived to function – and specifically the way it was perceived to function in the special circumstances of the royal or noble household. For it is crucial to recognise just how completely household drama – and especially the Tudor interlude – was a product of the households which produced it, both of the physical space in which it was performed, and of what we might term the moral economy of household life and the special relationships between patron,

---

[3] See Greg Walker, *Plays of Persuasion* (Cambridge, 1991), *passim*.

clients, and artists to which that economy gave rise. What follows will consider each of these issues in turn.

DRAMA IN THE GREAT HALL

As Stephen Orgel has pointed out, the presence and position of the sovereign, watching the play, formed a major part of the cultural significance of the Stuart masque and the French royal ballet.[4] But this principle was neither a seventeenth-century innovation nor solely a product of a more sophisticated French court. The point was certainly made all the more evident by the development of perspective scenery, which provided material proof that the drama was focused primarily upon and for the privileged play-goers in the immediate royal entourage.[5] But the same dynamic, privileged relationship between principal spectator and dramatic spectacle was also at work in the household drama, in the interludes of Tudor England and, if Sir David Lindsay's original draft of *Ane Satyre of the Thrie Estaitis* is at all representative, of James V's Scotland too.[6]

With household drama we are looking, not at theatre in the round, but at theatre specifically in the rectangular: drama conceived for and enacted within the precise circumstances of the royal or noble great hall. It was presented within the particular boundaries formed by the standing spectators, servants, and attendants at the screens end of the hall (around the exits leading to the kitchens and departments of the household below stairs), the royal or noble party dining in state at the opposite, dais end of the hall, and the increasingly privileged diners seated between the two (on the benches ranged on either side of the playing area).[7] In purely practical terms, then, the royal or noble party, and the patron in particular, enjoyed a privileged viewpoint. Whereas the best seat at a modern soccer game might be high in the stands, level

---

[4] Stephen Orgel, 'The Royal Theatre and the Role of the King', in Guy Fitch Lytle and Stephen Orgel, eds., *Patronage in the Renaissance* (Princeton, 1981), pp. 261–73, p. 265. See also Stephen Orgel, *The Illusion of Power* (London, 1975), pp. 9–16.

[5] The principle was no doubt also more evident in a court society in which, even under Francis I, the level of ceremonial focus upon every action of the royal body was far more pronounced than in its English equivalent.

[6] Greg Walker, 'Sir David Lindsay's *Ane Satyre of the Thrie Estaitis* and the Politics of Reformation', *Scottish Literary Journal*, 16 (1989), pp. 5–17; and see pp. 117–62, below.

[7] This model obviously assumes that the location of the dais was at the end of the hall opposite the screens, as it was in most large halls. In smaller halls, in which the dais may have been placed on one side of the hall rather than at the end, a different dynamic would have applied. The contrast between privileged and unprivileged spectators and the space they occupied would, however, remain. See T. W. Craik, *The Tudor Interlude* (Leicester, 1958), p. 9.

with the centre spot, at a Tudor interlude, the best position from which to view the whole action in comfort was on the dais. From there, there would be no need to jostle to keep one's place, or to stretch and crane the neck to keep up with the fast-moving action. The action took place directly ahead. And that action was itself predominantly directed towards the dais.

A number of the surviving play texts of the period show a sophisticated awareness of the practical and social distinctions within this variegated audience (a point too readily overlooked, perhaps, by those who argue for the novelty of the social diversity of an Elizabethan playhouse audience).[8] Characters might draw moral distinctions between the different types of spectator, as in *The World and the Child*, where the vice figure, Folly, addresses himself to 'any man / That runneth in this rout' and 'all this meinie . . . / That standeth here about': clear references to the standing spectators at the screens end of the hall, while the virtuous Perseverance directs his prayers and benediction to 'all this similitude that seemly here sits': the elite diners on the benches.[9] The association of the (lower status) standing spectators with folly and evil is made most clearly by Nichol Newfangle, the vice in Fulwell's *Like Will to Like*, as the marginal direction and attendant dialogue make clear:

> *Here entreth Nichol Newfangle the Vice laughing, and [he] hath a knave of clubs in his hand which, as soon as he speaketh, he offereth unto one of the men or boys standing by.*

[8] For accounts which stress the diversity of the audiences drawn to the commercial playhouses, see A. Harbage, *Shakespeare's Audience* (New York, 1941); W. Cohen, *Drama of a Nation: Public Theatre in Renaissance England and Spain* (Ithaca, 1985), pp. 17–19; Jean E. Howard, *The Stage and Social Struggle in Early Modern England* (London, 1994), pp. 12–13; Martin Butler, *Theatre and Crisis, 1632–1642* (Cambridge, 1984), pp. 293–306; Andrew Gurr, *The Shakespearean Stage, 1574–1642* (3rd edition, Cambridge, 1992), pp. 215–22.

[9] *The World and The Child*, lines 522–3, 559–60 and 746, in J. S. Farmer, ed., *Six Anonymous Plays*, English Drama Society (London, 1905), pp. 178, 179 and 185. It is also notable that during their fight, while Folly seeks the support of the 'meinie' standing about, Mankind appeals to 'all this row', that is the more orderly, seated spectators, (lines 558–63). In Henry Medwall's *Fulgens and Lucrece*, written for performance in Cardinal Morton's household, and probably first produced *c.* 1497, one of the servants, 'A', draws attention to the allegedly limited attention span of the screens end audience, referring to the 'diverse toyes' 'mengled' with the more serious matter of the play to bring solace to the audience, especially 'The leste that stondyth here'; Alan H. Nelson, ed., *The Plays of Henry Medwall* (Cambridge, 1980), lines 43–4. It may also be that the well-known distinction in *Mankind*, between 'Ye sovereigns that sit and ye brethren that stand right up', indicates that this play, hitherto assumed to be the definitive example of the popular, travelling, interlude, was also written with a noble or gentle household audience in mind (*Mankind*, line 29, in M. Eccles, ed., *The Macro Plays*, EETS, o.s. 2 (London, 1969)). For similar boisterous identification of the vices with the standing spectators, see *Hick Scorner*, lines 297 and following, in I. Lancashire, ed., *Two Tudor Interludes* (Manchester, 1980); *Jack Juggler*, lines 858–67, in W. Tydeman, ed., *Four Tudor Comedies* (Harmondsworth, 1984); John Pickering's *Horestes* (1567), *RSTC* 19917, sig. Eii; and *Wealth and Health* (?1557), *RSTC* 14110, sig. Biii.

N. NEW: Ha, ha, ha, ha, now like unto like, it will be none other:
Stoop, gentle knave and take up your brother.　　　　(lines 37–8)

Equally, a character might single out the women among the audience for comment as in John Heywood's *Play of The Weather*, or in the same author's *The Four PP*, where a further social distinction is implied between the women on the benches and those on the dais.[10] But the solemn supplications, the petitions and the statements of political import, seem clearly to have been directed squarely at the dais. Thus, in the first version of *The Thrie Estaitis*, the Poor Man turned from the Player-King enthroned within the playing-space to address James V in the audience, so drawing the royal spectator into the drama for polemical and persuasive effect.

And where he [The Poor Man] was showed to the man that was king in the playe, he aunswered and said he was noe king. . . And then he loked to the king and said he was not the king of Scotland for there was another king in Scotland that hanged John Armstrang with his fellows, and Sym the Larde and many other moe [i.e. James himself].[11]

But beyond these specific allusions to more or less privileged spectators, the plays drew more widely upon the potential inherent in their symbolically rich arena. In the great hall of a Tudor palace or manor house the playing space itself, stretching from the crowded, disordered throng around the screens entrances, to the more decorous civility of the dais where the royal or noble party dined, attended by the sewers, carvers, cupbearers, and ushers provided both a microcosm of society itself and a moralised *mappa mundi*. At the dais, in the pageant of deference and order around the patron's board, stood a vision of Heaven presided over

---

[10] John Heywood, *The Play of The Weather*, line 249 and marginal note ('Here he poynteth to the women'), in R. Axton and P. Happé, eds., *The Plays of John Heywood* (Woodbridge, 1991): all references to Heywood's plays are to this edition. In *The Four PP*, Heywood has the Pedlar single out 'the women in this border' (line 1069), i.e. those elite female diners seated specifically along one of the rows of side-benches. See also, William Wager's *Enough is As Good as a Feast*, line 483, in W. Wager, *The Longer Thou Livest and Enough is As Good as a Feast*, ed. R. Mark Benbow (London, 1967); Ulpian Fulwell's *Like Will to Like* (?1568), *RSTC* 11473, lines 47–8 and 227; John Phillip's *Patient and Meeke Grissell* (c. 1569), sig. Fi(v); *The Trial of Treasure* (1576), in J. S. Farmer, ed., *Anonymous Plays* (London, 1906), p. 211; and Thomas Preston's *Cambises* (?1569), line 954, in J. Quincy Adams, ed., *Chief Pre-Shakespearean Dramas* (Cambridge, 1924). For the most striking and sexually explicit use of the motif, see Sir David Lindsay, *The Thrie Estaitis*, ed. R. Lyall (Edinburgh, 1989), lines 4438–41.

[11] BLMS Royal 7, Cxvi, ff. 137–9, letter from Sir William Eure to Thomas Cromwell of 26 January 1540, describing a performance of Lindsay's play at Linlithgow on the Feast of the Epiphany (see chapter 4, below). Note the lines directed towards Henry VIII, and specifically not to be spoken if he was not present, in Heywood's *Witty and Witless* (lines 675 and following). Meg Twycross, 'The Theatricality of Medieval English Plays', in R. Beadle, ed., *The Cambridge Companion to Medieval English Theatre* (Cambridge, 1994), p. 37–84, p. 77.

by God the Father in the form of the presiding patron.[12] Opposing it stood a tableau vivant of the sins of the world and a prefiguration of hell-mouth in the throng of disorderly, predominately male faces and bodies issuing from the entrances to the steam and heat of the kitchens, accompanied by the smells of oven, spit, broiling pans, spicery, buttery, and cellars of wine and ale.

An indication of the sights and smells of the kitchens can be gained from the injunction in the Eltham Ordinances of 1526 that,

for the better avoyding of corruption and all uncleanesse out of the King's house, whiche doth ingender danger of infection, and is very noisome and displeasant unto all the noblemen and others repairing unto the same; it is ordeyned, by the King's Highnesse, that the three master cookes of the kitchen shall have everie of them by way of reward yearly 20 marks, to the intent they shall provide and sufficiently furnish the said kitchens of such scolyons as shall go naked or in garments of such vilenesse as they now does, and have been accustomed to doe. . . that they of the said money may be found with honest and whole course garments, without such uncleannesse as may be the annoyance of those by whom they shall pass.[13]

Within this already inherently moralised social and cultural space, the movement of the actors was itself symbolically charged in the moral economies of the plays. Just as the outdoor arena designed for *The Castle of Perseverance*, bounded and overlooked by its scaffolds for God, The World, The Flesh, Belial, and Covetise, created a moralised space in which the assault upon the castle of Humanum Genus was mapped out, so the great hall offered similar potential for the moral 'differentiation of space'.[14] Characters falling into vice were lured towards the lower end of the hall, while their moral purification would logically have involved an opposite orientation towards the dais. When, for example, Mankind in *The World and The Child* is tempted into a fencing match with Folly,

---

[12] The iconographic effect would have been all the more powerful if the noble patron dined, in the royal style, under a canopied Cloth of State of the sort used in the household of the Fifth Earl of Northumberland. The Northumberland Household Books required 'Over the Highe dease in the Hall a selour of Arres, Counterfeat Arras or fyne Tapestry to be hongyn ovir the heed of the lorde and the laidy wheire they shall sit', Ian Lancashire, ed., 'Orders for Twelfth Day and Night *circa* 1515 in the Second Northumberland Household Book', *English Literary Renaissance*, 10 (1980), pp. 7–45, p. 30.

[13] Society of Antiquaries, *A Collection of Ordinances and Regulations Made for the Government of the Royal Household, Made in Divers Reigns* (London, 1790), p. 148.

[14] *The Castle of Perseverance*, in Eccles, *The Macro Plays*, EETS, 262; Walker, *Plays of Persuasion*, pp. 90–101. For a helpful exposition of the notion of the differentiation of acting space in a more general sense, see Richard Southern, 'The Technique of Play Presentation', in Norman Sanders, *et al.*, eds., *The Revels History of Drama in English, vol.* II *1500–1576* (London, 1980), pp. 71–99.

symbolising his corruption by the pleasures of the flesh, he is clearly drawn into the midst of the screens-enders, as Folly's appeals to the spectators for adjudication ('On all this meinie I will make me vouch / That standeth here about' (lines 559–60)) make clear.[15]

Entrances also paid due regard to the moral topography: to the identification of the screens end and its crowds with vice. Whereas virtuous or noble characters slipped unobtrusively into the acting space, or had a path cleared for them through the crowd around the screens by the other actors, the vices issued directly and noisily into and from the crowds of screens-enders voicing their arch variations of the popular 'make room!' device. They thereby both signalled their own low origins and didactically suggested the culpability of the mass of humanity around them by association. In so doing they frequently co-opted the standing spectators into the action through banter and comradely requests for the material essentials of a life of the flesh: light, meat, and, most significantly of all, alcohol.[16]

In *Magnyfycence*, Measure alerts the audience to the protagonist's readiness to enter with the declaration,

> Nowe pleaseth you a lytell whyle to stande:
> Me semeth Magnyfycence is comyng here at hand.   (lines 162–3)

thus clearing the way for a dignified royal entrance. Similarly, in Henry Medwall's *Fulgens and Lucrece*, 'B' draws the audience's attention to the impending arrival of the more stately characters of the main plot with the admonitory,

> Pees, no moo wordes, for now they come
> The plears [players] bene evyn here at hand.   (lines 188–9)

---

[15] See also Man's progress to the throne of Mundus and Worldly Affection in Henry Medwall's *Nature* (Alan H. Nelson, ed., *The Plays of Henry Medwall* (Woodbridge, 1980), pp. 191–261; all references to Medwall's plays are to this edition), which was surely placed towards the screens end of the hall so that the elite diners could have a clear view of its occupant. Magnyfycence's fall into adversity seems to enact the same movement. See *Magnyfycence*, line 2160 and following, in V. J. Scattergood, ed., *John Skelton: The Complete English Poems* (Harmondsworth, 1983).

[16] For light, see *Weather*, line 98; for alcohol, see *The World and the Child*, lines 647–52, where Folly seems to obtain a glass of beer from the crowd of spectators whom he addresses, and Lust's request that the pots be filled in *The Trial of Treasure* (Farmer, ed., *Anonymous Plays*, p. 207). In Medwall's *Nature*, one of the vices, Worldly Affection, calls for a stool from a 'pyld knave' in the audience (Nelson, ed., *Plays*, line 518). See also *King Darius* (in Farmer, ed., *Anonymous Plays*, p. 46), where Iniquity offers to buy a stool from the spectators on which Charity might sit; *Lusty Juventus*, line 57, where the hero offers to 'go to game' with any man in the audience; *Wealth and Health*, sig. Biii, where Shrewd Wit similarly offers to play mumchance 'for a grote or twaine' with any 'yonkers' in the crowd; and *Horestes*, sig. Eii, where Revenge, thwarted by the reconciliation of the kings, seeks employment from members of the audience.

Thus the screens-end crowd would be encouraged to make way for such figures, leaving them untouched – or at least relatively so – and so free of association with the culpable 'lower end' of the hall audience. [17]

By contrast, the vices continually draw attention to their interaction, and their boisterous physical association, with these symbolic representatives of the mass of base humanity. Pride, the vice figure in Medwall's *Nature*, is noisily outraged at the lack of deference shown him by the standing spectators as he pushes his way into the place, and so draws ample attention to his relationship with them.

> Who dwelleth here? Will no man speke?
> Is there no fole nor hody peke?
> Now by the bell, yt were almys to breke
> Some of these knaves brows!
> A gentylman comys in at the dorys
> That all hys dayes hath worn gylt sporys,
> And none of thys knaves nor cutted horys
> Byddys hym welcome to [the] house.
>
> Wote ye not how great a lord I am,
> Of how noble progeny I cam?
> My fader a knyght, my moder called madame,
> Myne auncesters great estatys . . .　　　　　(I, lines 723–34)[18]

17　See also John Rastell's *The Nature of The Four Elements*, line 144, in R. Axton, ed., *Three Rastell Plays* (Cambridge, 1979). It is also conceivable that, for the most spectacular entrances, an actor or actors may have been led into the hall by a yeoman waiter with a torch, as the disguisers were during the Percy household revels, for which see Lancashire, 'Orders for Twelfth Day', pp. 34–5. For other dignified entrances, see *King Darius* (in Farmer, ed., *Anonymous Plays*, p. 62), where the aptly named Preparation clears the way for Darius and his court; *Cambises*, line 122, where Counsel clears the way for Sisamnese's entrance with a cry of 'Behold, I see him now agresse and enter into place'; and *Impatient Poverty*, (1560) *RSTC* 14112.5, lines 978–9, where the Summoner makes room for Poverty to do penance about the place with a candle (L. Tennenhouse, ed., *The Tudor Interludes 'Nice Wanton' and 'Impatient Poverty'* (New York, 1984)). A nice mixture of the two topoi of dignified and undignified entrance is provided in *Horestes*, where Provision enters with the classic, comic 'make room!' device, making way for the noble characters who follow: 'Make roume and gyve place, stand back there a fore, / For all my speakinge, you presse still more. / Gyve rome I saye quickeley, and make no dalyaunce. / It is not now tyme, to make aney taryaunce: / The Kinges here do com, therefore give way.' (sigs. Div and v). A marginal direction makes explicit the action to follow: 'Enter Idumius & Provision comming wt his cap in his hand afore him & making way'. See Craik, *Tudor Interlude*, p. 20.

18　A similar arch indignation is shown by the goddess Fortune in Wager's *The Longer Thou Livest*: 'No God's mercy? no reverence? no honour? / No cap off? no knee bowed? no homage? / Who am I? Is there no more good manners?' (lines 1038–40); by Wealth in *Wealth and Health*: 'Why is there no curtesy, now I am come[?] / I trowe that all the people be dume / Or els so god helpe me and halydum / They were almost a sleepe.' (sig. Aii); and by Hypocrisy on the Cardinal's behalf in Nathaniel Woods' *The Conflict of Conscience* (1581), 4.1.

Yet he cannot resist pointing out his fashionable clothes and accessories for those same spectators' approval, thereby marking his association with them and theirs with him. Merry Report has similar difficulties in entering and exiting the place in John Heywood's *Play of The Weather*, with equally predictable results:

> let me go by ye.
> Thynke ye I may stand thrustyng amonge you there [?](lines 178–80)

> Now syrs take hede for here cometh goddes servaunt
> Avaunt cartely keytyfs avaunt
> Why ye dronken horesons wyll yt not be?
> By your fayth have ye nother cap nor kne
> Not one of you that wyll make curtsy
> To me that am squayre for goddes precyous body . . . (lines 191–6)[19]

The vociferous refusal to identify with the standing spectators serves, of course, only to make his association with them clear. And elsewhere he and the other vices are only too keen to signal their companionship and complicity with these same standing spectators, calling one of the torchbearers 'brother', asking 'frendes a felyshyppe, let me go by ye', and even appealing to, 'all such standyng by / As favour my parte'.[20]

The household interludes, then, drew much of their rhetorical and symbolic richness from their relationship with their physical and cultural environment. So much is also true, no doubt, of other forms of drama. But the distinctive circumstances of the Tudor household created conditions for drama different in important respects from those which gave rise to the other major forms of Renaissance theatre. The contrast is instructive.

---

[19] For other uses of the 'Make Room!' topos and its variants, see *Nature of the Four Elements*, lines 416 and 555–6 and 1332–4, Heywood's *Johan Johan*, lines 243–57 and *A Play of Love*, line 176; *Magnyfycence*, lines 991–6; *Youth*, lines 40–1 ('Aback fellows and give me room, / Or I shall make you to avoid soon') and line 97; *Hick Scorner*, lines 646–9 and 718 ('Make Room, sirs, that I may break his pate'); *Fulgens and Lucrece*, 1.193–4; Thomas Engelend's *The Disobedient Child* (1567), p. 80 (where Satan uses the device) and p. 65 (where the Son, having chosen the life of self-indulgence over that of study, signals his new fallen status by leaving in the manner of the vices: 'Room, I say, room, let me be gone') (in J. S. Farmer, ed., *The Dramatic Writings of Richard Wever and Thomas Engelend* (London, 1905)); *St John The Evangelist* (c. 1550), Biii (v); *Cambises*, lines 126–7; Wager's *The Longer Thou Livest*, lines 636–43 (where Wrath enters with 'Make room! Stand back in the Devil's name! / Stand back, or I will lay the[e] by the face!'); *Common Conditions* (Farmer, ed., *Anonymous Plays*, p. 218). For perhaps the earliest and most obviously moralised use of the topos, see Satan's entrance in the York Smith's Pageant of *The Temptation of Christ*, 'Make rome belyve, and late me gang! / Who makis here all this thrang? / . . . For sithen the firste tyme that I fell / For my pride fro heven to hell, / Ever have I mustered me emell emonge mannekynde' (R. Beadle, ed., *The York Plays* (London, 1982), lines 1–2 and 7–10).

[20] *The Play of The Weather*, lines 98 and 176; *A Play of Love*, lines 412–23.

CENTRALITY AND LIBERTY: LOCATING THE STAGE

In *The Place of the Stage*, Stephen Mullaney has argued that it was the geographical, social, and political marginality of the Elizabethan commercial playhouses, their location beyond the reach of full civic jurisdiction and beyond the pale of sober, civil society in degenerate Bankside, which gave the theatre of Kyd, Marlowe, and Shakespeare its cultural potency.[21] The thesis is an initially seductive one. London's 'Liberties' were, he argues, 'a borderland whose legal parameters and privileges were open-ended and equivocally defined'. They were 'the suburbs of the urban world, forming an underworld officially recognised as lawless. . . and so could serve as privileged or exempt arenas where the anxieties and insecurities of life in a rigidly organised hierarchical society could be given relatively free reign'.[22] By siting themselves in these areas, the theatres thus appropriated the licence traditionally associated with the Liberties: 'Effectively banished from the city by increasingly strict regulations, popular drama translated the terms of its exile to its advantage'. 'While an integral part of Elizabethan culture, the stage was also set apart from that culture, displaced from it to a degree that would be crucial to the development of a new and ideologically mobile drama.'[23]

But, before one accepts too readily this association between cultural marginality and liberty, Bankside and ideological freedom, it is important to pause for thought. Were the Liberties, and Bankside in particular, really as notoriously – and practically – lawless as Mullaney insists? At his most extreme he presents them as more akin to a wasteland from science fiction than a recognisable suburb of the capital ('The licentious, dangerous, unclean, or polluted was cast out of the City, but was then maintained as such and even placed on public display . . . what London saw when it gazed out into the Liberties were things without a proper place in the communities, things that in a certain sense had already exceeded the limits of community.'[24]) But beyond this general exaggeration, there are a number of questionable procedures implicit in the model. Implicitly to equate all the Liberties, and thus all the playhouses, with the atypical conditions of Bankside, where stood many of the hospitals, prisons, and brothels of London, is itself questionable, particularly as over half of the popular commercial theatres were not situated there but to the north of the river. And the account given of Bankside is itself highly selective. Citing the authority of John Stow's *Survey of London*,

---

[21] Mullaney, *The Place of the Stage*, pp. 1–10 *et passim.*   [22] Ibid., p. 21.   [23] Ibid., pp. 23 and 30.
[24] Ibid., p. 21.

Mullaney describes a strange, nightmarish underworld of anarchy and corruption ('As we follow Stow around the City's perimeter, we encounter a heterogeneous collection of outcast things . . . sources of anxiety and dread, potentially unsettling or discomforting.'[25]) But this seems a curious reading of Stow's text. Far from reflecting a horror at the unsettling liminality of the Liberties, what the *Survey* describes as it takes its readers through Southwark and along the Thames-side is frequently a prosperous, and in many ways highly respectable suburb, well-integrated into the social and commercial economies of the City as a whole. Rather than dwell upon the lazar houses and brothels, Stow draws attention to the episcopal palaces, the court of justice, the five parish churches with their monumental memorials to the generations of noble and gentle benefactors who worshipped there, the royal mint, the former town houses of four wealthy abbots, the 'many fair inns for receipt of travellers' and many fair houses for gentlemen.[26] The differences of emphasis between Stow's reading of the suburbs and Mullaney's rereading are both general and particular. The latter makes much of the 'foreigners' graveyard' known as 'No Man's Land', offering this nickname as an apt description for the Liberties as a whole, repository for the nameless and placeless of the capital. Yet he neglects to reflect on Stow's further revelation that the original site of the graveyard was enclosed in 1348 and became the grounds of a chapel 'which is now enlarged and made a dwelling-house, and this burying plot is become a fair garden, retaining the old name of Pardon Churchyard'.[27] On closer inspection what is presented by Mullaney as exotic and horrific can appear rather more mundane and even homely.

And if Mullaney overstates the grotesque, carnivalesque lawlessness of the Liberties, he also underestimates the potential for social tensions elsewhere. By offering a binary opposition between a supposedly ordered society within London's walls and a lawless, ungovernable one beyond, he effectively elides the very real social stresses and strains to be found elsewhere in the City, and so overemphasises the importance of

---

[25] Ibid., p. 39.
[26] H. B. Wheatley, ed., *John Stow: The Survey of London* (London, 1987), pp. 361–7. Indeed, one of Stow's chief complaints about the suburbs, as Mullaney acknowledges, is the walling off of large areas of the Liberties to create pleasant gardens and summer houses for prosperous citizens. Ibid., pp. 381–2, Mullaney, *The Place of the Stage*, p. 46. Recent work on Southwark by historians has tended to confirm the view that it was more respectable than recent accounts suggest. See, for example, J. Boulton, *Neighbourhood and Society: a London Suburb in the Seventeenth Century* (Cambridge, 1987), especially p. 280 and following, which focus on the remarkably high degree of public piety exhibited by parishioners in the suburb. I am grateful to Dr G. W. Bernard for this reference.   [27] Stow, *Survey*, p. 384.

the theatres in generating and reflecting disorder. As recent work has shown, there were tensions and antagonisms between social groups within the City, and within its elite institutions, equally as significant as those between the City and its suburbs. If one were able to ask a Londoner of the 1590s what he or she thought the major threats to social stability were, they would have been likely to cite the incipient violence between apprentices and the servants of gentlemen, the armed clashes between the citizens and the Inns of Court over the latter's privileges and exemptions, or the disputes between the aldermen and local gentlemen over their respective contributions to the upkeep of the City. The uncertain cultural status of the public theatres may well have been fairly low on his or her list of anxieties.[28]

But of most immediate interest here is not the limitations of the general model, but the specific antithesis which Mullaney seeks to create between the playhouse drama and the other forms of theatre (including the interlude drama, which is our current concern) that preceded it. For Mullaney, this earlier stagecraft fitted 'comfortably into the gaps and seams of the social fabric: no matter how agonistic or inquisitive, it was fully circumscribed by the structures of authority and community.'[29] Only with the advent of the commercial theatres in the Liberties, it is asserted, did this comfortable symbiosis between drama and political authority break down. Unlike the temporary, contained misrule of the pre-playhouse drama, the stage in the Liberties was incontinent and uncontained.

A social and cultural distance was thus established when popular drama took liberties with its royal license and appropriated the Liberties of the City. In so doing it gained a different kind of license; a liberty that was at once moral, ideological, and topological: a freedom to experiment with a wide range of available perspectives on its own times.[30]

But, as what follows will argue, the stage did not have to relocate itself physically to the edges of society in order to gain such licence. Such thinking reflects the fashionable concentration upon the marginal as the seat of all that is interesting in cultural history far more than it does the realities of life in early modern England. In practice, the earlier interludes enjoyed a considerable freedom to explore political issues precisely

---

[28] See, for example, Ian Archer, 'The Nostalgia of John Stow', in David L. Smith, Richard Strier, and David Bevington, eds., *The Theatrical City: Culture, Theatre, and Politics in London, 1576–1649* (Cambridge, 1995), pp. 17–34, p. 20, and Ian Archer, *The Pursuit of Stability: Social Relations in Elizabethan London* (Cambridge, 1991).   [29] Mullaney, *The Place of the Stage*, p. 48.
[30] Ibid., p. 84.

because of their location within the great halls of the political elite. It was their very *centrality*, politically if not geographically, which created its own cultural power, as it brought into being a licensed, ludic space at the very heart of the political nation, in the royal household or the courts in miniature of the provincial nobility.[31]

Mullaney's further point that 'Elizabethan drama came into being only by dissociating itself from the community to which it owed its livelihood' again raises difficulties in the light of the close and necessary symbiosis between the commercial theatres and the communities of, often elite citizens which provided their income and livelihood.[32] Yet the notion is again useful, if only as it provides a contrast with the cultural dynamic apparent in the operation of household drama. For household drama, far from dissociating itself from its origins, vociferously asserted its stake in the communities which fostered it, claiming its place in the culture of the household, and with it, as we shall see, that opportunity to offer good counsel which was its licence to speak.

DRAMA AND THE HOUSEHOLD: GOOD COUNSEL AND ARTISTIC LICENCE

When the Tudor royal or noble household, the extended family of the lord, gathered together for signal occasions such as a formal banquet or feast accompanied by an interlude and other entertainment, it was a distinct cultural event, with its own rules, codes of practice, and, I would want to stress, theoretical justification. As Mark Girouard observes, such an occasion marked 'the supreme moment when the lord, his household and his guests feasted together, and demonstrated the strength and unity of the household and the wealth and generosity of its lord.'[33] More importantly still for our purposes, perhaps, it was also the occasion upon which the household most obviously presented itself, to itself as much as to outsiders, *as* a household; a single body with its own identity and purpose.

It is important to note that I am not primarily speaking here of the household as an administrative and political machine, still less of that sub-department of the court specifically called the *Household* (that is, the court 'below stairs', in contradistinction to the *Chamber*, the court 'above

---

[31] See Walker, *Plays of Persuasion, passim.*   [32] Mullaney, *The Place of the Stage*, p. 56.

[33] M. Girouard, *Life in the English Country House* (Harmondsworth, 1978), p. 34. See also M. Thompson, *The Medieval Hall: The Basis of Secular Domestic Life, 600–1600AD* (Aldershot, 1995), especially pp. 115 and 156.

stairs'). I am speaking of that body of men (and that they were predominantly men is easily forgotten) united by their membership of the king's
or a nobleman's affinity (in medieval terms his *familia*), not all of whom
necessarily held a specific household office, but all of whom were bound
to the patron by ties of friendship, kinship, service, or obligation more
immediate than simply those of subject to political overlord. And I am
interested less in what membership of that body meant in administrative
terms to an individual (did it bring with it *bouche* of court or livery, or
carry military obligations, etc.?), and more in what it meant in intellectual and cultural terms, and so what it means for an understanding of
great hall drama.

In the midst of his household the patron was in a real sense 'among
friends'. The gathering of his 'special friends', servants, and clients
existed somewhere between a public and a private occasion. As a public
affair it functioned, as Girouard notes, as a powerful demonstration of
the lord's magnificence, his capacity to summon, retain, and dominate a
body of men, many of whom were themselves rich and powerful patrons
in their own right. As a private occasion it was an assembly of those
individuals in whom the sovereign or magnate placed his supreme trust,
and a symbolic enactment of the reciprocal relationship between the
patron whose social and cultural function was to govern and provide for
the affinity, and the affinity whose purpose was to serve and advise the
patron.

In his household, then, the King or nobleman was in a unique
position to demonstrate his own power and wealth and to project his
own views.[34] But he was also uniquely exposed to counsel and advice.
For when, on such signal occasions as a public feast or visit to the chapel,
the patron played the role of the *pater familias* most obviously, so his
household men took on the role of his 'special friends' and counsellors
most obviously too. And each role presented both opportunities and
obligations, rights and responsibilities.

If there was one thing that the voluminous advice literature of the
Renaissance and late medieval period was clear about, it was the role
and responsibilities of those counsellors and 'special friends' who made
up the innermost circles of a prince or nobleman's retinue and household. Both Sir Thomas Elyot and Baldesar Castiglione agreed that the
goal and purpose of all their precepts for educating the perfect courtier
or inferior governor was to produce a man who could give good counsel

---

[34] See below, pp. 69–71.

to his prince or lord. For Castiglione, 'The end of the perfect courtier . . . is, by means of the accomplishments attributed to him . . . so to win for himself the mind and favour of the prince he serves that he can and always will tell him the truth about all he needs to know, without fear or risk of displeasing him.'[35] For Elyot 'the ende of all doctrine and studie' was, 'good counsayle, wherunto as unto the principall poynt, which Geometricians do call the Centre, all doctrines . . . do sende their effectes.'[36]

The model they are working from is a familiar one. Whereas the court of the tyrant was characterised by the dominance of flatterers, who pandered to his wishes, affirmed his every suggestion and kept silent at his abuses, the court of the wise ruler was characterised by the presence of such shrewd, upright counsellors, unafraid to speak out even if it should embarrass the monarch. Hence Castiglione has Ottaviano Fregoso advise the prince to choose from among his subjects, 'several of the noblest and wisest gentlemen whom he should always consult, and . . . he should give them free leave and authority to tell him their opinion on any subject without hesitation; and he should so behave towards them that everyone would realise he wanted to know the truth about everything and detested lies.'[37] But it is important to note the complexity of what is being said. As Fregoso's artful balancing of the private and public aspects of the issue reveals, the acceptance of good counsel was not just a moral or political duty for the governor, it was a public demonstration of his fitness to rule. Thus the prince not only privately offered those wise counsellors the opportunity to advise him, but publicly signalled ('to everyone') that he had done so. Part of the self-projection of the lord as a good ruler relied precisely upon promoting the image of a stable, well-ordered household in which good counsel was readily offered and readily heeded.[38]

The role of the scholar and artist as moral tutor, the close association between drama and religious instruction, the fool-like licence of the

---

[35] Baldesar Castiglione, *The Courtier*, ed. and trans. G. Bull (Harmondsworth, 1976), p. 284. For useful accounts of the politics of good counsel in the early modern period, see J. A. Guy, 'The Henrician Age', in J. G. A. Pocock, G. J. Schochet, and L. G. Schwoerer, eds., *The Varieties of British Political Thought, 1500–1800* (Cambridge, 1994), pp. 13–46; and J. A. Guy, 'The Rhetoric of Counsel in Early Modern England', in Dale Hoak, ed., *Tudor Political Culture* (Cambridge, 1995), pp. 292–310. See also Walker, *Plays of Persuasion*, pp. 51–9, and 'Setting a Good Example: Art, Politics, and Ideals in Early Tudor Court Culture', in G. Walker, *Persuasive Fictions: Faction, Faith, and Political Culture in the Reign of Henry VIII* (Aldershot, 1995), pp. 101–21.

[36] Sir Thomas Elyot, *The Boke Named The Governour* (London, 1907), p. 293. See also Lindsay's *The Thrie Estaitis*, lines 564–9.   [37] Castiglione, *The Courtier*, p. 306.

[38] See, for example, Elyot, *The Governour*, p. 119.

player to take liberties not permissible in more 'serious' forms of discourse; all contributed to the freedom of the playwright to address the failings of his patron in dramatic form. But underlying each of these and providing the ground rules upon which the politics of household performance and reception operated, was this notion of good counsel, and the relationship between good lordship and good service which it represented. Thus, the lord who wished to be seen as fulfilling the ideal not only sought out the truth from the wisest and fittest counsellors, but also let it be seen and recognised that he was doing so, that he was the sort of patron who sought such advice, even if that meant at times exposing himself to unwelcome admonition and criticism.

Good counsel and good lordship were two sides of the same coin. The patron anxious to augment his honour by projecting an image of the one, had thus to show evidence that he promoted and welcomed the other. Hence, he needed at key moments to grant the license to give free and if necessary harsh counsel to (some at least of) those about him. Chief among such moments were those at which the household was at its largest, gathered for the Holy Days of Christmas and Easter, festivals whose associations with spiritual renewal and penitential self-examination ideally suited such a purpose. That these occasions were also the main seasons for the performance of drama, a form with its own tradition of offering moral and spiritual instruction, gave the playwright all the qualifications to seek and fulfil the role of good counsellor.

Stephen Mullaney, as we have seen, places great emphasis upon the fact that the Elizabethan public theatres were set up in the 'Liberties', beyond the City walls.[39] But many of his conclusions have, if anything, greater relevance for household drama than for the commercial theatres. For the royal household and the provincial noble households were themselves in this sense 'liberties' (perhaps the most significant liberties of all in the Tudor period), paradoxically set, not beyond the reach, but under the very gaze of royal and aristocratic authority.

NEGOTIATING ROYAL AUTHORITY: STATECRAFT AND STAGECRAFT

The dictates of the ideal and the needs of practical politics complemented each other admirably in this respect for a number of Tudor dramatic patrons, most notably, perhaps, Henry VIII. The maintenance of his

---

[39] Mullaney, *The Place of The Stage*, pp. 42–4 *et passim*.

royal honour was a crucial factor in Henry's political calculations, and he knew how to utilise the notion of good counsel to that end. As I have argued elsewhere, he used it at crucial moments in the reign, such as the expulsion of the Minions in 1519 or the collapse of the Amicable Grant of 1525, as a means of escaping the consequences of political mistakes.[40] By accepting the criticisms or appeals of subjects as well-intentioned good counsel, and symbolically declaring his intention to reform himself in line with it, Henry cast himself as the hero of his own Morality drama, as the innocent who had been misled by the evil counsel of others, but who was now, thanks to the truth-telling of his newer and wiser advisers, able to see the folly of his earlier ways. Henry was never shy about admitting the mistakes he had made in the past, provided he could do so with honour intact, for, like Oliver in Shakespeare's *As You Like It*, he could claim

> 'Twas I. But 'tis not I. I do not shame
> To tell you what I was, since my conversion
> So sweetly tastes, being the thing I am. (4.3.134–6)[41]

Thus Henry might encourage good counsel in order both to advertise his virtue in general terms and to serve specific political ends. But this strategy was not without its risks, for it opened up the possibilities for political debate.[42]

Thomas Wyatt might, with good cause, lament that, in Henrician England, '*circa Regna tonat*' ('around the throne the thunder rolls').[43] But in the eye of that thunderstorm was a place of at least relative and conditional security, in which it was possible for the counsellor well-versed in the rules of the game and the mind of his sovereign, to articulate the dangerous utterance, to speak the otherwise unthinkable criticism. As what follows will suggest, a king like Henry VIII (or, as we shall see, James V) might employ political drama for his own ends at times, but he could not always ensure that the counsel it offered would be amenable to his own ends. Once the floodgates of counsel had been opened, the stream unleashed could not always be channelled in safe directions.

Chapter 3 of this book will provide an extensive demonstration of this principle in action in the work of John Heywood, who produced a number of interludes at the Henrician court which both appealed to the

---

[40] See Walker, *Plays of Persuasion*, pp. 231–4.   [41] *As You Like It*, Arden Edition (London, 1975).

[42] For a fuller examination of the possibilities for negotiation inherent in Henrician court culture, see Walker, *Persuasive Fictions*, pp. 14–23, 101–21 .

[43] R. A. Rebholz, ed., *Sir Thomas Wyatt: The Complete English Poems* (Harmondsworth, 1978), p. 155.

king in terms likely to gain his approval and offered him pointed counsel on questions of religious policy. Another example of the same process, this time from the Scottish court, will be studied in the fourth chapter, with its close study of Sir David Lindsay's interlude *Ane Satyre of the Thrie Estaitis*, played before James V at Linlithgow in 1540. Here again the performance of the play seems to have involved a subtle mediation and negotiation between the wishes of its royal patron and the playwright. As Thomas Bellenden, a religious reformer, told William Eure, Cromwell's agent in Scotland, the play was put on at the behest of the king and his reforming counsellors, and played before the king, queen, and councillors spiritual and temporal: 'and the hoole matier wherof concluded upon the Declaracion of the noughtines in Religion / the presumpcion of bishops, the collucion of the spiritual courts and the misusing of priests.'[44] At the end of the performance, James V made direct use of its impact upon his clerical guests to push for ecclesiastical reform.

After the said interlude was finished the King of Scots did call upon the Bishop of Glasgow . . . and diverse other bishops / exorting them to reform their factions and manners of living / saying that unless they did so he would send six of the proudest of them unto his uncle of England and as those were ordered so he would order all the rest that would not mend.[45]

Thus far, then, the play can be seen very much as court propaganda – an act of policy, directly contributing to James V's attempts to bully the church into self-renewal. But this is only part of the story. From what we know of the play, its seems to have been fashioned to urge the king to go beyond the sort of Erasmian reforms which he would readily countenance and which he referred to in his remarks to the Bishop of Glasgow, and take further steps towards a more evangelical religious settlement. Through the figure of the Poor Man (who brought James directly into the discursive space of the drama through the direct address to him cited earlier) the play sought to tie the king to a definition of political virtue centred upon the suppression of error: a reforming, correcting kingship some way beyond James' current political position and desires.

The play thus provides evidence of a complex negotiation between the desires of the king and those of the playwright and his reforming backers. James had his own immediate political needs met by the performance: he got his frightened bishops, his cue to chastise them, and

[44] BL MS Royal 7, Cxvi, ff. 137–9, printed in D. Hamer, ed., *The Works of Sir David Lindsay of the Mount* (4 vols., Edinburgh, 1936), II, pp. 2–6.   [45] Ibid., pp. 2–3.

a strong dramatic endorsement of his reforming stance played out before an audience of his chief political advisers and supporters: all this while he appeared to take on good counsel from Lindsay and thus demonstrated his own political virtue. But in doing so he also found himself publicly associated with a policy of continued reformation which he may have found rather less palatable, a situation which left him with less room to manoeuvre in both the domestic and the international arena than he would otherwise have desired. The licence of the household playwright might, then, prove more substantial than its granter bargained.

It is, consequently, important to read household drama in the light of the particular conditions created by this form of licence, as only by doing so can the many nuances of its function and reception be appreciated. There is a tendency among critics to see the drama of the early Tudor court or noble household as a much less politically and culturally sophisticated literary form than the poetry and prose produced in the same environments. Whereas scholars have been able to detect evidence of ideological subversion, self-reflexivity, and even outright criticism of established orthodoxies in the sonnet, pastoral poetry, or verse satire, household drama has generally been presented as a rather crude vehicle for royal and aristocratic views and values. Where scholars have considered the early Tudor interludes in political terms, the assumption has generally been that they fulfilled a nakedly propagandistic function, transmitting ideas in one direction only, from patron-producer to client-audience. The case has been argued most recently by Suzanne Westfall, who asserts that

> The themes of household revels communicated the attitudes of the patron, thus allowing the nobleman to educate and influence those within earshot in the ideas he considered proper. [Hence] . . . Theatre became, for the Tudor nobleman, a means to secure the loyalty of his domestic army, a loyalty that both reflected and reinforced the patron's political and economic power.[46]

The same reasoning, albeit in a more theorised form, is present in much of the New Historicist analysis and the cultural historiography of the Tudor court and of early modern elite societies generally. Stephen Greenblatt, for example, talks of patrons having 'the means to enforce their elaborate, theatrical, ceremonies of pride', Stephen Mullaney of 'orchestrated manifestations of power, studied representations of auth-

---

[46] Suzanne R. Westfall, *Patrons and Performance: Early Tudor Household Revels* (Oxford, 1990), pp. 207 and 11.

ority and community'.[47] But this aspect of household spectacle represents, as we have seen, only part of the equation governing its performance. Despite Mullaney's confidence, it is interesting to note just how *few* household plays (and even ceremonies) prove, on close inspection, to be simple demonstrations of power, majesty or policy, and how many reveal themselves to be moves or stages in a complex negotiation *for* power, or for influence over its use.[48]

Westfall's notion of a widening circle of dramatic indoctrination, from patron to household and thence to the wider community beyond ('Once a troupe received a script from its patron and performed it for his household, they set off to communicate it to other audiences', she argues[49]) consequently neglects perhaps the most crucial cultural functions of household drama. We know frustratingly little about the precise mechanics of dramatic commissioning and production in this period. Despite the comprehensive archival researches undertaken for the Records of Early English Drama project, which have added considerably to our knowledge of the staging, financing, and performance of early drama, precise information about the ways in which specific plays were selected for performance at court or in a noble household remains elusive. But what little is known suggests that troupes did not receive their scripts directly from their patrons in the way that Westfall's model suggests. The plays were generally the work of members of what might be termed the didactic and entertainment departments of the household: the Chapel staff, musicians, or tutors. Such individuals, and the functions they represented, existed at one remove from the patron himself, subject to his authority, but also licensed by the theory of the good counsellor to maintain at least the appearance of a sturdy independence from his every whim.

[47] Stephen Greenblatt, *Renaissance Self-Fashioning* (Chicago, 1980), p. 14; Mullaney, *The Place of the Stage*, p. 23. See also Guy Debord's observation that 'Spectacle is the existing order's uninterrupted discourse about itself . . . it is the diplomatic representation of hierarchic society to itself, where all other expression is banned' (G. Debord, *Society of the Spectacle* (Detroit, 1977), p. 23), a statement which similarly seems to underplay the negotiative aspects of much household spectacle in particular and the operation of aristocratic and royal patronage in general.

[48] Interestingly Mullaney does allow such a negotiative function to one form of pre-theatrical dramatic activity, the reception provided for Elizabeth I by the City on the eve of her coronation. Citing Clifford Geertz's formulation that 'The symbolism of the Progress was . . . admonitory and covenantal: the subjects warned, and the Queen promised', Mullaney observes that 'They [the City's pageant-makers] did not merely pay tribute to their royal audience; they also subjected her, as it were, to didactic and even prescriptive allegories on the arts of government. While they invited Elizabeth's response, they also shaped and qualified that response, eliciting vows of a peaceful, harmonious, and above all Protestant rule from the incipient queen.' Mullaney, *The Place of the Stage*, p. 11.

[49] Westfall, *Patrons*, p. 122. See also ibid., pp. 203 and 151.

Certainly, as we have seen in the case of Lindsay's *Satyre*, and as I have argued elsewhere, many household plays did in part represent their patron's attitudes and preoccupations.[50] But the latter were not reflected directly or uncritically in performance. The playwright may have taken his sovereign's known views and positions as the basis of his drama. But what is most interesting about such plays is not that they took up those views, but what they did with them having taken them up: how they deployed them and, quite literally, played upon them, to pursue their own persuasive ends.

When and if the plays were subsequently taken on tour, it would certainly be their general themes, the bold, primary colours, which would be their most obvious aspect to a non-household audience. But at the original performances, within the patron's household, the subtler textures and shadings, the variations upon the central themes, would be most evident.[51] These would be the means by which the primary persuasive purpose of the plays would be carried out. For it is vital to recall that the household was not simply a vehicle for lordly authority, a plastic medium for enacting its master's will. Household membership involved *reciprocal* bonds between lord and client, and aroused expectations from below as well as from above. In this respect the plays represent as much a message from the household playwright to the patron as from the patron to the gathered household. And there was something in the exchange for each of them.

On the level of morality, the playwright could offer sharp rebukes to his patron over his failings, and the patron, by receiving the rebuke well, could signal his desire for moral and spiritual reform. Hence, to return to our initial examples, the author of *Godly Queene Hester* could present a misguided and foolish king brought to eventual wisdom by the counsel of his queen, and point up the moral to his courtly audience:

> My lordes by this fygure ye may well se,
> The multitude hurte by the heades necligence,
> If to his pleasure so geven is he,
> That will no paine take nor dilligence,
> Who careth not for his cure ofte loseth his credence.   (lines 1162–6)

[50] Walker, *Plays of Persuasion*, pp. 223–36.
[51] As Meg Twycross has observed in a related context, 'There was no such thing as casual theatre-going: each of these plays was the centrepiece of a special occasion for a close-knit community . . . a great hall play was initially written for a household group who knew each other's quirks and foibles, and who were sensitive to status and ceremony. Both [the mystery plays and the great hall plays] were "community theatre" in the true sense.' Twycross, 'Theatricality', pp. 37–8.

Similarly Skelton could have Adversyte pointedly inform the ruined Magnyfycence and the audience that

> I stryke lordys of realmes and landys
> That rule not be [i.e. by] measure they have in thyr handys,
> That sadly rule not theyr howsholde men.   (lines 1938–40)

and have his royal protagonist, a clear type for Henry VIII, show evidence of most of the seven Deadly Sins in an Herodian display of boastful rage and lustful desire, and finally have him vomit in the midst of his Presence Chamber in a signal demonstration of his lack of kingly self-control. And the author of *Hick Scorner* could confront that master of the advantageous marriage, Charles Brandon, duke of Suffolk, with the complaint that

> Widows doth curse lords and gentlemen,
> For they constrain them to marry with their men,
> Yea, whether they will or no.
> Men marry for good[s], and that is damnable,
> Yca with old women that is fifty and beyond.
> The peril now no man dread will.
> All is not God's law that is used in land.   (lines 109–15)[52]

Thus the playwright, by speaking boldly, advertised his capacity to play the good counsellor and moral teacher, and the patron, by listening attentively, advertised his maturity and virtue.

On the level of practical politics, the playwright, as one aspect of his function, addressed the issues which concerned his patron, thus forwarding his general political ends.[53] But, as a licensed truth-teller, he was also free to do more than this. For, as Mullaney perceptively observes, licence is a slippery concept. Having begun life as an act of authority, it can quickly become a source of challenge, a transgression of the implied boundaries of permission.[54] And in recognising this fact we should avoid the trap of assuming that this criticism was inevitably circumscribed and neutralised by the courtly and aristocratic contexts in

---

[52] W. W. Greg, ed., *The New Enterlude of Godly Queene Hester* (Louvain, 1904); *Magnyfycence*, lines 1457–1514, 1560–9, 1726–34; *Hick Scorner* in Lancashire, *Two Tudor Interludes*. For a fuller treatment of these plays and themes, see Walker, *Plays of Persuasion*, pp. 37–132.

[53] See, for example, the powerful endorsement of the expulsion of the Minions offered in *Magnyfycence*, the condemnation of the newly disgraced Cardinal Wolsey and the support for royal government without favourites in *Hester* and Heywood's *Play of The Weather*, and the mockery of Charles Brandon's rival for the Suffolk dukedom, Richard De la Pole, in *Hick Scorner*. See Lancashire, *Two Tudor Interludes, passim*, and Walker, *Plays of Persuasion*, pp. 37–132.

[54] Mullaney, *The Place of the Stage*, p. 43.

which it was uttered. New Historicists, almost as an article of faith, have stressed the capacity of royal or noble authority to 'contain apparently subversive gestures, or even to produce them in order to contain them'.[55] They have argued that any criticism, however seemingly potent, is so contained within the structures of authority that it is co-opted even as it is being produced. Indeed, Stephen Greenblatt memorably suggests that the production of apparent subversion may well have been the very condition of royal or aristocratic power during the Renaissance.[56] But this notion of an untroubled and seamless operation of lordly authority does not allow for the real possibilities for political negotiation which the licence of household drama created. For the idea of good counsel opened up a discursive space, a 'liberty', in which some of the normal political prohibitions and inhibitions were relaxed. And perhaps the greatest advantage of this liberty for the playwright was the elasticity of its boundaries. Having claimed the freedom to offer good counsel, the playwright was then free to bring within its purview whatever issues he chose to define as relevant.

By defining the suppression of monastic houses and the limitation of episcopal independence as issues of good lordship, by implying that they were evidence of Cardinal Wolsey's alleged failure to be a good counsellor to his king and a good guardian of the Church, the author of *Godly Queene Hester* thus claimed the liberty to advise the sovereign on religious policy, an issue on which he otherwise had no obvious right to speak, and so could re-open a debate on that policy at the heart of the court. Similarly, by tendentiously redefining auricular confession as a threat to national security, John Bale claimed in *King Johan* a right to urge and co-opt Henry VIII to further radical religious reform in the guise of counsel supporting current foreign policy.[57] And, as we shall see in the following chapters, similar strategies were followed by John Heywood in his courtly interludes (in which pointed advice about religious policy is offered in the form of moral instruction) and by the dramatists of the mid-Tudor period and the reign of Elizabeth I, who raised and discussed crucial political questions with relative freedom through their careful employment of the role of dramatic good counsellor. In each instance the notion of counsel generally supportive of the patron's

[55] Louis A. Montrose, 'Professing the Renaissance: The Poetics and Politics of Culture', in H. Aram Veeser, ed., *The New Historicism* (London, 1989), pp. 15–36, p. 21.
[56] Greenblatt, 'Invisible Bullets', pp. 18–47.
[57] Walker, *Plays of Persuasion*, pp. 102–32 and 169–221.

political position allowed the expression of distinct and antipathetic political ideas.

Thus a careful study of Renaissance household drama would focus, not simply upon the correlations between the major preoccupations of a play text and the political agenda of its patron, but upon how those agenda were addressed in the specific context of the play, and thus how the patron's attitudes were subtly refracted rather than simply reflected in the good counsel which that play offered. We should thus refocus our attention on the element of process at work here and look not primarily at the apparently contradictory elements of confrontational criticism or affirmative compliment to be found in the plays, but at the way these two are combined in a strategy of engaging persuasion.[58]

Critics have misidentified the political impact of the household drama partly, then, because they have searched in it for the wrong things. Because the drama does not confront the political orthodoxies of the court and its presiding patrons head-on, it has been interpreted as politically quiescent. Because the texts were not sites of obvious ideological conflict they have been read as instruments of royal authority.[59] But political engagement can be effected by more means than one. The household plays did not so much offer an alternative ideology as attempt to (re)define the practical implications of a shared ideology of good lordship already in existence. What did it mean in practice to be a Good Lord or a virtuous sovereign? The answers which household drama offered to such questions sought to cajole and persuade its royal and noble audiences to undertake far-reaching and radical political action. Thus its results could be as fundamental as any challenge to royal policy or aristocratic hegemony conducted on the level of ideology – more so, perhaps, as where the ideals were shared between playwright and patron and what was at issue was their implementation, there was room for manoeuvre, for negotiation, and thus for change. With direct con-

---

[58] The distinction was identified in M. Butler, *Theatre and Crisis, 1632–42* (Cambridge, 1984), p. 3 and taken up most effectively in Sharpe, *Criticism and Compliment.*

[59] The limitations of this position are perhaps revealed most obviously in Jean E. Howard's recent analysis of the political role of the commercial theatres (*Stage and Social Struggle*, pp. 5–14). The choice offered there is a stark one: the stage, it is claimed, either operated in the service of 'established power, whether one defines established power as the monarchy, the Anglican church, or the male sex', or 'it enacted ideological contestation as much as it mirrored or reproduced anything that one could call the dominant ideology of a single class, class faction, or sex'. The possibility that negotiation over the use of power need not be conducted on the level of ideology, that negotiation with the sovereign, or other powerful patrons might not necessarily involve an attempt, whether conscious or unconscious, to undermine their authority, is apparently not considered.

frontation, on the other hand, there could be only the statement and restatement of mutually exclusive principles: an exchange in which the royal or noble patron, challenged in the heart of his domestic space, would not and could not yield.

CHAPTER 3

John Heywood and the politics of contentment

Perhaps no finer example of the paradoxical nature of the politics of household drama can be found than the career of John Heywood. The most consistently courtly of Tudor dramatists, Heywood was also in many ways a thoroughly 'oppositional' playwright, profoundly out of sympathy with the religious reforms of the 1530s and 1540s. Indeed, he came perilously close to dying for his beliefs in 1543, when he was condemned for denying the Royal Supremacy in the aftermath of the Prebendaries Plot.[1] Yet his opposition to royal policy took place, in all but the latter instance, at court and in the royal household where he found employment throughout both the Reformation period and the Marian reaction. And his dissent was expressed, not in factional in-fighting or secret conspiracy, but in the more public forum created by the production of courtly drama and the circulation of literary manu-scripts. Through these means he made articulate appeals for the con-tinuation of the old order aimed at the courtly community and, in the late 1520s and 1530s, chiefly at Henry VIII himself. Only after the return to protestantism under Elizabeth was he prompted to enter self-imposed exile in 1564, and only then after he had provided at least one dramatic entertainment for the new queen.

THE PLAYWRIGHT

Heywood was born around 1497, perhaps, as his most recent editors suggest, in Coventry, where he may have begun the association with the Rastell family, and through them with Thomas More, which was to colour his early dramatic career. Certainly by 1519 he was at court,

---

[1] For accounts of Heywood's career, see Richard Axton and Peter Happé, eds., *The Plays of John Heywood* (Woodbridge, 1991), pp. 1–10; A. W. Reed, *Early Tudor Drama: Medwall, the Rastells, Heywood, and The More Circle* (London, 1926); R. W. Bolwell, *The Life and Works of John Heywood* (New York, 1966).

receiving quarterly wages as a singing man.[2] And from this point onwards his name appears frequently in the household accounts, providing evidence of a lucrative and varied career as an entertainer and household servant. On 12 February 1521 he was granted the rents from lands in Essex which had reverted to the crown.[3] In 1525 he received a payment of £6 13s 4d as a 'player of the virginals', and at Christmas 1528 he began to collect an annual pension of £10, which he seems to have received consistently for at least the next twenty-three years. Further references to him as a musician, actor, and dramatist continue through the 1530s, as do signal marks of royal favour, both direct and indirect. On 20 January 1530 he was presented as Common Measurer in the Mercers' Company, a privilege granted at least in part on the strength of his courtly connections, as is suggested by a note in the Town Clerk's records that 'at the contemplacion of the Kynges letter, John Heywoode be admitted into the liberties of this citie'.[4] Those connections are even more evident in his receipt of a gift from the king of a 'gilte cuppe with a cover weing xxiii oz.' on New Year's Day 1533, a clear indication that Heywood managed to retain royal favour at a time when other religious conservatives were beginning to feel Henry's wrath. Later in 1533 there is equally clear evidence of the fruits of his dramatic labours, for John Rastell's son William, the printer of More's dialogues and polemical tracts, began to publish Heywood's interludes at this time. He began with *Johan Johan*, issued anonymously on 12 February, and *The Pardoner and The Friar* (again printed anonymously on 5 April), and continued with *The Play of the Weather* (1533), *A Play of Love* (1534), and probably also *The Four PP*.[5]

Further literary and dramatic endeavours can be glimpsed in the household accounts and other surviving records from this period. In 1534 Heywood wrote a ballad in praise of Princess Mary, daughter of Henry VIII and Katherine of Aragon (a significant political gesture in the year that she was formally deprived of her royal title and her place in the succession). And in 1537/8 he was evidently providing both music and drama for Mary's household.[6] In March 1538 he produced an

[2] Axton and Happé, eds., *Plays*, p. 2. A. W. Reed, *Early Tudor Drama*, p. 9. Heywood married Joan Rastell, the daughter of John Rastell and the niece of Sir Thomas More, at some point before 1523. [3] Axton and Happé, eds., *Plays*, p. 3. [4] Reed, *Early Tudor Drama*, p. 46.

[5] For the likelihood that a now 'lost' edition of *The Four PP* was printed by Rastell at this time, see Axton and Happé, ed., *Plays*, p. 6. See also A. Fox, *Politics and Literature in The Reigns of Henry VII and Henry VIII* (Oxford, 1989), pp. 251–2.

[6] Axton and Happé, ed., *Plays*, pp. 5–8; W. R. Streitberger, *Court Revels, 1485–1559* (Toronto, 1994), pp. 149–52.

interlude, performed before the princess by child actors (almost certainly from St Paul's), while at Shrovetide in the following year he was producing a 'Masque of King Arthur's Knights' both at court and in the household of Thomas Cromwell. Later in the 1540s he devised an interlude on 'The Parts of Man' for performance in the household of Archbishop Cranmer. Given the political and religious tensions existing in the later 1530s, the range and breadth of Heywood's popularity is remarkable. To perform plays in the household of the disinherited Princess Mary, whose support for her mother's case and the catholic faith had taken her into a lengthy period of royal disfavour, and those of Cranmer and Cromwell, the architects of many of the reforms which the princess opposed, suggests an ability to cross political divisions which few other courtiers of the period could boast.

Indeed, Heywood has long attracted admiration from modern critics for just this capacity to rise above the religious divisions blighting the reign. His survival through three changes of monarch, and at least as many alterations in religious policy, has been attributed to a characteristic geniality which enabled him to submerge his own religious conservatism beneath a 'merry', sociable demeanour. Critics have spoken of his 'charitable disposition' and of a perhaps naive but 'good-natured balance of mind, religious tolerance and lack of factionalism'.[7] But, as what follows will suggest, Heywood was far from indifferent to religious disputes, still less naive about them. He was as strongly committed to catholicism as many of the more overtly partisan of his contemporaries. What his long career suggests is that he found other means to express his religious principles and to defend them, means which take us to the heart of the literary and dramatic politics of the Henrician court and the controversies of the early years of the English Reformation.

THE PLAYS

Although it is not possible categorically to establish that any one of Heywood's plays was performed before the king, their milieu is resolutely courtly. In the case of *Witty and Witless*, which seems on stylistic grounds to have been the earliest of them, it is clear that Heywood envisaged a performance at court, as he added three stanzas addressing Henry VIII with the marginal proviso that 'Thes thre stave next folowyng in the Kyngs absens are voyde' (following line 675). And

---

[7] B. A. Milligan, ed., *John Heywood's Works and Miscellaneous Short Poems*, (Urbana, 1956), p. 296; Axton and Happé, eds., *Plays*, p. 2.

Heywood's court service in the 1520s and 1530s, during which time he was responsible for the performance of other lost plays at court, also provides the most likely occasions for performance of the rest of his surviving dramatic output.[8]

Witty and Witless

Heywood's conservative religious credentials were made evident in this, probably his first, interlude, which took the venerable form of a debate between a wise man and a fool over the respective merits of wisdom and folly. It is generally assumed that the play predates the most heated phase of the Reformation controversies in England, being written as early as 1523–4. But this may be too early. It is possible that the additional stanzas directed to the king make specific reference to the Supreme Headship of the church, and that the play should thus be included with *The Pardoner and The Friar, The Four PP, Love,* and *Weather* as works of the early years of the Reformation Parliament. When Jerome, the play's spokesman for religious truth, turns to the audience and commends their wisdom, he singles out the king for special attention:

> Yf the glos of Gods schyne not bryght eche way
> In them, who havyng a realme in governall
> Set forthe theyre governans to Gods glory all,
> Charytably aydynge subjects in eche kynde,
> The schynyng of Gods gyfts wheer schall we then fynde?
>
> And of this hye sort the hy hed most excelent
> Ys owr most loved and drade supreme soferayne,
> The schynynge of whose most excellent talent
> Ymployde to Gods glory above all the trayne
> Syns wytt wantyth here recytall to retayne,
> And that all hys faythfull fele the frewte of hys fame.
> Of corse I pray pardon in passyng the same. (lines 678–89)

The conspicuous conjunction of 'hy hed most excelent' with 'supreme soferayne' in the following line could well be a pointed allusion to the king's claim to the title of 'sole protector and supreme head of the English church and clergy', first voiced on 7 February 1531 in the king's demand for a clerical subsidy. If this is so, then the play – or perhaps

---

[8] See Greg Walker, *Plays of Persuasion: Drama and Politics at the Court of Henry VIII* (Cambridge, 1991), pp. 134–6.

more plausibly only the additional stanzas aimed at the king – must be redated to February 1531 or later.[9] Whether this is accepted or not, however, what is clear is that Heywood used the play to offer the court a highly orthodox account of Christian wisdom, stressing the efficacy of good works at a number of points (lines 587, 625, 628, 637), and placing his concluding words, as we have seen, in the mouth of a figure with the highly significant name of Jerome: a clear allusion to the saintly compiler of the Vulgate Bible.[10] Moreover, the latter's final appeal to the king to act as an impartial father to his people 'charytably aydynge' his subjects whichever side they favoured in the play's central dispute, voices a call for tolerance in disputatious times which will be taken up again in each of his subsequent interludes.

The Pardoner and The Friar

This play, a dramatic *tour de force*, brings together a preaching friar and a pardoner in vociferous contention for the attention of the audience: the latter being addressed as if they were a parish congregation. Both men seek to convince their hearers of the superiority of their own brand of religion in order to monopolise their charitable offerings. But, as Richard Axton and Peter Happé have recently argued, the play offers more than simply a virtuoso piece for two roguish vice-figures.[11] It presents a dramatic analogue to the religious controversies of the period from the first session of the Reformation Parliament in 1529 to the Royal Supremacy of 1533. For, in the figure of the Friar, Heywood provides an ironic pastiche of the evangelical reformer, critical of the practices and apparatus of the established church, and (hypocritically) determined to assert the primacy of the Scriptural word. While in the Pardoner one sees a parodic representative of that same established church. In many respects the latter is a conventional type of anti-clerical satire, familiar to readers of Chaucer or Langland, with his fraudulent relics and extravagant claims for the powers of his bulls. Yet he is also, in his repeated stress upon papal authority, and his willingness to use the disciplinary

---

[9] As the earliest (manuscript) text of the play dates from the early 1540s and is not a holograph (see Axton and Happé, eds., *Plays*, p. 4; and P. Happé, ed., *Two Moral Interludes*, Malone Society Reprints (Oxford, 1991)) it is impossible to tell whether the royal stanzas were part of the original text. It is quite possible that they were added to an earlier play to 'bring it up to date' with a pointed allusion to the king's claim, if Heywood knew a performance before the court was impending. On 11 February 1531 Convocation finally granted Henry the title 'singular protector, supreme lord, and even, so far as the law of Christ allows, [even] supreme head of the English church and clergy'.   [10] See Axton and Happé, eds., *Plays*, p. 34.   [11] Ibid., pp. 39–42.

apparatus of the church to silence his opponent, a figure drawn directly from the controversy of the late 1520s and early 1530s: a personification of the worst alleged abuses of orthodox religious practice, careless of criticism and determined to continue in his own corrupt ways.[12] In the dramatic conflict between the two (in which both actors speak simultaneously in a rising cacophony of contending claims and accusations, culminating in a stand-up fight), Heywood creates a powerful image of the fruitless and destructive power of religious strife, and its capacity to corrupt its practitioners, confuse the laity, and ultimately destroy the fabric of the parish community.

The play begins with the entry of the Friar, who greets the audience with what appears to be a sincere blessing ('Deus hic! The holy trynyte / Preserve all that nowe heere be' (lines 1–2)). But, as his heavily rhetorical declaration of his calling (more sales pitch than sermon) will soon reveal, he is no virtuous ascetic, but an all-too-worldly performer, offering his version of salvation only to those who are prepared to pay for it.

Echoing a claim frequently made by the evangelicals, to be preaching a faith based upon the scriptural purity of the early apostolic ministry, he declares that he has come

> The gospell of Chryst openly to preche,
> As dyd the appostels by Chryst theyr mayster sent
> To turne the people and make them to repent. (lines 16–18)

And the overtones of evangelicalism are further strengthened as he talks of offering the peace of Christ only to those houses 'worthy and *electe*' (line 43; my emphasis), echoing a key term in the reforming theology of Luther and Tyndale.[13] Similarly, there is more than a hint of the conventicle or secret meeting of the 'godly' to his account of how he found his way to this congregation, led by word of mouth to what promised to be a gathering of like-minded believers.

> And as I cam hether, one dyd me tell
> That in this towne ryght good folke dyd dwell,
> Which to here the worde of God wolde be glad.

---

[12] In his *Practice of Prelates* (1530), Tyndale was to claim that the clergy used the apparatus of the church courts to maintain their own vicious lifestyles: 'whatsoever soundeth to make of your bellies, to maintain your honour, whether in the Scripture, or in your own traditions, or in the Pope's law, that ye compel the lay-people to observe: violently threatening them with your excommunications and curses, that they shall be damned, body and soul, if they keep them not.' W. Tyndale, *Exposition and Notes . . . Together with The Practice of Prelates*, ed. H. Walter, Parker Society (Cambridge, 1849), pp. 242–3. On Heywood's Pardoner, see D. Boocker, 'Heywood's Indulgent Pardoner', *English Language Notes*, 29 (1991), pp. 21–30.

[13] For this suggestion, see Axton and Happé, eds., *Plays*, p. 40.

And as sone as I therof knolege had,
I hyder hued me as fast as I myght,
Entendyd by the grace of god almyght . . .
Here to make a symple colacyon.   (lines 63–8, 70)

Against the gospel-centred rhetoric of the Friar is set the conventional catholicism of the Pardoner, who enters at this point, signally blessing the company by 'God and saynt Leonarde' (line 79). Where the Friar found his authority to preach in the biblical word, the Pardoner grounds his in the papal text, 'this blessed pardon / Whiche is the greatest under the son, / Graunted by the Pope . . .' (lines 89–91). And, where the Friar cited only divine sanctions for his activities, the Pardoner immediately stakes a claim to the highest earthly authorities of all, bulls from the Pope and a warrant from the king:

. . . fyrst ye shall knowe well that I com fro Rome –
Lo, here my bulles, all and some!
Our lyege lorde seale here on my patent
I bere with me my body to warrant,
That no man be so bolde, be he preest or clarke,
Me to dysturbe of Chrystes holye warke.   (lines 97–102)

There then follows a powerful dramatic metaphor for the religious discord unsettling the nation as a whole, and the capital in particular in the period of the Reformation Parliament.[14] As the Friar begins to expound scripture in one part of the place, the Pardoner begins to declare the potency of his bull simultaneously in another (lines 195–204 and following), the two speaking at the same time until they turn angrily upon each other directly, the Friar being interrupted on the phrase 'in scrypture eke' (line 210), by the Pardoner's oath 'by the mas[s!]' (line 211). The exchanges continue for a further 100 lines until the Pardoner loses his temper and attempts to bring the full weight of ecclesiastical censure to bear to silence the Friar, declaiming a sentence of excommunication upon him.

Why despysest thou the Popes mynyster?
Maysters, here I curse hym openly,
And therwith warne all this hole company
By the Popes great auctoryte,
That ye leve hym and herken unto me!
For, tyll he be assoyled, his wordes take none effecte –
or out of holye chyrche he is now clene rejecte.   (lines 305–11)

[14] For the religious dissension in London at this time, see S. Brigden, *London and the Reformation* (Oxford, 1989), pp. 172–215.

But the Friar is unabashed and the attempt at repression only provokes further dissension.

> FRIAR: My maysters, he dothe but gest and rave –
> It forseth not for the wordes of a knave!
> But to the worde of God do reverence,
> And here me forthe, with dewe audyence.   (lines 312–15)

And thus the debate continues, with Heywood providing further juxta-positions of signal doctrinal issues to make clear to the audience the sort of controversy he is parodying (as the Friar announces that 'our lorde in the gospell sheweth the way' (line 529), for example, the Pardoner assures his audience that 'ye shall now here the Pope's auctoryte' (line 530)). The combatants mouth pastiche tags of evangelical and conserva-tive rhetoric until their dispute degenerates into open conflict, with each abusing the other's calling, seeking to incite the audience to rise up against them, and finally taking matters violently into their own hands.

> FRIAR: What? Sholde ye gyve ought to pratyng pardoners?
> PARDONER: What? Sholde ye spende on these flaterynge lyers
> FRIAR: What? Sholde ye gyve ought to these bolde beggars?
> PARDONER: As be these bablynge monkes and these Friars
> FRIAR: Let them hardely labour for theyr lyvynge:
> PARDONER: Which do nought dayly but bable and lye.
>   (lines 436–41)

> FRIAR: I say, wylt thou nat yet stynt thy clappe?
>   Pull me downe the pardoner with an evyll happe!
> PARDONER: Maister Friar, I holde it best
>   To kepe your tonge while ye be in rest.
> FRIAR: I say, one pull the knave of his stole!
> PARDONER: Nay, one pull the Friar downe lyke a fole!
> FRIAR: Leve thy railynge and babbelynge of Friars,
>   Or, by Jys, Ish'lug the by the swete eares.   (508–15)

Only the entrance of the parish curate, aghast that his church should be 'polluted' with violence, breaks up the ensuing brawl. But, rather than bringing a sense of order and justice to the proceedings at the close of the play, the Parson's entrance only sets up a final ironic reversal. It is he, the legitimate authority in the parish, and 'Neybour Prat', the parish constable whom he summons from the audience to help him, who are routed by the two villains, who forget their differences and unite to fight the newcomers. Thus *The Pardoner and The Friar* is unique among Hey-wood's moral interludes in that it ends, not in harmony, but in bitter division, with the disputants exchanging threat and malediction as they leave the place.

> FRIAR and PARDONER: Than adew, to the devyll, tyll we come
> agayn!
> PARSON and PRAT: And a myschefe go with you bothe
> twayne!   (640–41)

Here the point seems to be that this is not a dispute which is amenable to rational solution and eventual accommodation. When conducted in a spirit of ill will, it, like its chief adversaries, will 'come agayn' in vengeance.

It is not clear exactly when Heywood wrote *The Pardoner and The Friar*, nor when precisely it was first performed. Suggestions have placed it as early as 1521 (or earlier) and as late as 1532–3.[15] On the basis of the doctrinal content mentioned above, a date after 1529 seems logical. But, beyond this, the precise moment of production is less significant, for the contention which prompted the play was a constant factor in the period from 1529 to 1533.

Hostility to the church seemed to the Imperial ambassador, Eustace Chapuys, to be widespread among the noblemen at court as the Reformation Parliament met for its troubled first session. Rumours were circulating during October 1529 that the church's temporal possessions would be seized by Act of Parliament, and the first day of the session was marked by the provocative distribution of Simon Fish's fiercely anticlerical tract *The Supplication for the Beggars* on the streets of Westminster.[16] Once Parliament opened, the debates quickly grew heated as members in the Commons began to 'shewe their grudges' and to 'comon of their griefes wherewith the spiritualitie had before tyme grevously oppressed them, both contrarie to ye lawe of the realme, and contrarie to all righte'.[17] In response, Bishop Fisher spoke out in the Lords against the bills introduced to limit mortuary fees, probate charges, and clerical

---

[15] See Axton and Happé, eds., *Plays*, pp. 38–40.
[16] *LP*, IV (iii) 6011; C. Haigh, *English Reformations: Religion, Politics, and Society Under the Tudors* (Oxford, 1993), pp. 96–7.
[17] Hall, p. 765. A document recently discovered in Berkeley Castle by Dr Richard Hoyle and plausibly identified as a petition to the 1529 session of the Reformation Parliament suggests that the extent of anti-clerical proposals aired during the first session may have been far wider than the resulting legislation would suggest. The matters debated seem to have included a possible subjugation of all ecclesiastical jurisdiction to royal control for a period of seven years, and a proposal that the heirs of the founders of religious houses be enabled to recover their lands if they were dissatisfied with the uses to which the recipients were putting their revenues. R. Hoyle, 'The Origin of the Dissolution of the Monasteries,' *Historical Journal*, 38 (1995), pp. 275–305, especially pp. 284–5.

pluralism, comparing the current situation to that in Bohemia at the time of Hus, and talking of a lack of faith among the Commons. And, during the debate on the Pluralism Bill, the prelates in the Lords were said to have 'railed on the commons of the common house, and called them heretikes and scismatikes'.[18]

By 13 December 1530, Chapuys was reporting back to his Imperial master that 'nearly all the people here hate the priests'.[19] Such statements cannot be taken as definitive evidence of impending legislation. But what they do indicate is the state of heightened tension which existed between the clergy and laity over the issues of practical and doctrinal reform at the time: a tension which was to exercise Heywood in each of his subsequent interludes.

The Play of Love

As Axton and Happé have claimed, this play may well have been devised for performance, not at the royal court itself, but at the Inns of Court, perhaps specifically in Lincoln's Inn, in 1529/30, to mark Sir Thomas More's elevation to the chancellorship after the fall of Wolsey. Certainly More's new-found prominence in legal circles could only have helped to find patronage for members of his family and circle in the Inns. And the play's frequent use of legal terminology, and its possible parodic allusion to Wolsey's mannerisms while sitting in the prerogative courts, mark it out as a drama particularly well suited for performance before an audience of lawyers.[20]

But, even if the play was written for a performance in Lincoln's Inn early in More's chancellorship, there is little in it to mark it out as a factional piece. Certainly there is little evidence of it playing up to any supposed 'hatred' of Wolsey among the common lawyers.[21] Other than the possible passing glance at the cardinal's background and manner, there is little which is satirical or vitriolic in the play. Rather, it continues the strategy of condemning such hostility, contention, and division which was begun in *The Pardoner and The Friar*.

The play is essentially an extended 'moot' or legal debate concerning

[18] Hall, p. 767.   [19] *CSPSp*, IV (i), 228.

[20] See Axton and Happé, eds., *Plays*, p. 46. For the possible allusion to Wolsey, see below, pp. 86–7.

[21] For the suggestion that the play reflected the lawyers' hatred of Wolsey see Axton and Happé, *Plays*, p. 46 and R. J. Schoeck, 'Satire of Wolsey in Heywood's *Play of Love*', *Notes and Queries*, 196 (1951), pp. 112–14. For a more measured analysis of the cardinal's relationship with the common lawyers, see J. A. Guy, *The Cardinal's Court* (Hassocks, 1977), *passim*, and P. J. Gwyn, *The King's Cardinal: The Rise and Fall of Thomas Wolsey* (London, 1990), pp. 104–43.

the respective torments and pleasures of different attitudes towards and experiences of love. The play begins with a soliloquy in rhyme royal from Lover not Loved, the conventional Petrarchan lover, who bemoans the toils and agonies of his unrequited passion for an unnamed mistress. Surely, he claims, to love someone who does not return one's love is the worst state that a human being could suffer. This claim is immediately rejected by the second character to enter the place, Loved not Lovyng, a woman in precisely the same situation as Lover not Loved's mistress. She replies that to be forever pursued for love by someone one hates is a much worse case. The couple then argue over the sorrows of their own particular conditions for some 182 lines until, realising that neither will yield to the other, they agree to seek 'some man indyfferent / Indyfferently to heare us, and so gyve judgement' on their claims (lines 237–8).

The two then leave the place in search of this neutral arbitrator, making way for the arrival of the other two characters in the drama, Lover Loved and No Lover nor Loved, who immediately fall into disputation over which of them enjoys the happier state, he who is fulfilled emotionally in a relationship with a mistress who shares and returns his love, or he who is entirely free of emotional commitments, maintaining a cynical indifference to women and seemingly provoking a similar response from them in return. After much debate this couple also agree to seek a judge to try their claims, and the four contrasting antagonists are brought together in the place when each pair agrees to judge the merits of the others' claims.

It is at this point that No Lover nor Loved, the play's Vice figure, offers what may well have been a parodic allusion to Wolsey's courtroom mannerisms. Taking on the role of judge with a flamboyant display of mock seriousness, No Lover disappears from the place, only to reappear in a seat of judgement (in the gallery or on the dais?), claiming that he has been to confession in the interim, for,

> I never syt in justyce but ever more
> I use to be shryven a lyttell before,
> And nowe syns that my confessyon is done
> I wyll depart and come take penaunce sone.
> When conscyens prycketh, conscyens must be sercht by God
> In dyschargyng of conscyens or els gods forbod;
> Which maketh me mete when conscyens must come in place
> To be a judge in every comen case.
> But who may lyke me his avaunsement avaunt?

Nowe am I a judge and never was serjaunt,
Which ye regarde not much by ought that I see
By any reverence that ye do to me.   (lines 801–12)

The references to confession, the stress upon conscience, and the expectation of reverence despite a lack of legal training ('Nowe am I a judge
and never was serjaunt') seem likely references to Wolsey, the church-
man-lawyer who, without legal training or qualifications, presided as
Lord Chancellor over the, so called, prerogative courts of Chancery and
Star Chamber, the 'conscience' courts where the judge's discretion
rather than Common Law precedent determined judgement. But the
allusion is taken no further. It cannot be used to suggest that No Lover
'is' Wolsey, or stands for him at other points in the play. This is simply a
comic 'turn', in which the Vice momentarily adopts what might arguably have been a 'Wolseyan' manner to gain a laugh from a knowing
audience. The reference is soon forgotten in the continuing comic
debate which follows. It would thus be misleading to consider *Love* as in
any sense an anti-Wolsey play, or see this speech as in some way
providing the centrepiece of the drama. What the play as a whole is, far
more obviously, is another in a series of plays from Heywood's pen
warning against the destructive effects of contention and lauding its
reverse, a tolerant accommodation of differing viewpoints. Thus the
play ends, unlike *The Pardoner and The Friar*, but like all Heywood's
subsequent interludes, with harmony and reconciliation rather than
confrontation and conflict. None of the contending characters gains
precedence at the end. The 'oddly valent' pair,[22] Lover not Loved and
Loved not Loving, are eventually judged by their evenly valenced
counterparts to be equal in suffering. As Lover Loved tells them,

In peysing your paines my consciens doth alowe
A just counterpaise, and thus your paynes be
Ajudged by us twaine one paine in degre.   (lines 1486–8)

Similarly Lover Loved and No Lover nor Loved are deemed co-equals
in pleasure. As Lover not Loved declares, 'I judge and awarde / Both
these pleasures of yours as one in regarde' (lines 1528–9).

These even-handed judgements are readily accepted by the various
supplicants. As Lover Loved concludes,

Wel syns I thinke ye both without corrupcion,
I shall move no mater of interrupcion.   (lines 1530–1)

[22] The phrase is Axton and Happé's (*Plays*, p. 24).

The only moment of mild dissension is provided by No Lover, who asks whether he might not still think that he has the best position of all of them (lines 1532–3). But his voice is quickly absorbed into the harmonious resolution as Loved not Loving broadens her response into a general lesson on humility and social conformity.

> Affeccion unbridled may make us al thynke
> That eche of us hath done other wronge,
> But where reason taketh place it can not sinke
> Syns cause to be percial here is none us amonge;
> That one hed that wolde thinke his owne wit so strong
> That on his judges he myght judgement devise,
> What judge in so judging coulde judge hym wyse? (lines 1534–1540)

The message is taken up and expanded by each of the speakers in turn, first by Lover Loved's declaration of a wider significance to their conclusion:

> Thus not we foure but al the worlde beside
> Knowledge them selfe or other in joy or payne,
> Hath nede of contentacion for a gyde;
> Havinge joy or payne, content let us remayne.
> In joy or payne of other fee we disdaine;
> Be we content welthe or woo, and eche for other
> Rejoyse in the tone and pyte the tother. (lines 1557–63)

Finally Lover not Loved, who had begun the play with a self-centred complaint at his own plight, ends it with a general homily for the audience on the social and spiritual virtues of contentment.

> Syns such contencion may hardly acorde
> In such kynde of love as here hath ben ment,
> Let us seke the love of that lovyng Lorde
> Who to suffer passion for love was content.
> Wherby his lovers that love for love assent
> Shall have in fyne above contentacyon
> The felyng pleasure of eternall salvacyon.
>
> Which Lorde of Lordes, whose joyfull and blessed byrth
> Is now remembred by tyme presentyng
> This accustomyd tyme of honest myrth,
> That Lorde we beseche in most humble meanyng
> That it may please hym by mercyfull hearyng
> Thestate of his audyens longe to endure
> In myrth, helth, and welth, to graunt his pleasure.
> AMEN   (lines 1564–78)

Such seemingly harmonious reconciliations of difference were to mark each of the later interludes from Heywood's pen.

The Play of the Weather

More obviously a play about the role of the king in settling disputes among his subjects is *The Play of The Weather*, the most clearly courtly of Heywood's moral interludes. As I have considered the political implications of the play at length elsewhere, I shall treat it rather more briefly than its counterparts in what follows.[23] But its importance for an appreciation of the political dimensions to Heywood's drama is such that I shall recap some of the argument here.

Briefly, the play concerns the arrival on Earth of Jupiter, king of the gods, who – having dissolved a factious session of the Olympian parliament, which had degenerated into a row over how best to regulate the weather – had taken into his own hands absolute control over the elements.[24] He has now arrived on earth to hear the suits of his mortal subjects on how the weather should be organised for the benefit of all. The play itself represents each of these mortal suitors in turn, as each begs the god-king for totally unreasonable preference in the allocation of weather. The water-miller begs for unceasing rain to drive his mill, the laundress for baking sun to dry and bleach her clothes, the small boy for never ending snow for snowballs, and so on. Finally, faced with such partisan and self-seeking petitions, Jupiter returns to the heavens, resolved to ignore all advice and to determine the weather himself, giving each of his subjects only what they deserve.

Such a summary of the plot, given in isolation, does little to indicate the play's political import. But when considered in the light of contemporary events, its function as an allegory becomes clearer. The play takes as its central premise the view that a conscientious monarch needs to dispense with the factious and partial advice of both his parliament and his courtiers and trust instead to his own considered judgement. And it portrays the education of Jupiter in the wisdom of that view, showing him frustrated, first by the intractable wrangling of a divided parliament, and then by the selfish counsels of his courtiers and subjects. And in 1529–33, when the play was conceived, this message was clearly relevant to Henry VIII, who had witnessed the first sessions of the Reformation Parliament and was posing as mediator between, on the

---

[23] See Walker, *Plays of Persuasion*, pp. 133–68.
[24] Ibid., pp. 147–54, 164–7. For what follows, see pp. 164–8.

one hand, the reforming, 'anti-clerical' Commons and radicals at court, and, on the other, the conservatives on his bench of bishops and his council. Indeed, as careful scrutiny of the play reveals, the absolutist rhetoric which Jupiter employs may well have been modelled upon Henry's own declarations and actions at this time.

Simply put, having decided that Cardinal Wolsey had let him down over the crucial matter of the 'divorce' from Katherine of Aragon, Henry clearly had one of his not-infrequent crises of conscience over his role in government. As a result he began to reassert himself openly in the administration of the realm, and especially in the prosecution of his 'Great Matter' in Rome. He seems to have decided that there would be no more 'favourites' or chief ministers with wide-ranging executive powers like Wolsey, but a strong personal monarchy resting on the traditional basis of royal government, a broadly based council. As Edward Hall (who can generally be relied upon to reflect both royal policy and the rhetoric in which it was articulated) recorded,

The Kinge whiche after twentie yere past, had bene ruled by other, and in especial by the Cardinal of Yorke, began now to be a ruler, and a Kynge, yea a kyng of suche wytte, wisedome and pollicie, that the lyke hath not reygned over this realme.[25]

From this moment on, Henry loudly proclaimed his personal control of government business. On 1 October 1529, the Bishop of Bayonne complained to Francis I that 'I do not see that I can for a long time speak with the King, who at present takes the management of everything'.[26] In January 1530, Henry assured the Spanish ambassador that he was no longer prepared to tolerate the alleged oversights of Wolsey's administration:

At that time . . . those who had the reins of government in their hands deceived me, many things were done then without my knowledge, but such proceedings will be stopped in the future.[27]

Eventually Henry's initiative was to give way to other pressures on his time. But in August 1530 it was still being reported that Henry chose 'to know and superintend everything himself'.[28]

Henry's declarations had a profound effect upon the mood and style of the court. Those who had previously worked through Wolsey's special relationship with the king and talked in terms of chief ministers and leaders of the Council now adopted a more egalitarian style. Hence the Duke of Norfolk informed the Spanish ambassador that there would

---

[25] Hall, p. 759.   [26] *LP* IV (iii) 5982.   [27] *CSPS*, V, p. 250.   [28] Ibid., IV, p. 601.

no longer be a single dominant voice among the king's councillors, and the drafters of the list of articles tabled against Wolsey in 1529 condemned the cardinal for stifling free discussion at the Council table and seeking to monopolise royal favour.[29]

This change in governmental style and rhetoric is central to any political reading of *The Play of The Weather*. What Heywood seems to have done is take up and exaggerate this rhetoric of royal independence. In so doing the playwright reminded the king and his court of Henry's new resolution, and hinted that he should pursue it to its logical conclusions. If he intended to rule personally, he did not need to countenance either the destructive debates of a divided Parliament or the partial advice of partisan courtiers. He should settle the religious debates which had arisen on his own initiative. A performance of *Weather* at court, at the centre of Henry's household, would, then, certainly have appealed to the king's current preoccupations and served his immediate political ends. It allegorised and applauded his decision to rule more directly himself, and so both affirmed his position within the court, the government, and the wider realm, and served a warning to the gathered courtiers of the need to conform to this approach to government. But to see the play simply as royal propaganda would be to miss half of its political significance – and probably the most important half at that. For Heywood's aim was clearly not simply to pander to royal wishes, but to shape those wishes and hence royal policy, in directions he himself favoured. As we shall see, the playwright's interest in personal monarchy at this time probably had less to do with abstract principles or flattery, and far more to do with the need to deprive the radical opponents of the established church and traditional catholic practices of the potent weapon which Parliament was providing them. Hence the terms in which Jupiter's personal monarchy is presented at the close of the play. The god-king leaves the playing place to return to Olympus determined, not to work closely with a loyal council or a compliant parliament, but to close his ears to all advice, withdrawing to his palace to rule at his own discretion.

The Four PP

The last of the interludes, *The Four PP*, continues this exploration of contemporary politics and the role of the Supreme Headship, developing the argument a stage further. The play begins as the first of the Ps,

---

[29] Lord Herbert of Cherbury, *The Life and Reigne of Henry the Eighth* (London, 1649), pp. 268–9.

the Palmer, enters the place, offering a sincere blessing on the company, and begging the audience's indulgence.

> Nowe God be here! Who kepeth this place?
> Now by my fayth I crye you mercy!
> Of reason I must sew for grace,
> My rewdnes sheweth me [now] so homely.   (lines 1–4)

He introduces himself and his vocation, listing the many shrines to which he has travelled in his peripatetic life. Unlike the Pardoner in *The Pardoner and The Friar*, however, the Palmer's declaration of his 'profession' does not serve to undercut the sincerity of his initial blessing. Despite the inclusion in this catalogue of a number of the saints familiar to readers of anti-clerical literature, including 'Saynt Uncomber', 'Saynt Roke', and 'St Tronion' (Chaucer's 'St Ronyon'), the Palmer remains a resolutely orthodox and only very lightly ironized figure. If he has a fault, it is enthusiastic over-credulity (as his naive responses to a number of the Pardoner's fraudulent relics later reveal) rather than anything more culpable.[30] He has travelled, he assures us, only 'As pylgrymes do of good intent' (line 12). There is no hint of the Wife of Bath's worldly motives about his diligent journeying. And there is nothing of the idolatrous misdirection of worship condemned by reformers in his careful explanation that he has called upon the Saints,

> Prayeng to them to pray for me
> Unto the blessed Trynyte,
> By whose prayers and my dayly payne
> I truste the soner to obtayne
> For my salvacyon grace and mercy.
> For be ye sure, I thynke surely,
> Who seketh sayntes for Crystes sake –
> And namely suche as payne do take
> On fote to punyshe [their] frayle body –
> Shall therby meryte more hyely
> Then by any thynge done by man.   (lines 53–63)

It is only in this final assumption of superior virtue that the Palmer errs, and significantly it is at this point that the Pardoner enters to challenge him. For, as in the other interludes, it is the claim to exclusivity, whether, as here, to virtue, to pleasure or suffering as in *Love*, or to the

---

[30] The Palmer's moral authority in relation to the other characters is underlined in dramatic terms by the fact that only he among the characters uses elevated verse forms, beginning the play speaking in quatrains and concluding it with two stanzas of rhyme royal (Axton and Happé, eds., *Plays*, p. 19).

right to determine the weather, as in *Weather*, which represents the greatest threat to the society of Heywood's plays.[31]

As the Pardoner points out, although the Palmer's vocation is no doubt sincerely practised, his claims for its superiority involve an implicit, un-christian, attack upon all other forms of devotion, chiefly in this context, the Pardoner's own profession. As he later claims to the third of the Ps, the Potycary,

> ... yf he [the Palmer] coulde avow [his claims] true,
> As good to be a gardener,
> As for to be a pardoner! (lines 339–41)[32]

Consequently a dispute arises between the two, with both claiming the pre-eminence of their own form of devotion, until the Pardoner's grandest claim for his own powers provides the cue for the next character to enter and deflate his pomposity with an irreverent question.

> PARDONER: Geve me but a peny or two pens
> And, as sone as the soule departeth hens,
> In halfe an houre or thre quarters at moste
> The soule is in heven with the Holy Ghost.
> *Potycary enters*
> POTYCARY: Sende ye any soules to heven by water?
> PARDONER: If we dyd, syr, what is the mater?
> POTYCARY: By God, I have a drye soule shulde thyther
> I praye you let our soules go to heven togyther! (lines 147–54)

The dispute is then widened, and a more macabre element added, as the Potycary claims, with carnivalesque pragmatism, that it is his profession that is the most effective in despatching souls to heaven. For, unless the body dies the soul cannot be released, and this former is a service most ably performed by the lethal admixtures prepared by apothecaries. His sinister logic is inescapable.

---

[31] In *Love*, for example, it is only when Lover not Loved claims that 'I sey and wyll veryfy / Of all paynes the most incomparable payne / Is to be a lover not lovyd agayne' (lines 61–3) that Loved not Lovyng enters to contest his claim. Similarly No lover nor Loved enters to dispute with Lover Loved only when the latter avers that 'the hyest pleasure that man may obteyne / Is to be a lover beloved agayne' (lines 300–1).

[32] The reference to a gardener as the touchstone of worthlessness here may well have a satirical point. In April 1532, Stephen Gardiner, bishop of Winchester, had provoked Henry VIII's anger and earned himself a period in the political wilderness by drafting a robust defence of clerical independence in response to the Commons' Supplication Against the Ordinaries. In 1532/3, then, Gardiner might indeed appear to provide an example of political marginality and inconsequentiality. See Walker, *Persuasive Fictions*, pp. 17–18; G. Redworth, *In Defence of The Church Catholic: The Life of Stephen Gardiner* (Oxford, 1990), pp. 35–9.

PARDONER: If ye kylde a thousande in an houre space,
　　When come they to heven, dyenge from state of grace?
POTYCARY: If a thousande pardons about your neckes were teyd,
　　When come they to heven yf they never dyed?　　(lines 186–9)

Thus the dispute threatens to end in acrimonious deadlock.

PARDONER: The longer ye dwell in communicacion,
　　The lesse shall you lyke thys ymagynacyon,
　　For ye may perceyve even at the fyrst chop
　　Your tale is trapt in such a stop
　　That at the leste ye seme worste then we.

POTYCARY: By the masse, I holde us nought all thre.
　　　　　　　　　　　　　　　　　　(lines 197–202)

It is only the arrival of the final P, the Pedlar, that breaks the cycle of claim and counter-claim. He assumes no superiority for his trade, and thus steers the debate away from spiritual salvation towards anti-feminist satire, where all three (male) combatants can find common ground. But even here the Pedlar gives the first indication of his role as moderator and pacifier in the group, as he steps in to halt the raucous sexual badinage about pins and pin-cases, and suggest that the disputants might wish to buy something from his box of wares.

Let womens maters passe and marke myne.
What ever theyr poyntes be, these poyntes be fyne,
Wherfore, yf ye be wyllynge to bye,
Ley downe money, come of quyckely.　　(lines 279–82)

But, any suggestion that the Pedlar is simply a mercenary is quickly dispelled as, on hearing that the others are 'but beggers . . . [and] no byers' (line 284), he concludes merrily,

Well, though thys journey acquyte no coste,
Yet thynke I nat my labour loste,
For by the fayth of my body
I lyke full well thys company . . .

Who may nat play one day in a weke
May thynke hys thryfte is fame to seke.　　(lines 287–90; 293–4)

To mark this declaration of fellowship, the company join together for a song. But this brief, harmonious reconciliation proves premature, as the Pardoner then recalls the theological dispute which had initially provoked them. Which of the three *is* the most effective in sending souls to heaven? The question will not go away, and the disputants seek the Pedlar's arbitration as a disinterested outsider. This prompts the latter's first direct attempt to reconcile the group in mutual tolerance and respect – an attempt based upon a refusal to measure the merits of others' virtue.

> I neyther wyll judge the beste nor worste,
> For be ye bleste or be ye curste
> Ye know it is no whyt of my sleyght
> To be a judge in maters of weyght.
> It behoveth no pedlars *nor proctours*
> To take on them judgement as doctours.
> But yf your myndes be onely set
> To worke for soule helthe, ye be well met.
> For eche of you somwhat doth showe
> That soules towarde heven by you do growe.
> Then yf ye can so well agree
> To contynue togyther all thre,
> And all you thre *obey on wyll,*
> Then all your myndes ye may fulfyll
> As yf ye came all to one man.
> Who shulde goo pylgrymage more than he can?
> In that, ye, Palmer, as debite
> May clerely dyscharge hym, parde;
> [to Pardoner] And for all other syns ones had contryssyon
> Your pardons geveth hym full remyssyon.
> And then ye, mayster potycary,
> May sende hym to heven by and by.   (lines 382–403; my italics)

The plea for reconciliation and accommodation seems general enough, but the reference to 'proctours' not taking it upon themselves to be doctors suggests a sideswipe at the common lawyers and burgesses in Parliament seeking to legislate on matters of ecclesiastical law and practice. While the hope that all three might obey 'on[e] wyll' might well be read in the light of the king's claims to arbitrate the disputes between clergy and laity (ultimately formalised in the Royal Supremacy) as a plea for general obedience to the authority of the sovereign and an end to disputation.

But, in the context of the play this plea is doomed to fail, for none of the disputants is prepared to subject himself to the rule of the others. And, the Pedlar is not yet prepared to impose a settlement in the interests of justice, as his willingness to countenance the claims of the Potycary (a spoiling candidate if ever there was one) as well as the more legitimate religious figures suggests. It is clear that there *is* a moral hierarchy within the combatants. The Palmer, for all his naiveté, is a sincere practitioner of his vocation. The Pardoner, for all his evident insincerity, *may* have genuine powers of remission and thus could fulfil a genuine spiritual function. Only the Potycary's position is both insincere and of no spiritual merit. His role in the debate is simply to mock the claims of the others through his worldly cynicism: a representative of the most negative form of anti-clericalism. Yet this moral scale remains implicit at this stage. It is not clear which of the three will win the debate, or the terms on which it will be conducted. To this point the Potycary's quick wits have given him the edge in the dispute, and his bawdy humour engages the audience's sympathy. Thus, when the Pedlar suggests that the dispute be conducted, not in the realm of pseudo-theology, but through a lying contest – he who can tell the most outrageous lie shall have lordship over the other two – it seems quite possible that the moral hierarchy will be inverted and the Potycary triumph.

Faced with the prospect of such a competition the two 'professional' liars, the Potycary and the Pardoner, jump at the opportunity to display their skills. The Palmer offers a more humble submission to the will of the judge.

> Sir, I well neither boost ne brawl,
> But take suche fortune as may fall,
> And yf ye wynne this maystry
> I wyll obaye you quietly.
> And sure I thynke that quietnesse,
> In any man is great rychesse
> In any maner company
> To rule or be ruled indifferently. (lines 474–81)

Thus, if there remain any doubts concerning the characters' respective moral worth, they are removed by the way each submits himself to the terms of the lying competition. The Palmer here aligns himself with the Pedlar as a figure of stability, fair judgement ('I muste and wyll be indifferent' (line 646) the Pedlar tells the Potycary when the latter tries to bribe him with a jar of fine marmalade), and obedience to established authority. His watchword here is 'quietness', as it had been, tacitly, earlier, when he refused to condemn either the Pardoner or the Potycary outright. He offers little opposition to the Pedlar's attempts at accommodation. Indeed, as we shall see, he brings about the final reconciliation himself through an act of accommodating generosity.[33]

Against these two moderating influences stand the more energetic and, initially at least, more dramatically engaging figures of the Pardoner and the Potycary. These two consistently reject the notion of reconciliation and push their own claims to pre-eminent virtue evermore vigorously until they are finally thwarted. Significantly, the Pardoner picks up the key word in the Palmer's submission and flatly rejects it in favour of a more aggressive strategy. 'Quietness', he claims, is a beggar's doctrine.

> By that bost thou semeth a begger in dede.
> What can thy quyetnesse help us at nede?
> Yf we shulde starve, thou hast nat, I thynke,
> One peny to bye us one potte of drynke. (lines 481–4)

It is, he claims, the vigorous marketing of his pardons that will bring the riches necessary for a comfortable life. Thus he displays his relics for the admiration of the others, an assertive act which only prompts the Potycary to show his wares in retaliation. Again, only the intervention of the Pedlar brings them back to the matter in hand.

The contest itself, after a brief false start in which the Potycary tries to claim victory by default, proves a masterful display of Rabelaisian storytelling. First, the Potycary spins a tale concerning administering a medicinal 'clyster' to a female patient which was subsequently ejected with such force that it destroyed a castle ten miles away. Then the Pardoner tells of a journey into hell in search of the soul of a dead female 'friend', in the course of which he obtained her freedom, as the devils were glad to be rid of her. In each case the grotesque realism of the impossible narrative embellishes a worthy contender for the title of best lie. But it falls, significantly, to the Palmer and his policy of 'quietness' to carry the day. For his modest interjection at the close of the Pardoner's story that he found the devils' attitude incredible (for 'in all the places where I have ben, / Of all the women that I have sene, / I never sawe nor knewe, to my consyens, / Any one woman out of Paciens' (lines 1000–3)) provokes his opponents to concede spontaneously that they have never heard a greater lie.

The Palmer is thus declared the victor. But the first act of his supremacy is, characteristically, to abrogate his authority over the other

---

[33] Significantly it is the moderating spokesmen for 'quietness' that are Heywood's own creations, the more combative Pardoner and Potycary he drew from his chief source *La Farce d'un Pardonneur, d'un Triacleur, et d'une Tavernier* (see Axton and Happé, eds., *Plays*, p. 42).

two. Thus, as in Heywood's other moral interludes, the characters are brought back at the end to the same position as they occupied at the outset, albeit with a new sense of the value of the status quo ante. As the Pedlar points out for the audience's benefit,

> Now be ye all evyn as ye begoon:
> No man hath loste nor no man hath woon.   (lines 1137–8)

But, having tasted, albeit only briefly, subjugation to the will of another, the roguish Pardoner and Potycary are better prepared to appreciate the benefits of an accommodating society in which no one approach claims superiority. Hence the Pedlar can now bring about a lasting reconciliation in which each of the two contending spiritual vocations has its legitimate place. As the play shifts from comic to didactic mode, he turns to each of the other characters in turn. Addressing the Palmer, he acknowledges and affirms his vocation, giving a clear statement of the value of pilgrimages undertaken for the correct motives.

> I do perceyve that pylgrymage
> Is chyefe the thynge ye have in usage,
> Wherto in effecte for love of Chryst
> Ye have, or shulde have bene, entyst,
> And who so doth with suche intent
> Doth well declare hys tyme well spent.   (lines 1141–6)

Similarly the Pardoner is encouraged to practice his profession on the same terms.

> And so do ye in your pretence,
> If ye do procure thus indulgence
> Unto your neyghbours charytably,
> For love of them in God onely.
> All thys may be ryght well applyed
> To shewe you both well occupyed.   (lines 1147–52)

And the Pedlar concludes his declaration to the clerical combatants with a ringing endorsement of the multitude of legitimate approaches to God available within an orthodox framework.

> For though ye walke nat bothe one waye,
> Yet walkynge thus, this dare I saye:
> That bothe your walkes come to one ende.
> And so for all that do pretende,
> By ayde of Goddes grace, to ensewe
> Any maner kynde of vertue –

As some great almysse for to gyve,
Some in wyllfull povertie to lyve,
Some to make hye wayes and suche other warkes,
And some to mayntayne prestes and clarkes
To synge and praye for soule departed –
These with all other vertues well marked,
All though they be of sondry kyndes,
Yet be they nat used with sondry myndes,
But as God only doth all those move;
So every man, onely for his love
With love and dred obediently
Worketh in these vertues unyformely.
Thus every vertue, yf we lyste to scan,
Is pleasaunt to God and thankfull to man.
And who that by grace of the holy goste
To any one vertue is moved moste,
That man by that grace that one apply
And therin serve God most plentyfully.   (lines 1153–76)

One kynde of vertue to dyspyse another
Is lyke as the syster myght hange the brother.   (lines 1185–6)

Finally the anti-clerical Potycary is confronted directly and his position rejected. When he quips that he thanks God 'I use no vertue at all' (line 1188), the Pedlar condemns this is 'of all the very worste waye!' (line 1189). Significantly the latter acknowledges not only the dramatic appeal of the Potycary's antics, but also the theological appeal of his assertively sceptical position.

I suppose ye dyd saye true,
In that ye sayd ye use no vertue.
In the whiche wordes, I dare well reporte,
Ye are well beloved of all thys sorte [i.e. the audience],
By your raylynge here openly
At pardons and relyques so leudly.   (lines 1195–200)

But he rejects a positive response to the Potycary as both presumptuous and wrong-headed. In response, and speaking directly to the audience as much as to the chastened Potycary, he offers a measured defence of good catholic practice, tempered with a frank acceptance of the existence of abuses. There are both good and bad pardoners, true and false relics. The problem lies in telling them apart. In such an uncertain world he advocates not the iconoclastic criticism of the reformers, figured in the cynicism of the Potycary, but modesty and caution. Demonstrably fraudulent relics may in good conscience be rejected and ignored. But where fraud cannot definitively be established it is both more prudent and more Christian to approach the matter in a spirit of generosity, leaving judgement to those in the best position to determine the truth: the church authorities.

> For [the Pardoner's] and all other [relics] that ye knowe fayned,
> Ye be nother counceled nor constrayned
> To any suche thynge in any suche case
> To gyve any reverence in any suche place.
> But where ye dout, the truthe nat knowynge,
> Belevynge the beste, good may be growynge.
> In judgynge the beste no harme at the leste;
> In judgynge the worste, no good at the beste.
> But beste in these thynges it semeth to me,
> To make no judgement upon ye.
> But as the churche doth judge or take them,
> So do ye receyve or forsake them.
> And so be sure ye can nat erre,
> But may be a frutfull folower.   (lines 1202–16)

It is left to the Palmer to offer a concluding prayer which, while resolutely orthodox, offers a gesture towards accommodation in the mixture of grace and works in its salvific formula. He begs that,

> to our reason God gyve us his grace
> That we may folowe with fayth so fermely
> His commaundementes, that we maye purchace
> Hys love, and so consequently
> To byleve hys churche, faste and faythfully
> So that we may accordynge to his promyse
> Be kepte out of errour in any wise . . .   (lines 1221–7)

> Besechynge our lorde to prosper you all
> In the fayth of hys churche universall.   (lines 1233–4)

THE POLITICS OF CONTENTMENT

It is the premise, or the recurring pattern, of these interludes that the attempt to establish overall superiority in the play-community leads only to fruitless contention, whereas the eventual acceptance of equality – or of a plurality of states and conditions in which there is no single victor –

results in the greatest happiness for all. It is the claim to supremacy (whether in fortune or sorrow as in *Love*, in determining the weather as in the play of that name, or in securing salvation for others as in *The Pardoner and The Friar* and *The Four PP*) which is the prime cause of dissension and disruption in each of Heywood's 'debate' plays. And it is also the claim to supremacy, of course, which was at the heart of the disputes between Henry VIII and Rome, between Henry and the English clergy, and between Parliament and the church, reformers and conservatives, as they unfolded in the early 1530s.[34]

To write and perform these plays at court in the period 1528–32, and still more to publish them in 1533/4, in the period leading up to the declaration of the Royal Supremacy, were thus profoundly political acts. But what it is vital to notice is not simply that these plays address the issues of authority, religious division, and reform at a time when they were both sensitive and contentious, but that they did so in particular and distinct ways. *In The Pardoner and The Friar*, as we have seen, Heywood offered a powerful vision of the disruptive effects of religious strife and issued an implicit warning of the dangers to the whole commonweal if it was not resolutely and effectively suppressed. In the futile efforts of the Parson and Neighbour Prat one sees reflected the impotence of the parish community when faced with the intrusion of disputes beyond their control or understanding. Their failure provides the 'worst-case' scenario against which the harmonious reconciliations of the other plays may be judged.

In *Weather*, Heywood offered a solution to the problems of division raised in *The Pardoner and The Friar*: a solution based upon determined royal intervention to halt civil strife. It is only Jupiter's resumption of absolute power over the weather which cuts through the tangle of self-interested claims and restores stability and prosperity for all. In this play at least, the incipient notion of a royal supremacy offers the prospect of an end to division and contention. In *The Four PP*, however, the claim to supremacy itself becomes part of the problem. Although the text is recognisably of a piece with *Weather, Love, Witty and Witless*, and (the anti-type) *The Pardoner and The Friar*, in that division is only

---

[34] The preamble to the Act in Restraint of Appeals (1533) made explicit the royal claim that

The see apostolic, most ambitiously aspiring to be supreme lordes of all the world, forgetting the holy steppes and examples of their good predecessours which nothing els desired but the advauncement of the lawes of God, th'increase of the catholik faithe and of vertue, good example, and good lif in the people, have now within fewe yeres devised and practysed as well to amplifie their wordly honor and possessions as their auctoritie, power, prehemynence, and jurisdiction nott only within this realme but in many other sundry provinces and contreys of the worlde. (*LP* IV 120)

ended by the imposition of a solution by an outside party to whose judgement the contending forces submit, it is notable that in this play it is the Palmer's relinquishing of his newly won sovereignty, rather than his exercising of it, which brings harmony. The play itself ends similarly, with a lesson in humility and the bold assertion that the church should be left to prune the corruption in its own branches. Neither the Palmer nor the Pedlar take it upon themselves to discipline the corrupt Pardoner.

Taken together, then, Heywood's political interludes represent a call for royal intervention in the religious and political debates taking place as the Reformation Parliament met for its first sessions, a call designed to appeal to the rhetorical and political stance currently adopted by Henry VIII. Throughout this period the king's professed position was that of mediator between the contending parties, the concerned monarch anxious to root out dissension and restore good order to the commonweal. No doubt his motives were a volatile mixture of a sincere desire for social and confessional stability and a pragmatic desire to steal the moral high ground and tactical advantage in his struggle for the 'Divorce'. But the net result was to provide a model of disinterested, concerned kingship to which both reformers and conservatives could appeal for support with some hope of success.[35]

During the first session of Parliament, Henry had intervened on a number of occasions to short-circuit debate and reduce rancour. After the bill capping probate fees had run into difficulties in the Lords, with the clergy reportedly both 'frowning and grunting' at its provisions, a joint committee of the two houses was established to consider the issue.[36] But this, too, could not reach agreement. At this point the king had new compromise bills drafted which avoided the more contentious criticisms of principles and toned down the hostile rhetoric of the originals. When the bill outlawing pluralism aroused similar opposition, Henry again stepped in to establish another committee to consider the issue away from the contentious atmosphere in both chambers.

The idea that the king might prove the best champion that the church could find would also have gained strength from his evident orthodoxy

---

[35] That the royal stance was recognised outside the immediate court is clear from the account of events produced by one London citizen, who, noting the proposal to establish a joint committee of laymen and clergy to consider legislation on clerical jurisdiction, observed that the body would contain equal numbers of laity and clergy 'and the kyng to be umpere'. J. A. Guy, 'The Political Context of *The Debellation*', in J. A. Guy, C. H. Miller and R. McGugan, eds., *The Complete Works of Thomas More* x, *The Debellation of Salem and Bizance* (New Haven, 1987), p. lxiv.

[36] Hall, p. 766.

in these years. In 1529 and 1530 Henry was actively involved in the campaign against heterodoxy, issuing proclamations against heretical books in each year, and informing Chapuys on 15 October 1530 that he intended to introduce a much stricter rule against heresy.[37] The appointment of Thomas More as lord chancellor in succession to Wolsey is often read as an anti-clerical move, placing a layman in a position traditionally occupied by clerics. But it might well have been read at the time as a more balanced gesture: a shot across the bows of both the more ardent defenders of the church and the more vocal reformers. For More, although a layman, was a staunch defender of the church and opponent of heresy, whose appointment might easily be seen as a signal that a new campaign against heterodox opinions was being planned with royal approval.

Henry's demand to be styled Supreme Head of the Church is often plausibly cited as a turning point in his relationship with the clergy. From this point, it could be argued, the clergy could be under no illusions as to their sovereign's aggressive motives towards them. But, again, it is not evident that things would have appeared so clear cut at the time. The pressure placed upon Convocation was certainly intense, but it was not unique. The Commons, too, faced Henry's wrath over the same issue. When members petitioned the king through Speaker Audley for inclusion in the General Pardon for involvement by association in Wolsey's Praemunire, hinting that they might not pass the Pardon of the Clergy if they were not also included in its provisions, they gained short shrift from Henry. He angrily retorted that he would be 'well advised' before he would pardon the laity, and menacingly observed that he could pardon the churchmen on his own under the Great Seal if the Commons were unco-operative. The delegation returned to the Lower House 'very sorrowful and pensive'.[38]

By 1530–1 the 'Divorce' issue was proceeding apace, and enormous pressure was applied to the church in England and the papacy in Rome to achieve it. But this issue was not directly and necessarily linked to the religious divisions creating so much heat in Parliament and alarming conservatives like Heywood and More. The 'Divorce' question and the debate over the headship of the church which was so obviously linked to it still cut across confessional divisions at this stage. Leading reformers like Luther and Tyndale could still oppose the king's Great Matter while

---

[37] *CSPSp*, IV (i) 460. As late as February 1533 the Papal Nuncio was invited to attend Parliament to witness the knighting of the new speaker, Humphrey Wingfield (*CSPSp*, IV (i), 1047).
[38] Hall, p. 774, *LP* V, 171.

conservatives like Gardiner and Norfolk supported the Supremacy. Under such circumstances putting the reform of the church into royal hands could still appear a safer prospect than seeing it devolve upon the common lawyers in the House of Commons. Thus, when southern Convocation spoke of the king as the defender of the church against lay hostility in the prologue to the Subsidy bill of February 1531, this may well have been more than simply wishful thinking.[39]

There was, then, good cause for Heywood to assume that appeals to Henry couched in the language of moderation and accommodation might find a ready ear. But his plays do more than simply echo royal rhetoric concerning the need to impose an end to contentious disputes. Seizing the licence afforded the dramatic good counsellor, Heywood offers the king clear advice on how to use his power once he has intervened. Implicit in *Weather* and explicit in *The Four PP* is a plea for the church to be left alone to bring about the reforms which all sides in the debates accepted were necessary.[40] In each case it is necessary to impose an end to the disputation from the outside. But it is also notable that the external authority, having brought about a reconciliation, determines to leave the situation much as it was before the dispute began. In *Weather*, Jupiter takes it upon himself to reward each of the suitors with favourable weather according to their deserts. But as each is now equally determined to conduct him or herself in the best interests of the com-

---

[39] *LP* IV (iii) 6047 (3). The prologue spoke of the laity's 'late raging agenst the same [church] and personages of the prelates of the clergie with their famous lyes and cursed bokes and workes everywhere dispersed to th'intent to blemishe and hurte the estimacion of the said prelates and clergie and to bring them into common hatred and contempt' and described how 'thy most wise and excellent majeste . . . hath [so] confounded and repressed them, that now their presumptuous boldness beginnith to rebate'. Again, prior to the Submission of the Clergy, when the prelates objected to a bill drafted by Cromwell subordinating Convocation to Parliament, Henry intervened to ensure that he alone and not Parliament was recognised as head of the church. See J. Guy, 'The Henrician Age', in J. G. A. Pocock, ed., *The Varieties of British Political Thought, 1500–1800* (Cambridge, 1994), pp. 13–46, p. 27.

[40] It is clear that from 1529–30 onwards it was accepted by all parties that some degree of ecclesiastical reform was both necessary and inevitable. On 6 December 1529, Henry told ambassador Chapuys that, although Luther had gone too far in doctrinal matters, his criticisms of clerical abuses had merit, and that he, Henry, hoped 'little by little to introduce reforms and put an end to scandal' (*CSPSp*, IV (i), 224). During 1530, Bishop Stokesley was energetically putting such ideals into practice in the diocese of London, initiating investigations aimed at weeding out inadequate priests (Brigden, *London and the Reformation*, p. 62). Other conservative figures had also argued for ecclesiastical and monastic reform in the period, including John Colet, Cardinal Wolsey, John Longland, and Thomas Starkey. See C. Harper-Bill, 'Dean Colet's Convocation Sermon and the Pre-Reformation Church in England', *History*, 73 (1988), pp. 191–210; P. J. Gwyn, *The King's Cardinal: The Rise and Fall of Thomas Wolsey* (London, 1990), pp. 265–353; M. Bowker, *The Henrician Reformation: The Diocese of Lincoln Under John Longland, 1521–1547* (Cambridge, 1981), pp. 7, 17–28, 108–9; Thomas Starkey, *A Dialogue Between Pole and Lupset*, ed. T. F. Mayer, Camden Society, 4.37 (1989), pp. 103–4; Hoyle, 'Origin of the Dissolution', pp. 280–2.

monweal, it is clear that no drastic alteration of the climate will be necessary. As Merry Report cheerfully concludes, 'Syrs, now shall ye have the wether even as yt was' (line 1240). And in *The Four PP* the Palmer's refusal to use his new-found authority is even more obvious. As we have seen, no sooner has he gained 'lordship' but he hands it back to his 'vassals', paving the way for the Pedlar's exhortation that no outsider should take it upon himself to reform ecclesiastical abuses. Thus Heywood gives the court a positive analogue for the role of the king in settling religious debate. But he makes it abundantly clear that, having suppressed the disorder, the king would be best advised to leave things as they stand. For the playwright the Royal Supremacy should lead to reformation from within not without.

Given Henry's oft-stated desire for an end to divisiveness, Heywood's advocacy of consensual politics was hardly a radical step. Indeed both conservatives and reformers can be found making a claim for royal support by adopting the call for an end to rancorous debate in these years. But behind each appeal lay more pragmatic, self-interested agenda. When a parliamentary common lawyer drafted a bill to put before the Commons in 1531, he couched it in terms which appealed directly to Henry's dislike of contention, proposing to establish thereby the 'encrease of love, amytie and good agreement betwene the spiritualtye and the temporaltie'.[41] The bill deplored the current rift between the clergy and laity and proposed that it be made illegal for members of either group to malign the other. But, behind this pluralist lanuage lay a series of practical proposals which would have stripped the church of many of its privileges and powers.[42] Similarly the Supplication against the Ordinaries, which passed the Commons on 18 March 1531, was a thoroughgoing assault upon clerical rights and immunities, yet it too was couched in the language of reconciliation, complaining of the 'grett inquyetacion and breche of your [majesty's] peace within this your most catholique realme' and lamenting that 'much discord, variance and debate hath risen, and more and more daily is like to increase and ensue amongst the universal sort of your said subjects, as well spiritual as temporal, either against other'.[43] In early 1533 Christopher St German

---

[41] S. E. Lehmberg, *The Reformation Parliament, 1529–1536* (Cambridge, 1976), pp. 120–1, *LP* v 50. The author was probably Christopher St German, the common lawyer. See Guy, 'Context', pp. xxiii *et passim.*

[42] Among the proposals the draft suggested that the clergy should be barred from forming associations to protect their worldly privileges, a stipulation which could have struck to the heart of ecclesiastical jurisdiction and government. Guy, 'Context', p. xlii.

[43] Lehmberg, *Reformation Parliament*, p. 140.

was still ostensibly deploring the ill-will between the clergy and laity in his *Treatise Concerning the Division Between the Spirituality and the Temporality* and posing as a peacemaker between the two in a tract which was actually a fierce denunciation of clerical jurisdiction, immunities, and alleged malpractices.[44]

Thus the politics of quietness and contentment had a wider currency than simply Heywood's dramatic canon. But the playwright was to prove its most earnest and consistent advocate. He was still advocating the necessity for accommodation long after it had ceased to be a rallying point for reformers, and he was to argue for it not only before the king but in other contexts as well, most remarkably of all, perhaps, in an interlude performed in the household of Archbishop Cranmer in the aftermath of the Prebendaries Plot.

Although the text of this interlude is now lost, it is possible to determine its basic outline, and to see that it, like the interludes of 1529–33, was a further endorsement of the politics of toleration. Thomas Wythorne, Heywood's one-time amanuensis, recalled in his autobiography how Cranmer had requested an interlude from Heywood's pen.

at the request of doktor [Thomas] Cranmer, lat a[rchb]yshop of Cantorbury, hee [Heywood] mad a sertayn enter[lude] or play, the whiche waz devyzed upon the parts of man, at the end wherof hee lykneth and applieth the sirkumstans therof to the universal estat of Chrystes church.[45]

Why Cranmer should have made such a request is unclear. Perhaps, as Axton and Happé suggest, the play may have been a peace offering

---

[44] St German, *A Treatise Concerning the Division Between the Spirituality and Temporality* (1533), printed in J. B. Trapp, ed., *The Complete Works of Thomas More*, ix (New Haven, 1979), pp. 176–212. The introduction states that 'This lyttell booke declareth dyvers causes, wherby division hath rysen betwene the spiritualtie and temporaltie: and partly sheweth, howe they maye be brought to a unit[y]' (sig. Aii). The tract itself begins with a lament couched in similar terms of regret and even-handedness. 'Who may remember the state of this realme now in these dayes, without great hevynes and sorow of herte? For whereas in tymes past hath reygned charite, mekenes, concorde and peace, reygneth nowe envye, pryde, division and stryfe: & that nat only betwene lay men and lay men, but also betwene religious and religious, and betwene preestes and relygyous, and that is yet more to be lamented, also betwene preestes and preestes' (sig. Aii). The reforms offered as a solution to this enmity would, however, amount to a thoroughgoing assault upon the legal and social positions of the clerical estate. The perceived enmity between the spirituality and the temporality was also deplored at about the same time by an anonymous commentator who noted that 'as the spirituality and the temporality be not, as it is thought, at such perfect love, friendship, and amity as appertaineth, the temporality to scan the temporality, thinking verily that they may have acquired a great deal more than reason would require, the spirituality again supposing all such matter and language rather to spring and proceed of malice than for any zeal of the commonwealth' (BL Cotton MS Cleopatra EIV, f. 212, cited in Hoyle, 'Origin of the Dissolution', p. 276).

[45] J. M. Osborne, ed., *The Autobiography of Thomas Wythorne* (Oxford, 1961), pp. 13–14.

from the playwright to the archbishop in the aftermath of the Prebenda-ries Plot, an attempt to ease his return to favour in court circles after his condemnation and public recantation of treasonable plotting against the Royal Supremacy in 1542.[46] Alternatively Cranmer's approach (and Whythorne's account suggests that the initiative did come from the archbishop and not the playwright) might have been prompted by a desire to test the author's newly avowed compliance with the Suprem-acy. Was he trying to secure form Heywood a public statement of orthodoxy or, failing that, trap him into producing public evidence of catholic sympathies? Whichever was the case, it is characteristic of the playwright that he responded to the commission with a play fully in the spirit of *The Play of Love* and *The Four PP*, a drama which called for a tolerant accommodation of difference for the overall benefit of the Christian commonweal, a commonweal here figured literally as the body politic. For, as Wythorne describes in a later part of his autobi-ography, *The Parts of Man* took the form of a dramatic debate involving a disputation between Reason and Will over which of them should govern human activity. First Reason argued that only his presence distin-guished Man from the beasts, then the claim was challenged by Will, 'who dispiuteth with reazon for the siuprem government in Man, whereupon in the end thei both ar dryven to graunt that man kan do nothing withowt will, and without reazon Man kan do no good thing.'[47] Even when writing for the most influential and committed spokesman for reform, then, Heywood was determined to make the case for the religious *via media*, for in this lay the heart of his dramatic and political strategy.

HEYWOOD AND MORE: THE POLITICS OF PUBLICATION

Heywood thus used the opportunities provided by his position as a playwright writing for the household of both king and archbishop to make the case for pacification and reconciliation in the most effective way available to him. He did so, not primarily because of any innate generosity of spirit or sense of fair play (although he may well have possessed both in good measure), but because he seems to have con-cluded that a policy of 'quietness' and reconciliation was the most effective means of safeguarding the traditional rights and status of the catholic church in England and, with them, the central tenets of the

---

[46] Axton and Happé, eds., *Plays*, p. 8.   [47] Osborne, *Autobiography*, p. 74.

orthodox faith in which he believed so passionately. In this, he was pursuing a strategy distinctly at odds with that pursued by Sir Thomas More, the man with whom he is so often linked.

It is something of a critical commonplace to note Heywood's close associations with the More–Rastell circle, and to read remarks in a number of his plays as supportive of More's own position in the early 1530s.[48] Indeed the very decision to publish those plays from William Rastell's press in 1533/4 has itself been described as 'part of an energetic campaign . . . to support Thomas More after his resignation as Chancellor in his private stand for the old beliefs and loyalties'.[49] As Heywood's most recent editors have suggested, there are sufficient telling coincidences of phrase and argument between Heywood's interludes and More's polemical writings to suggest that Heywood was aware of the latter's work (and probably vice versa) and that his own writing was informed by it.[50] But, what too great a concentration upon the similarities of detail between the two authors' work obscures is the profound difference in their overall strategies. Both men were striving to defend the church and traditional religious practice in their work, but they did so in markedly different ways. While Heywood was crafting eloquent and genial testimonies to the benefits of accommodation: opposing confrontation and dispute, More was actively pursuing a policy of confrontation, exposing and attempting to exterminate heresy through both the printed word and the official machinery of investigation and punishment available to him as lord chancellor.

While More expressed open hostility to the idea of religious diversity, throwing tract after polemical tract onto an already extensive canon of European contentious literature, Heywood, as we have seen, took a softer line. Taking his cue from Henry VIII's own pronouncements about arbitrating between the church and its critics, he made the case for the suppression of contention from above, and thus for royal protection for the church while it reformed itself from within. He sought not the toleration of heresy, but its removal by gentler means. Thus he offered the prospect that all the contending parties might be welcomed back into the broad and diverse confraternity of the universal catholic church. In so doing he engaged with the king's own oft-stated desire for harmony within the commonweal, presenting the current dissension as the work of an over-zealous few.

The marked contrast between the two writers' approaches can be

---

[48] Axton and Happé, eds., *Plays*, pp. 6–7; Reed, *Early Tudor Drama*, pp. 82–7.
[49] Axton and Happé, eds., *Plays*, pp. 6–7.   [50] For the similarities, see ibid., p. 39.

judged from the works published by Rastell between 1532 and 1534. While Heywood's plays move towards reconciliation and consensus, the very titles of More's texts (many of which are paradoxically written in one of the most consensual forms, the dialogue, in which two contesting opinions are gradually reconciled to a single view) proclaim their hostile, confrontational intent. More despatched *The **Confutation** of Tyndale's Answer* (1532), *The **Debellation** of Salem and Bizance* (1533), *A Letter **Impugning** the Erroneous writings of John Frith* (1533), and *The Answer to a Poisoned Book* (1533).[51] And this aggressive attitude was reflected in his practical activities as lord chancellor. As the church came under increasing criticism in parliament for the severity of its punishment of heretics and for the manner of its proceeding *ex officio* against laymen in its courts, More made no effort to moderate his allies on the episcopal bench or to appease reforming opinion. Indeed he acted in an increasingly provocative manner, using and occasionally abusing the powers at his disposal to pursue the fight against heresy, imprisoning and interrogating suspects in his own home, instigating high-profile trials of leading reformers, and overseeing humiliating ceremonial recantations for those found guilty of handling forbidden books.[52]

In Autumn 1531 More arrested the book-dealer George Constantine and held him in the stocks in his porter's lodge at Chelsea until he broke free and escaped abroad in early December. From Constantine he obtained the information which enabled the arrest and trial of the Benedictine monk Richard Bayfield, who was burned at the stake at Smithfield on 4 December. Another victim of the flames that December was the leather-seller John Tewkesbury, who had also been imprisoned by More prior to his trial, as had James Bainham who was to be burned in April 1532. All of this, however provocative, was within the law. More questionable was the Ccancellor's use of the court of Star Chamber to investigate the events surrounding the controversial burning of Thomas Bilney in Norwich in August 1531. Here it is hard to avoid the conclusion

---

[51] My emphasis in each case. More's conception of his own role as the antithesis of Heywood's ideal was to be made obvious in *The Debellation* (1533). There he represents himself as a martial champion of orthodoxy belligerently defending the lists against all comers. He had, he boasted, chased Christopher St German's *Salem and Bizance* (notionally 'Jerusalem and Byzantium') back to their own countries, 'And if the Pacifier [St German] conveie them hyther againe, and tenne suche other towns with them, embatailed in such dialogues; Sir Thomas More hath undertaken to put himself in thadventure alone against them all', *English Works* (1557), p. 929. For a perceptive exposition of More's stance in the polemical tracts, see A. Fox, *Thomas More: History and Providence* (Oxford, 1982), pp. 128–98.

[52] Guy, *Public Career*, pp. 141–74; R. Marius, *Thomas More* (London, 1984), pp. 386–406; R. W. Chambers, *Thomas More* (London, 1935), pp. 275–82.

that More was misusing his authority to summon witnesses to an *ex officio* enquiry merely to destroy Bilney's reputation as a steadfast reformer and so deprive the evangelicals of a martyr.[53]

At precisely the point that Heywood was devising his dramatic expositions of the dangers of religious contention, then, his 'ally' More was probably the most prominent advocate of religious antagonism in the land. It is hard, therefore, to read Heywood's plays as unequivocal defences of either More or his policies. Unlike More's texts, Heywood's dramas argue, not that heresy should be suppressed, but that contention itself should be eliminated. Both the aggressive anti-clerical and the reactionary catholic come in for criticism in *The Pardoner and The Friar* and *The Four PP*. And it is disputatiousness and special pleading *per se* which are condemned in *Weather*, rather than any particular shade of opinion.[54] Such a strategy clearly rests on the premise that an end to debate at a time when the tide seemed to be running with the reformers was in the church's best interests, and so, as we have seen, is hardly impartial. But it nonetheless condemns the kind of polemical partisanship practised by More along with the militant anti-clericalism of the parliamentary common lawyers and the evangelicals.

In the light of the distinctly different strategies pursued by the two men, it is possible to see the publication of Heywood's interludes in 1533–4 as a rather more complex and interesting matter than is often assumed. Rather than simply offering support for More's stance, Rastell's decision to print the plays, and the manner in which he did so, read rather as an attempt to qualify and eventually to distance himself from

---

[53] G. Townsend and S. R. Cattley, eds., *The Acts and Monuments of John Foxe* (8 vols., London, 1837–41), IV, pp. 619–55, 688–93, 697–705; Guy, *Public Career*, pp. 170–1, Greg Walker, 'Saint or Schemer?: The 1527 Heresy Trial of Thomas Bilney Reconsidered', *Journal of Ecclesiastical History*, 40 (1989), pp. 219–38, revised and reprinted in Walker, *Persuasive Fictions: Faith, Faction and Political Culture in the Reign of Henry VIII* (Aldershot, 1996), pp. 143–65.

[54] Interestingly, Heywood's son, Ellis was to continue this same strategy in his account of More's thought and conversation in the dialogue *Il Moro*, published in Italian in 1556. In this text, dedicated to Cardinal Pole, the younger Heywood recrafted a vision of More as the accommodating humanist which he had ceased to be by the 1530s at the latest. As the dialogue's modern editor observes, Heywood has his More fulfil precisely the function which his father had employed to resolve the disputations in his interludes. 'After each [debater] has had his say, More defines the problem of happiness and proposes the solution which has evaded the others . . . The others cling tenaciously to partial notions . . . and are unhappy, while More is happy precisely because he has moved beyond these partial insights to a more comprehensive vision of human happiness'. *Il Moro: Ellis Heywood's Dialogue in Memory of Thomas More*, ed. and trans. Roger Lee Deakins (Cambridge, MA, 1972), p. xiv. I am very grateful to Mark Robson of the University of Leeds for this reference.

the full rigour of the former chancellor's position, as close scrutiny of the chronology of events suggests.

Having resigned the chancellorship on 16 May 1532 (the day after the formal Submission of the Clergy), More subsequently devoted himself to opposing what he saw as the dangerous follies of heresy and anti-clerical-ism through the tracts noted above. In this he found a ready ally in William Rastell, who was to publish all More's polemical texts written in this period. More was, however, walking a fine line between the freedom of the private citizen to engage in debate about subjects which were not officially prohibited, and the sort of wilful opposition to government policy which could be interpreted as treasonable. In writing against Will-iam Tyndale in the two parts of *The Confutation of Tyndale's Answer* (1532 and 1533), More was able to maintain the polite fiction that he was not entering into the political debate or opposing the drift of royal policy directly, merely refuting the errors of an acknowledged heretic. But in turning his ire against Christopher St German in *The Apology* and *The Debellation of Salem and Bizance*, he was pursuing an altogether more dan-gerous strategy. As John Guy has argued, in taking on St German, More was knowingly attacking a man who enjoyed support among members of the king's council.[55] Thus, although he strenuously denied opposing the crown or intervening in politics, it is unsurprising that the government took an increasingly sceptical and suspicious line. By January 1534, Cromwell was investigating rumours that More was writing a riposte to the official propaganda published in *The Articles Devised By the Whole Con-sent of the King's Most Honourable Council* (December 1533). At this point William Rastell was questioned about his involvement in More's cam-paign, and had to deny any knowledge of a new, anti-governmental work. By 21 February, More was under investigation for more directly treasonable activities. He was accused of Misprision in the Act of Attain-der laid before the House of Lords against Elizabeth Barton, the Nun of Kent, who had fomented opposition to the royal 'divorce' through vi-sions and prophecies. More's name was subsequently removed from the act, but this was only a temporary reprieve. On 17 April he was arrested and taken to the Tower for refusing to take the oath attached to the Act of Succession, and was not to emerge again until his execution on 6 July 1535.

At the same time that he was printing More's increasingly incendiary

---

[55] Guy, 'Context', pp. xxii-xxviii.

tracts, Rastell was, as we have seen, also publishing the more amiable, accommodating interludes of Heywood. The presentation of the two sets of texts is informative. During 1532 and early 1533 it is clear that More's dialogues were enjoying the full confidence and endorsement of the printer. The two parts of *The Confutation* were printed with an elaborate title page, framed with the monumental proscenium arch generally employed by Rastell for his more prestigious publications, and proclaiming the works as 'made by Syr Thomas More, Knyght, lorde Chauncellour of Englonde'.[56] The more contentious *Debellation*, published later in the same year, was, however, a considerably less impressive affair. Its title page was framed by a far less impressive ornament, and simply announced the name of the work.[57] While this may in part be explained as the result of haste on the author's part to have the text published as quickly as possible, while the polemical iron was still hot, it is equally possible that this apparent downgrading of More's work might reflect a desire on the printer's part to distance himself from the work. Anxious at the increasingly anti-governmental stance that his uncle was taking, Rastell may well have desired to play down the close association between himself and the works which was evident in the earlier texts. Perhaps significantly, Rastell was to use the monumental arch decoration again in 1533, this time on his edition of Fabian's *Chronicle*, the title page of which proclaimed a sentiment which was rather more politically conformist. The text was advertised as

Fabyans Chronycle: newly prynted wyth the cronycle, actes, & dedes done in the tyme of the reyne of the moste excellent prynce kyng Henry the vii father unto our most drad soverayne Lord Kynge Henry the VIII. To whom be all honour, reverence, and joyfull contynaunce of his prosperous reygne, to the pleasure of god and wele of his realme. AMEN[58]

Was Rastell consciously proclaiming his loyalty to the crown at a time when he felt himself to be under unwelcome scrutiny from above? Interestingly, just as More's texts were being presented in a less prestigious manner by Rastell, Heywood's interludes were enjoying the opposite fate. In 1533 Rastell printed *John Johan* and *The Pardoner and The Friar* in cheaply made editions, without title pages and which did not name their author. Such lack of preliminary apparatus is perhaps easy to explain, given the low status of dramatic publishing in this early period.

---

[56] *RSTC* 18092, sig. Ai, and *RSTC* 18080.   [57] *RSTC* 18081, sig. Ai.   [58] *RSTC* 10660, sig. Ai.

But what followed is less explicable. The next interlude to be printed, *The Play of The Weather* (1533) was given a title page with minor ornaments, and named Heywood as its author. *A Play of Love*, printed on 15 January 1534, was not only given a title page and an author, but was given the ornamental arch that had previously been reserved for substantial works like Fabian's *Chronicle*, More's earlier texts and the *Registrum Omnium Brevium Judicialium*.[59] The contrast between the first and last of the Heywood interludes published by Rastell is remarkable. What had prompted this remarkable change in status in the space of less than twelve months? No doubt a number of explanations are possible. But a weather eye on the political situation by printer and author alike seems the most likely. Just as the government was turning its attention upon More in a serious fashion and beginning to investigate his collaborators, Rastell altered the look of the most oppositional of the texts which he published for his uncle, making it appear less significant and less like the work for which he expected the greatest market and the greatest financial and professional profit. At the same time he began to increase the status of the interludes written by another member of his family and circle – interludes which spoke for a wholly less contentious and more politically acceptable form of religious and political conservatism. This process ended in the printing of *A Play of Love* in a format hitherto reserved for only the most prestigious of his editions, a format which proclaimed the text to be more central to the work of his press. Within little more than a month of the publication of *Love*, Rastell was himself being interrogated by Cromwell, and More was accused of misprision of treason. That the former escaped any further repercussions while the latter was less fortunate perhaps owed something to the timely advocacy of the more accommodating Heywoodian line by the Rastell press. Far from marking unqualified support for More's political stance, then, the printer's decision to publish Heywood's interludes how and when he did might more plausibly be read as an attempt to indicate differences in opinion between printer and author, and within the More circle itself over the wisdom of the former chancellor's stance.

Indeed, given the Erasmian moderation of the writings of others in the More circle at this time, most notably Thomas Elyot, whose dialogues and treatises consistently argued from classical models for an accommodating political culture which would neutralise the radicalism

[59] *RSTC* 20836 (1531).

of demands for reform,[60] it might well be argued that it was More himself, rather than Heywood, who was out of step with the mood and strategic thinking of the circle around him at this time. Which of the two men was pursuing the more effective strategy in defence of traditional beliefs and practices is a moot point. In the short term, of course, both were to fail, and More was to pay for directly opposing the royal will with his life in 1535. Heywood at least survived the reign, and indeed was to prosper in the next until he could laud the return of catholicism at the accession of Mary. But it would be unwise to see the strategy of 'quietness' and accommodation as simply the product of a desire for self-preservation, or a naive and misplaced faith in Henry VIII's innate religious conservatism. With hindsight Heywood's pleas for reconciliation can appear hopelessly misguided, a doomed attempt to square the circle of loyalty to the crown and allegiance to an international church whose days in England were numbered. But hindsight obscures as much as it reveals. It can, for example, create the impression that each of the measures undertaken in the course of the Reformation Parliament, from the first bills limiting ecclesiastical privileges to the Royal Supremacy itself, was a logical step on a predetermined march towards a separate and independent Church of England, hostile to Rome and inclined doctrinally towards the reformed churches of Germany, Switzerland, and Scandinavia.[61] But this was not the case. Henry VIII clearly did not intend a formal and institutional schism when he called the Reforma-

---

[60] Greg Walker, 'Thomas Elyot and the Politics of Accommodation: *The Defence of Good Women*', in Walker, *Persuasive Fictions*, pp. 178–203. Elyot (described by Stapleton as among More's 'friends and companions in the pursuit of polite literature', Thomas Stapleton, *Tres Thomai* (Douai, 1588), ed. and trans. P. E. Hallet as *The Life and Illustrious Martyrdom of Sir Thomas More* (London, 1928), p. 44) was to make his differences with More explicit in a number of communications with Thomas Cromwell. In *c.* 1537 he asked Cromwell to 'lay apart the remembraunce of the amity betwene me and Sir Thomas More, which was but *usque ad aras* ['up to the altars': i.e. a merely private friendship rather than a political alliance], as is the proverb, consydering that I was never so moche addict unto him as I was unto truthe and fidelity towards my soveraigne lord, as Godd is my juge' (BL Cotton MS Cleopatra E IV, f. 260). In 1534 he had spoken of his friendship with religious conservatives more generally, informing Cromwell that his own desire for reform had caused 'no little contencion betwixt me and suche persones as ye have thowght that I have specialy favored, even as ye also didd, for some laudable qualities which we supposed to be in them. But neither they mowght persuade me to approve that which both my faith and my raison condemned, nor I mowght dissuade them from the excusing that which all the world abhorred. Which obstinacy of bothe partes relentid the grete affection betwene us and withdrewe our familiare repayre' (BL Cotton MS Cleopatra E VI, f. 254). See S. E. Lehmberg, *Thomas Elyot: Tudor Humanist* (Austin, TX, 1960), pp. 15 and 150.

[61] For possibly the most extravagant assertion of this teleological argument, see J. C. Bryant, *Tudor Drama and Religious Controversy* (Mercer, 1984), p. 1: 'As far back as the coming of William the Conqueror to the throne of England there appeared a breach between church and state that could never mend. It was destined to result in Henry VIII's reformation of the church in England.'

tion Parliament in 1529, still less when he made the first moves to dissolve his marriage in 1527–8. What he wanted was a divorce from Katherine of Aragon which was honourable, public, and universally recognised. Those signs of incipient 'imperial' ambition which some critics have detected earlier, in his redrafting of the coronation oath, or the naming of ships for the royal navy, suggest more a proper sense of royal dignity and diplomatic sabre-rattling than any long-term intention to assert jurisdictional claims against Rome.[62]

And while the *primum mobile* of royal policy remained the desire for a divorce, recognition of the king's right to marry Anne Boleyn, and the legitimisation of their subsequent offspring, the eventual reconciliation of political and religious loyalties, was not an implausible expectation for conservatives like Heywood. As Henry had no real desire to establish a fully reformed faith in England for its own sake, the possibility that a compromise might be reached with Rome, or with the English clergy, which would give Henry what he wanted and leave the church and its doctrine substantially intact, was always present. Any one of a host of imponderable factors could have radically altered the train of events which hindsight now imparts with an air of inevitability. Had Katherine of Aragon (or indeed Anne Boleyn) died of natural causes in 1529, 1530, or even 1532; had Henry's volatile passions been redirected back towards Katherine or towards another mistress who set her sights rather lower than a royal marriage;[63] or had the king heeded subtle papal hints that a bigamous marriage to Anne in 1528 could break the deadlock and be sorted out legally once Imperial tempers had cooled, then the need to push the divorce demand until the joints linking England to Rome were shattered would have been removed. Conversely, had Clement himself died in this period and been replaced by a pontiff less sensitive to Imperial pressure; had a sufficient weight of continental scholarly opinion swung behind Henry's case to make a papal judgement in Katherine's favour impossible; or had the aged Archbishop Warham not lived on until 1532, and had his successor, or his fellow bishops, taken the view that an annulment of the royal marriage was within the

---

[62] For 'Imperial' precedents earlier in the reign, see W. Ullmann, 'This Realm of England is an Empire', *Journal of Ecclesiastical History*, 30 (1979), pp. 175–203.

[63] The seemingly unlikely possibility of Henry's returning to Katherine and so enabling a political and religious rapprochement received serious support in May and June 1531. Sermons were delivered at court on the issue, prominent individuals spoke out against divisiveness and in favour of Katherine, and the Dukes of Norfolk and Suffolk were said to feel that the time was ripe to 'strive to dismount the King from his folly', *LP* v 238 and 287. See C. Haigh, *English Reformations*, p. 110.

remit of the domestic ecclesiastical courts, then a settlement of royal demands might have been reached without a schism. In either case it would then have been possible for the reform of the church which all sides agreed was necessary to have been conducted in an atmosphere far less charged with diplomatic and political implications. In such circumstances the sort of modest moral and financial reforms enacted in the parliamentary session of 1529, and those put in train by Convocation in 1531, might well have marked the end rather than the beginning of the English Reformation. Consequently Heywood's intelligent, good-humoured dramatic appeals for national and confessional reconciliation might now be read, not as the products of a naive, misguided, optimism, but as effective contributions to the debates at court, and prime examples of that policy of quietness and accommodation which was to be the 'spirit of the age'.

CHAPTER 4

Acting government: Sir David Lindsay's 'Ane Satyre of the Thrie Estaitis'

With Sir David Lindsay's panoramic political, social, and religious satire *The Thrie Estaitis* we move to a different court and a later time period to that covered by the plays of John Heywood.[1] But the foci of our interests remains the same: household drama and the politics of performance. For Lindsay's play provides a valuable example of a household play written for a different but closely related political culture. Moreover, it is doubly revealing of the politics of performance in the early Renaissance, for it existed in not one but two forms, the first an interlude performed indoors before James V at the royal palace of Linlithgow in 1540, the second performed in the open air, first on Castle Hill, Cupar, Fifeshire on 7 June 1552, and then on the Greenside Playfield, Calton Hill, Edinburgh on 12 August 1554. On both the latter occasions, Scotland was without an adult king and administered by a regent. And, on the last occasion at least, that regent, the queen dowager, Marie of Guise, was present at the performance. A comparison of the two versions of the play, insofar as this is possible, can, then, tell us much about how a political drama adapts itself to the very different circumstances of, first a household performance before a reigning monarch and, second, an outdoor performance before a far wider cross-section of the political community in a realm without an adult monarch upon whom to focus. What follows will attempt to draw out the political implications of each

[1] I am grateful for the help and advice offered by Dr John J. McGavin of Southampton University and my colleague at Leicester, Dr Elaine M. Treharne, who read various drafts of parts of this chapter, and to my students and colleagues at the University of Leicester, especially David Salter, for sharing their thoughts on Lindsay's work with me, both inside and outside the seminar room. I am also greatly indebted to Glen Thomas of the University of Queensland for his tireless labours on my behalf in the university library during the heady three-week period when I could afford (thanks to an administrative error) the services of a research assistant. Carol Edington's excellent study of Lindsay's political and poetic career, *Court and Culture in Renaissance Scotland: Sir David Lindsay of the Mount* (Amherst, 1994) appeared after this chapter was substantially completed, but I have referred to it, and where possible engaged with its arguments, in the footnotes which follow.

performance and account for the often profound differences between the two.

SIR DAVID LINDSAY OF THE MOUNT

Lindsay the courtier

Sir David Lindsay of the Mount (*c.* 1486–1555) is a fascinating subject for study. Courtier, diplomat, herald, poet, dramatist, and companion of the young King James V, he was a thoroughly courtly figure – perhaps the most thoroughly courtly poet of the sixteenth century.[2] He was the eldest son of David Lindsay of the Mount, whose family estates were centred on Cupar in Fife, but from early in his life the centre of his own activities was the royal household. He was probably the 'one called Lindsay' whose name appears in the Exchequer Rolls for 1508 as '*in averia quondam domini principis*' (that is, in the household of the infant Prince James who lived for less than a year and died on 17 February 1508).[3] And his close association with drama and courtly entertainment also began early in his career. He took part in a play before James IV and Queen Margaret Tudor at Holyrood Abbey during October 1511, for which he was provided with a specially made coat.

ij$\frac{1}{2}$ elnis blew taffatis and vi quartaris yallow taffatis to be ane play coit to David Lindesay for the play playt in the King and Quenis presence in the Abbay.[4]

But it was after James IV's untimely death in the Scottish military defeat at Flodden in 1513 that Lindsay was to cement his uniquely close relationship with the Scottish monarchy.

His first official post in the household of the infant James V was that of usher. But, as the description of his duties offered in his later poem, *The Dreme* (1528), addressed to the adult king, reveals, his relationship with his young sovereign was to be far deeper and wider-ranging than this initial appointment would suggest.

> Quhen thow wes young, I bure ye in myne arme,
> Full tenderlie tyll thow begouth to gang,
> And in thy bed oft happit the full warme;
> With lute in hand, syne, sweitlie to the sang;
> Sumtyme, in dansing, feiralie I flang;

---

[2] See D. Hamer, ed., *The Works of Sir David Lindsay of the Mount* (4 vols., Edinburgh, 1936), IV, pp. ix–liv.   [3] Ibid., p. 246, no. 24; Edington, *Court and Culture*, p. 13.   [4] Ibid., p. 246, no. 26.

And, sumtyme, playand fairsis on the flure;
And, sumtyme, on myne office takkand cure;

And, sumtyme, lyke ane feind, transfegurate;
And, sumtyme, lyke the greislie gaist of gye;
In divers formis oft tymes, disfigurate;
And, sumtyme, dissagyist full plesandlye.
So, sen thy birth, I have continewalye
Bene occupyit, and aye to thy plesoure;
And, sumtyme, seware, Coppare, and Carvoure,

Thy purs maister and secreit Thesaurare,
Thy Yschare, aye sen thy Natyvitie,
And of thy chalmer cheiffe Cubiculare,
Quhilk, to this houre, hes keipit my lawtie.   (lines 8–25)[5]

And with James' growth into adolescence and manhood, Lindsay adapted and continued his personal service, reading and telling the young king stories of classical heroes and heroines, political prophecies and popular fables (lines 29–49).

What Lindsay here describes (even if he exaggerates some of the detail for comic effect) is a relationship which goes far beyond simple courtly service, bordering on surrogate fatherhood and certainly encompassing the roles of personal entertainer, informal tutor, guardian, and friend. And it is this uniquely intimate relationship with his sovereign that was to dominate his life until James' death in 1542, and give his work in this period its pre-eminent quality as household literature.

Except for a brief exclusion from court in the mid-1520s, during the temporary ascendancy of Archibald Douglas, Sixth Earl of Angus, Lindsay remained *'familiarius domini regis'* throughout this period.[6] And this household focus dominated his literary output. All his extant poems and dramatic works reveal an explicit focusing on the person of the king or (more rarely) the queen, whether through formal dedications, direct addresses, or acknowledgements of a royal commission. The poem that we have already glanced at, *The Dreme*, begins with a preparatory epistle to the 'Rycht Potent Prince, of hie Imperial blude' (line 1), and ends with a direct demand that the king take reform of the church and common-

[5] J. Small and F. Hall, eds., *Sir David Lyndesay's Works*, EETS, o.s. 11, 19, 35, 37, and 47 (5 parts reprinted in 2 vols., New York, 1969). All references to Lindsay's works other than *The Thrie Estaitis* are to this edition.

[6] See Hamer, ed., *Works*, IV, pp. 246–7. For a helpful account of the centrality of the court and the person of the king to Lindsay's thinking generally, see Edington, *Court and Culture*, pp. 1, 11, 15, and 115.

weal into his own hands. *The Complaint* (*c.* 1529) is again addressed to the king, and is written to be delivered in the Presence Chamber, as the reference to 'yow, my Lordis, that standis by' (line 109) makes clear. *The Testament of the Papyngo* (1530) concerns the death of the king's parrot, and contains an epistle from the dying bird to James himself and another to her brother at court. His other poems of the reign – a description of a mock joust supposedly witnessed by the royal couple, the 'complaint and public confessioun' of one of the king's dogs, an appeal to the king against the extravagant 'syde taillis' of contemporary fashion, and a reply to a (lost) flyting written by James himself – similarly show clear evidence of their household origins. Each piece, moreover, reflects the particular license of household production in its capacity both to honour its royal recipient and also to seek, through the offering of good counsel to influence and persuade him too.[7] This is nowhere clearer than in the dramatic pageant designed by Lindsay to greet Marie of Guise on her arrival in St Andrews on 10 June 1538. The pageant, performed at the New Abbey Gate, both welcomed the French princess as an honoured guest and the future Queen of Scotland, and also made quite clear what was expected of her by her loyal subjects. As she approached the gates, a great cloud descended, which divided to reveal an angel who handed her symbolic keys to the realm ('in signe and taikan that all the heartis of Scotland was oppinit to the ressawing of hir grace'), but also presented her

Witht certane wriesouns and exortatiouns maid be the said Dawid Lynsay into the quens grace instructioun quhilk teichit hir to serve her god, obey hir husband, and keep hir body clene according to godis will and commandement.[8]

By 1532, Lindsay had also taken on a new role which was to formalise and extend his special relationship with the king, with kingship itself, and with the political nation more widely. By this time he had certainly become Snowden Herald, and may well also have assumed (as deputy) the highest heraldic office, that of Lyon King of Arms, a role which he was to perform in his own right from 1540. As a herald – and more obviously as Lyon King – Lindsay's role at court, and his role specifically as a courtly writer, took on powerful new resonances.

As Janet Hadley Williams has noted, the office of Lyon King gave Lindsay responsibility for the ceremonial aspects of court life and also

---

[7] See Edington, *Court and Culture*, p. 206.
[8] Robert Lindsay of Pitscottie, *The History and Chronicles of Scotland*, ed. Æ. J. G. Mackay (3 vols., Edinburgh, 1899–1911), I, p. 379.

made him 'guardian and recorder of Scottish arms and pedigrees'.[9] This alone gave him a uniquely influential status at court and in the wider realm as a repository of chivalric lore and wisdom. But, more important still for Lindsay's role as a writer were the responsibilities of the office to act as the chief representative of the crown to the political nation and of the realm as a whole to the crown. In Parliament, Lyon King sat *ex officio* at the foot of the throne, at the king's right hand, and

> would convey to the monarch those formal messages brought to him by the heralds and pursuivants from the assembly. In complementary action, he would also proclaim to the parliamentary assembly the sovereign's own words. Such a role was pivotal, yet mediating; formal, yet deeply involved. Lindsay acted in place of the realm in addressing the King, as representative of the Crown in communicating to the people, and, by extrapolation, on behalf of the kingdom when furth of Scotland.[10]

Lindsay's formal, official voice – and, by implication, his less formal, poetic, voice – had thus a signal authority with which to address political issues on behalf of both king and commonweal. His office formalised and strengthened his freedom – indeed his obligation – as a household man, to bring political issues, and political counsel, to the ear of the sovereign.

Again, the crucial point here is the fundamental role played by the person of the king in this equation. Lindsay speaks for the realm, not in a merely general sense, but specifically to the king, and for the king, in turn, to his subjects. It is James V who provides the context for, and the meaning of, his political role. Consequently, the death of the king in 1542 posed almost unanswerable questions for Lindsay. On top of the, no doubt, profound psychological impact of the loss of an individual whom he had served, loved, and counselled for so long, the loss of an adult male sovereign removed the one fixed point in Lindsay's political landscape. What did a royal counsellor and the voice of the sovereign do when there was no adult monarch to counsel and speak for? It was with the implications of this question that Lindsay was to struggle for the remaining thirteen years of his life.

As David Reid has tellingly suggested, the preparatory Epistle to *Ane Dialog betuixt Experience and ane Courteour* (*c.* 1550) provides valuable evi-

---

[9] Janet Hadley Williams, 'Shady Publishing in Sixteenth-Century Scotland: The Case of David Lyndsay's Poems', *Bibliographical Society of Australia and New Zealand Bulletin*, 16 (1992), pp. 97–106, p. 98.

[10] Ibid., p. 98. For the roles and responsibilities of Scottish heralds, see Edington, *Court and Culture*, pp. 28–32.

dence of the author's discomfort at the thought of writing poetry of counsel in a realm without an adult sovereign to whom to address it.[11] Addressing his text, Lindsay laments,

> We have no kyng the to present, allace!
> Quhilk to this countre bene ane cairful cace;
> And als our Quene, of Scotland Heretour,
> Sche dwellith i France: I pray God saif hir grace.
> It war to lang for the to run that race,
> And far langer or that young tender flour
> Bryng home tyll ws ane Kyng and Governour,
> Allace, tharfor, we may with sorrow syng,
> Quhilk moste so lang remane without ane Kyng.   (lines 10–18)

Somewhat at a loss as to where else to despatch the *Dialog*, Lindsay addresses the Regency governors, 'James [Second Earl of Arran] our Prince and Protectour' (line 26) and 'his Brother [John Hamilton, Archbishop of St Andrews], our Spirituall Governour / And Prince of Preistis of this Natioun' (lines 27–8). But he seeks only their token approval, in order that the poem might be distributed more widely still.

> Than go thy waye quhare ever thow plesis best;
> Be thay [the governors] content, mak reverence to the rest.
>
> To faithfull Prudent Pastouris Spirituall,
> To nobyll Erlis, and Lordis Temporall.   (lines 35–38)

In the absence of a single, royal, addressee, Lindsay evidently had no clear sense of an addressee at all. Having here suggested that the poem should be despatched (albeit somewhat haphazardly) to the political elite, he goes on to redefine it later as a text for the commons, the 'unlernit knawis' who know no Latin (line 547).

> Quharefore to Colyearis, Cairtaris and to Cukis –
> To Jok and Thome – my Ryme sall be diractit.   (lines 549–50)

The sense of Lindsay making fun here at the expense of those quibbling clerks who will criticise his use of the vernacular to treat scholarly themes is unmistakable.

---

[11] David Reid, 'Rule and Misrule in Lindsay's *Thrie Estaitis* and Pitcairne's *Assembly*', *Scottish Literary Journal*, 11 (1984), pp. 5–24, pp. 8–9. 'It is as if didactic writing was a forlorn affair to him if it was not in some sense advice to his king.' Reid goes on, however, to argue for the centrality of Rex Humanitas as a figure of sound royal governance in the 1552–4 production of *The Thrie Estaitis*, performed during the minority, and absence, of Mary, Queen of Scots. As what follows will demonstrate, my own reading of the play reaches rather different conclusions from the same initial premise about Lindsay's reliance on the monarch.

Thocht every commoun may nocht be ane clerk,
Nor hes no Leid except thare toung maternall,
Quhy suld of god the marvellous hevinly werk
Be hid frome thame? I thynk it nocht fraternall.   (lines 552–5)

Yet, there also seems a genuine dilemma over where to direct so important a work in the absence of its natural recipient: a king. As the ambivalence of the references to 'Jok and Thome' and 'unlernit knawis' makes clear, Lindsay was not truly interested in educating the whole of society. His text is explicitly a courtly tract, and its counsel had meaning only within a courtly context. Thus the dilemma became all the more acute. Not only did Lindsay need to find a role as a counsellor without a king, he also needed to learn to function as a courtier and household man without a household in which to operate. As we shall see, it was a dilemma which informed (and frustrated) much of the 1552–4 production of *The Thrie Estaitis*.

Lindsay the reformer

Lindsay's precise religious inclinations have been the subject of much critical discussion. It has been suggested both that he was a consistently moderate figure, arguing for reform of the church from within rather than a reformation of it from without; *and* that he was a convinced reformer who, as the years passed became more and more convinced of the necessity for radical measures.[12] There is no doubt some truth in each assertion. Lindsay was never a radical protestant in the Knoxian mould. His demands for reform were always framed within the parameters of practical politics, and he remained silent on the most radical reforming doctrine of all, criticism of the miracle of the Mass. Yet neither was he wholly a conformist. It is important always to be aware of the context in which an individual's beliefs and opinions were developed and given expression, for context alone makes them either moderate or radical. The crucial context for the development of Lindsay's religious thinking in the period to 1542 was provided by the views of James V.

It has been argued that King James' own desire for reform from within the church was wholly reflected in Lindsay's thought and writings.[13] But this is surely misleading. It seems clear that, from the late 1520s onwards, Lindsay's own religious views, although in themselves

---

[12] Williams, 'Shady Publishing', p. 100; Edington, *Court and Culture*, pp. 28–32.
[13] Williams, 'Shady Publishing', p. 99; Claude Graf, 'Theatre and Politics: Lindsay's *Satyre of the Thrie Estaitis*' in A. Aitken, M. McDiarmid, and D. Thomson, eds., *Bards and Makars: Scottish Language and Literature: Medieval and Renaissance* (Glasgow, 1977), pp. 143–55, p. 147. For an account of James V's religious position, see Edington, *Court and Culture*, p. 51 and following.

only partially reformist, were in important respects distinctly more radical than those of his king. In *The Complaynt* (1529), for example, he was already attacking a number of central catholic practices as 'vaine traditiounis' of the clergy (line 418):

> As superstitious pylgrimages,
> Prayand to grawin ymages,
> Expres aganis the Lordis command.   (lines 421–3)

Consequently when, in the *Dialog* (of *c.* 1550), he turned upon the 'idolatrous' practices of the clergy in Edinburgh, it marked merely a change of tone rather than a fundamental shift in doctrinal position.

> Off Edinburgh the gret Idolatrye
> And manifest abominatioun,
> On thare feist day, all creature may se:
> Thay beir ane auld stock Image throuch ye toun, –
> With talbrone, troumpet, schalme, and Clarioun,
> Quhilk hes bene usit mony ane yeir bigone
> With preistis and freris in to processioun,
> Siclyke as Bell wes borne throuch Babilone.
>
> Aschame ye nocht, ye seculare prestis and freris,
> Tyll so gret superstitioun to consent?
> Ydolateris ye have bene mony yeris,
> Expresse agane the Lordis Commandiment.   (lines 2501–12)

Similarly, when Lindsay launched his attack upon the doctrine of Purgatory in the *Dialog*,[14] it was not without precedent. In the far less conducive atmosphere of 1528 he had already offered a highly ambivalent analysis of Purgatory during the cosmographic journey in *The Dreme*.

[14] Contrasting the 'catches' of the fishermen Apostles with those of the Roman clergy, Lindsay declared, 'Into thare [the clerics'] nett thay fangit ane fysche, / More nor ane quhaill worthye of memorye, . . . / That marvelous monstour callit Purgatorye. / Howbeit tyll ws it is nocht amyable, / It hes to thame bene veray profytable. / Latt thay that fructfull fysche eschaip thare nett, . . . / Adew the daylie dolorous Derigeis! / Selyre pure preistis may syng with hart full sorye, / Want thay that painefull palyce, Purgatorye. // Fairweill, Monkyre, with Chanoun, Nun, & Freir! / Allace! thay wylbe lychtleit in all landis: / Cowlis wyll no more be kend in kirk nor queir, / Lat thay yat fructfull fysche eschaip thare handis. / I counsall thame to bynd hym fast in bandis: / For Peter, Androw, nor Johne culde never gett / So profytable ane Fysche in to thare nett' (lines 4771–2, 4775–8, 4782–91).

> I purpose never to cum heir [Purgatory] agane;
> Bot, yit, I do beleve, and ever sall
> That the trew kirk can no waye erre at all.
> Sic thyng to be gret Clerkis dois conclude;
> Quhowbeit, my hope standis most in Cristis blud.   (lines 346–50)

While it is difficult to judge the precise limits of the ironic play in this passage, it is clear that on another central point of catholic doctrine Lindsay was at best ambivalent as early as 1528. Later he would go on to express more wholehearted criticisms of auricular confession and the attendant apparatus of penitence and absolution, and to adopt the rhetoric of the thoroughgoing reformer.[15]

> Unmercifull memberis of the Antichrist,
> Extolland your humane traditione
> Contrare the Institutione of Christ,
> Effeir ye nocht Divine punytione? . . .
> . . .
> Behald quhow your awin brether, now laitlye,
> In Ducheland, Ingland, Denmark, and Norowaye,
> Ar trampit doun, with thare Ipocrasye,
> And, as the snaw, ar meltit clenc awaye. (*Dialog*, lines 2573–6; 2593–6)

In the context of the royal politics of the 1530s, then, Lindsay was already significantly more sympathetic to reform than current policy sanctioned. And, it is this difference of position between the playwright and his sovereign that, as we shall see, gives the production of *The Thrie Estaitis* of 1540 much of its political interest.

THE 1540 INTERLUDE

The evidence

The evidence for the otherwise lost text of the 1540 production of *The Thrie Estaitis* is provided by a letter from Sir William Eure (an English agent in Scotland) to Thomas Cromwell, Henry VIII's Vicegerent-in-Spirituals. In this letter Eure gave a brief account of the play and with it enclosed a more detailed description provided by 'a scotts man of our

---

[15] See *Kitteis Confessioun* (written pre-1542, probably by Lindsay), lines 107–14, which attacks Lindsay's favourite targets, the friars, who 'dois the peple teiche and tyste, / To serve the Paip, the Antechriste', and counsels laymen rather: 'To the greit God omnipotent Confes thy syn, and sore repent; / And traist in Christ, – as wrytis Paule, – / Quhilk sched his blude to saif thy saule; / For nane can the absolve bot he, / Nor tak away thy syn from the.' See Edington, *Court and Culture*, pp. 158, 170, and 193.

sorte / being present at the playing of the saide enterluyde'.[16] Eure's
brief was to encourage those sympathetic to religious reform in Scotland, and to keep a weather eye upon the activities of James V, whose
religious inclinations were themselves of profound importance to Henry
VIII's foreign policy. Would James remain a loyal catholic and make
common cause with his French allies and the orthodox continental
powers against schismatic England? Or might he incline towards reform
and so be amenable to a more co-operative relationship with his southern neighbour? In the answer to such questions lay much of England's
future security, hence the close interest in them betrayed by the government's diplomatic correspondence. It is in this context that Eure wrote
to Cromwell from Berwick on 26 January 1540, to inform him that he,
Eure, had

hade diverse commynyngs with Master Thomas Bellendyn, one of the . . .
[C]oun[ce]llours for scotlande / a man . . . of gentle and sage conversacion /
specially touching the staye / of the spritualtie in scotlande.[17]

Gathering Bellenden 'to be a [man] inclyned to the soorte used in our
soverains Realme of England' (that is, a fellow reformer), Eure

dide soe largely breke with hym in thoes behalves / as to move to know of hym
of what mynde the king and counsaile of scotland was inclyned unto /
concernyng the busshope of Rome / and for the reformacion of the mysusing of
the spritualtie in scotlande.[18]

Bellenden's answer to this rather leading question merits more critical
attention than it has received to date from historians of both politics and
drama. It offers a number of intriguing suggestions, not only concerning
the nature and impact of the first version of Lindsay's *Satyre of the Thrie
Estaitis* (and, by implication, of political drama more generally), but also
about the early course of the Reformation in Scotland itself.

Bellenden's response, 'genttlie and lovinglie aunswered', began very
much in the way Eure desired. 'The king of scotts hym self', he claimed,

with all his temporall Counsaile was gretely geven to the reformacion of the
mysdemeanours of Busshops / Religious persones / and prests within the
Realme / And so muche that by the kings pleasour / he being prevey therunto
/thay have hade ane enterluyde played in the feaste of the epiphanne of our
lorde laste paste [i.e. 6 January] / before the King and Quene at Lighgive

[16] Eure's letter (BL MS Royal 7, C xvi, ff. 137–9) is printed in Hamer, ed., *Works*, II, pp. 2–6.
[17] Hamer, ed., *Works*, II, p. 2.   [18] Ibid.

[Linlithgow] / and the hoole counsaile sprituall and temporall / The hoole matier whereof concluded upon the Declaracion of the noughtines in Religion / the presumpcion of busshops / the collucion of the sprituall Courts / called the concistory courts in scotland / and mysusing of priests.[19]

There is much in this passage which is worthy of note, and we shall return to it in due course. But, what is perhaps most immediately interesting, and indeed surprising, is the fact that, when he sought to demonstrate the sincerity of the king and council's commitment to religious reform, Bellenden did so, not by pointing to proposed legislation or apposite royal declarations, but to the performance of an interlude. He asks that Eure measure James' seriousness by his willingness to allow the production at court of a play dealing with religious issues. No more striking exemplification could be found of the premise upon which this study is founded. The drama of the royal household, and of the political elite more generally, was not marginal to the political process but central to it. Nor were political concerns marginal to the playwright's interests. Dramatists were concerned with politics and politicians with drama: not least when, as here, the dramatist was himself a politician, with an intimate knowledge of both the processes of government and the mind of the king.

It is informative to note the terms in which Bellenden refers to the production ('by the kings pleasour / he being prevey therunto / *thay have had ane enterlude played*' (my italics)). It was not a matter of chance, or of the playwright's importuning, that the interlude was produced at this particular moment, but as the direct result of negotiation between the king, his counsellors, and the playwright. As the context makes clear, this act of patronage, amounting perhaps to a specific commission, was performed in the full knowledge that the resulting drama would be an anti-clerical, 'reforming' play. The 'thay' of the letter clearly knew what they wanted, and commissioned it. In this we see the dynamics of household drama at work in their most evident form. The play was produced from within the royal household by one of James V's most intimate and loyal household men. But the resulting drama, as we shall see, offered no simple articulation of royal wishes. In true household fashion it represented a dialogue – a negotiation – between the agenda of patron and client respectively.

There has been much debate over the early history of *The Thrie*

---

[19] Ibid.

Estaitis.[20] But it is now generally agreed that the 1540 interlude described
by Bellenden was written by Lindsay, and constitutes the earliest performance of a form of the play later presented in Cupar and Edinburgh
in 1552 and 1554. The precise relationship between the interlude and the
surviving texts remains, however, a contentious issue. Roderick Lyall
has argued strongly that, 'While it may well be that Lindsay wrote the
Linlithgow interlude, . . . the differences between this lost play and *The
Thrie Estaitis* are so great that it would be extremely rash to associate any
specific passage of the extant play with this earlier piece.'[21] There is little
doubt that this final point is sound. We do have only a general description of the 1540 interlude from which little can be gleaned about the text
itself on the level of language or verse structure. What is less clear,
however, is that there were major differences between the interlude and
the extant text in terms of the action and intellectual content of the
central dramatic set-piece: the gathering of the three Estates. Certainly a
number of important differences do seem to have existed between the
two plays. The 1540 text seems, as we shall see, not to have contained
any of the morality drama centred on Rex Humanitas which constitutes
the bulk of the first half of the surviving text, nor did it apparently
include the concluding act of the later play, the arrival of Folly and his
sermon. But, beyond that the changes seem more peripheral. The, so
called, Interlude between the halves of the later play is absent from
Eure's report (although he does say that there were 'interludes' of some
kind in the earlier play), as are the Pauper, Sowtar, Taylor, and their
wives, and the vices Flattery, Dissait, and Falset. In general the 1540 text
seems to have been, as one might expect of a shorter, indoor play, more
tightly constructed and more closely focused than its later incarnation
upon the business of the parliament which gives it its name. But, while
there are clear and signal differences between the two plays, there are
also enough crucial similarities to demonstrate that we are looking at a
single conception, an exploration of the same themes and problems in
two very different sets of circumstances. An investigation of the changes
between the two productions, and their implications for the political

[20] See, for example, John MacQueen, 'Ane Satyre of the Thrie Estaitis', *Studies in Scottish Literature*, 3
      (1965/6), pp. 129–43; Anna Jean Mill, 'Representations of Lyndsay's *Satyre of the Thrie Estaitis*',
      PMLA, 47 (1932), pp. 636–51, and 'The Original Version of Lindsay's *Satyre of the Thrie Estaitis*',
      Studies in Scottish Literature, 6 (1968/9), pp. 67–75; J. S. Kantrowitz, 'Encore: Lindsay's *Thrie
      Estaitis*, Date and New Evidence', *Studies in Scottish Literature*, 10 (1972), pp. 18–32, and *Dramatic
      Allegory: Lindsay's 'Ane Satyre of the Thrie Estaitis'* (Lincoln, NE, 1975); Roderick Lyall, ed., *The Thrie
      Estaitis* (Edinburgh, 1989), pp. ix–xiv (all references to the text of the play are to this edition).
[21] Lyall, ed., *Thrie Estaitis*, p. xii.

content and impact of the *Thrie Estaitis*, will constitute much of the remainder of this chapter.[22]

The politics of Reformation at the Court of James V

If we are to make anything of Thomas Bellenden's comments about the production of Lindsay's play, it is important first to establish a number of basic points. Initially we need to be clear about precisely what he meant when he wrote of the 'thay' who had the interlude played. Clearly he was talking of the king and Council, but who, in his view had the initiative in this collaboration? The syntax is ambiguous. Was he referring to the king and Council acting as one; or to reformers on the

---

[22] The 'nootes of the interluyde' provided by Bellenden's anonymous informant offer a detailed description of events in the play. The first figure to enter the place, he reports, was Solace, who seems to have combined a number of the features and functions of the Solace of the 1552–4 text, and Diligence, the Master of Ceremonies of the later drama. For, although the notes declare that his 'parte was but to make mery / sing ballettes with his fellowes / and Drinke at the interluydes of the play', they also point out that he had a general role as an apologist for the play too. For he 'shewede firste to all the audience the play to be played'. And the claim which he made for the text (that it 'was a generall thing / meanyng nothing in speciall to displeas noe man / praying therfor noe man to be angre with the same') accords exactly with the pre-emptive apologies offered by Diligence in the later text: 'Prudent peopill, I pray yow all, / Tak na man greif in speciall, / For wee sall speik in generall, / For pastyme and for play' (lines 70–3). Similar assurances are also offered by Correctioun's Varlet in his opening address to the audience: 'Sirs, thocht we speik in generall, / Let na man into speciall / Tak our words at the warst: / Quhat ever wee do, quhat ever wee say, / I pray yow tak it all in play / And judg ay to the best' (lines 1506–11). Then, as in the 1552–4 text, the King enters the place, followed in quick succession by a trio of courtly vices (here Placebo, Pikthanke, and Flatterye rather than the Placebo, Solace, and Wantonnes of the later text). The vices perform a series of conventionally boastful, *miles gloriosus* burlesques, before the Estates enter for the parliament. The chief difference with the ensuing meeting is the absence of Divine Correctioun and Gude Counsall, although the latter's role seems to have been performed by the related figure of Experience ('clede like a doctour / whoe sete thaym all down on the deis'). As in 1552–4, the chief business of the parliament becomes the hearing of the complaint of a member of the commons, here the Poor Man, who makes many of the points made by John the Common-Weill in the later play, against feudal dues and clerical exactions (specifically: mortuary payments and 'the herying of poor men / by concistorye lawe'), and the predatory promiscuity of 'busshopes / Prelettes / Abbotes / reving menes wifes and doughters'. When the Busshope protests against this litany of charges, seeking to charge the Poor Man with heresy, Experience steps in to protect him, confirming the truth of his allegations and adding to them others of his own. As Correctioun does to great effect in the 1552–4 text, Experience produces the New Testament and quotes from it the correct office and duties of a bishop (very likely, as in the later version, stressing the central importance of preaching and teaching to the episcopal office). But even this does not move Busshope from his opposition to the substantial reforms proposed by the parliament, which would curtail clerical wealth and influence. So, with a pragmatism bordering on cynicism, the other Estates point out the inconsequentiality of his resistance when it comes to a vote: 'And the Busshope said he wold not consent therunto / The Man of Armes and Burges said thay wer twoe / and he bot one / wherfor thair voice shuld have mooste effecte.' Again, all of this is repeated in the 1552–4 text, down even to Temporalitie's dismissal of Spiritualitie's protest: 'Wee set nocht by quhider ye consent or nocht / Ye are bot ane Estait and we ar twa, / *Et ubi major pars ibi tota!*' (lines 2839–41).

Council, such as Bellenden, acting with the king's connivance ('he [James] being privy thereto'); or to the king acting with the connivance of the Council? Are we looking, that is, at a court in which the king was the driving force behind political action – and thus the engine for religious reform – or one in which he was led towards decisions by his advisers and was thus less instrumental in the progress of reform? What follows in Eure's letter suggests answers to these questions.[23] It is important, however, to raise the issue here, and hold it in our minds. For, what Eure and Bellenden are describing is the political context which generated and shaped the early form of *The Thrie Estaitis*. To analyse the one is thus to provide the ground rules for the analysis of the other.

It is of interest to note how Eure reported Bellenden's further description of events, and to observe what he went on to say himself, for the latter in particular provides valuable evidence of how the political process operated at the court of James V.

Bellenden was, it seems, at pains to assure Eure that the interlude was successful in raising the question of reform at court. 'After the said enterlud fynyshed', he told him,

the King of scotts Dide call upon the busshope of Glascoe being Chauncellour and diverse other busshopes / exorting thaym to reforme thair facions and maners of lyving / saying that oneles they soe did / he wold sende sex of the proudeste of thaym unto his uncle of england / and as thoes wer ordoured soe he would ordour all the reste / that wolde not a mende.[24]

Here we see the king far more obviously in authoritative mood. But, perhaps more interestingly, the passage also contains a number of suggestive allusions to how religious policy was conceived at this time. Events in England were evidently closely observed in Scotland, as one might expect. Certainly they were sufficiently familiar for James to threaten his bishops with an audience with Henry, and they provided both a stimulus and a warning to interested parties in Scotland. That the determining role in the course of the English Reformation was played by Henry VIII was also perceived, and seems to have coloured James' actions. Indeed, in warning his prelates specifically to 'reforme thair facions and maners of lyving', James seems to have been pursuing a line parallel to that taken by Henry in his public attitude towards the English

---

[23] Edington, *Court and Culture*, p. 50, argues that the initiative may have been 'a more impetuous attempt to influence religious policy staged by a group of court evangelicals'. Eure's phrasing suggests, however, that the king was well aware of what was intended and, as what follows will argue, any attempt to influence policy was made within the conventions of 'good counsel' as defined in chapter 2, above.   [24] Hamer, ed., *Works*, II, pp. 2–3.

church. His interest was less in liturgical or doctrinal issues than in moral and political ones. The bishops must reform 'thair maners of lyving', their personal lifestyles and administration of their cures. Significantly, he also demanded that they reform their 'facions': their divisions. The damaging debates within the clergy over the need for reform, debates which paralysed church discipline and permitted the growth of lay heresy (perceived to be the real threat to the ecclesiastical and civil polity in England and Scotland alike), must be settled. Just as Henry VIII was currently doing through the royal proclamations and Acts of Parliament of 1538–42, James was taking this opportunity publicly to establish himself as the arbiter of religious disputes, and seeking to distance himself from both extremes of opinion.[25]

His threat to send some of his bishops to Henry for correction should not be read as a declaration of the intention to introduce a thoroughgoing protestant reformation into Scotland (not least because Henry VIII would hardly be the person to initiate (or even approve of) such a policy). James was simply using the readily available bogey-figure of Henry to frighten the bishops (however seriously or otherwise the remark was intended). And, significantly, he frightened them with the prospect of personal discomfiture, not with an assault upon the liturgy or the sacraments. It remained an enforced moral reform on essentially Erasmian lines which he was considering, not radical doctrinal innovation. Thus he subsequently threatened them with expulsion from royal service rather than expulsion from the church.[26]

James V was a king interested in reform of the church. But he would not swallow the more radical reforming message in its entirety. Consequently a tension existed between him and his more evangelical counsellors, as is evident from Eure's letter. Bellenden, whom Eure felt Cromwell would recognise as a fellow radical, was, it is clear, attempting to

[25] The policy of balancing the demands of both sides – and consequently unsettling both to strategic effect – can best be judged from the fact that, at the very time he was launching his scathing attack upon the Bishop of Glasgow and the clergy, James was also placing a shot across the bows of the reformers, by endorsing an Act of Parliament which stated that 'the auctorite of halikirk be mantenit and defendit in all their priveleg and liberteis as thai haif bene in our sovirane lordis tyme that now is and his predecessouris' (T. Thomson and C. Innes, eds., *The Acts of the Parliament of Scotland* (12 vols., Edinburgh, 1814–75), II, p. 358). For similar conclusions concerning James' 'pragmatic' and 'opportunistic' approach to religious policy, see Edington, *Court and Culture*, p. 51 ('Certainly no convert to the evangelical cause, he nevertheless acknowledged occasions on which it was expedient to volunteer limited support').

[26] Eure reported that 'I am alsoe advertised by the same Mr bellendyn / that the king of Scottes is fully mynded to expell all sprituall men frome having any auctoritie by office under his grace / either in household or elles where within the Realme / And Dailye studiethe and devisithe for that entente' (Hamer, ed., *Works*, II, p. 3); Edington, *Court and Culture*, p. 51.

persuade James to take up the reformers' cause by several methods. 'The same Master bellendyne', he told Cromwell,

haithe desired of me / to have an abstracte of all suche Actes, constitucions and proclamacions as ar passed within this the King / our Soverains Realme touching the suppression of religion / and gather[ing] unto the Kinges majestie suche other proffeites / as befor haithe been sp[ritual] with the reformacion of the mysdemeanours of the clergye / saying that h[e] trustethe to have the King his Master to studie the same.

Such documents should be conveyed to Bellenden 'by suche a pr[evy] persone as he by a secreate token whiche is devised bitwene hy[m and] me shall send unto me / for that purpose'.[27]

Unlike the commissioning of the interlude, in which the king and his reformist counsellors might collude in order to frighten the bishops out of their abuses, then, this was more obviously Bellenden's own project. He aimed secretly to obtain copies of the instruments of the Reformation in England with a view towards using them to persuade James to follow a similar course in Scotland. The material which he intended to use would play upon James' greed (and financial necessity) and his concern at clerical abuses (the clergy's 'proffeites' and their 'mysdemeanours'), rather than the theological issues at stake. Yet he remained unsure how this information would be received. Would the king even be willing to read it? Significantly Bellenden said that he only '*trustethe* to have the King his Master to studie the same': he did not *know* what James' reaction would be.

This caution on the part of a leading reformer is surely suggestive: as is his focus of attention. For all historians' interest in the Reformations in Britain as popular phenomena, Bellenden's concerns reveal that the Scottish Reformation, at least in its abortive, early form was (as it was in England) primarily a battle for the heart and mind of the sovereign, in which each side presented its arguments in terms best suited to gain royal approval. The struggle took place at court, taking the form (initially at least) of a genuine debate, the result of which was always in doubt until the monarch declared himself definitively. Scotland was experiencing at this time a period of flux in matters of religious policy, in which both the more reactionary prelates and the more advanced reformers made use of the theological *glasnost* to try to establish their cases and stamp their authority upon events, attempting to win the sovereign to their side, if not by persuasion, then by *fait accomplis*.

---

[27] Hamer, ed., *Works*, II, p. 2.

It is always tempting, as Jenny Wormald has suggested,[28] to see the Reformation struggle as a simple choice between two alternatives. Either the dominion of the catholic church would continue as before (perhaps with a little moral fine-tuning), or it would be superseded by a radical protestant alternative. Things would not, of course (as the previous chapter suggested), have looked that way at the time. In discussing the future of the church in Scotland, contemporaries were arguing very much in the dark, unclear as to what they may have been building, and what they were being asked to reform. What exactly *were* the central and essential tenets of the catholic faith and what were *adiaphora*, 'things indifferent', which might be altered or removed? Until the Council of Trent there was really no clear answer to many questions of detail. Some judgements had been made, such as the declaration of the centrality of the doctrine of Transubstantiation made at the Lateran Council of 1215. But there remained a great deal of confusion concerning other points. Thus the related question 'what was heresy?' was equally difficult to answer. Those on the ground made up the rules as best they could as they went along, and a strong lead from the crown could prove decisive (even without the kind of administrative schism which occurred in England) in determining what would constitute orthodoxy in a giving kingdom. Hence Bellenden's focus upon the king, and the attempts to win royal support by all shades of opinion.

At the same time that Bellenden was acquiring inflammatory material from Eure with a view to presenting it to James, Cardinal Beaton and his conservative allies were initiating heresy investigations, culminating in a series of burnings in 1539.[29] Then, in 1540 the cardinal cited one of James' own 'familiar servants', James Borthwick, on heresy charges. If Knox is to be believed, he subsequently presented the king with a long list of the names of leading laymen, nobles, and lairds, whom he claimed were suspect on religious grounds and whose property might thus be made forfeit under the heresy statutes.[30]

Just as Bellenden was trying to win James for reform by offering him the prospect of a lucrative spoliation of the church, so Beaton was wooing him for reaction by offering him the prospect of a spoliation of the wealth of rich lay 'heretics'. In the end, James swallowed neither bait

[28] Jenny Wormald, *Court, Kirk, and Community* (London, 1981), pp. 76–7. For the situation in England, see Greg Walker, *Persuasive Fictions: Faction, Faith, and Political Culture in the Reign of Henry VIII* (Aldershot, 1996), pp. 123–42.

[29] M. H. B. Sanderson, *Cardinal of Scotland: David Beaton, c. 1494–1546* (Edinburgh, 1986), appendix 3.

[30] John Knox, *History of the Reformation in Scotland*, ed., W. C. Dickinson (2 vols., Edinburgh, 1949), I, p. 34.

and opted for a continuation along a middle way. As George Buchanan succinctly observed, 'The different factions pointed out the riches of their opponents, as a booty ready for him when ever he chose: and he, by agreeing alternately with either, kept both in a state of suspense between hope and fear.'[31] On the one hand, he continued to milk the church through unprecedented new taxation and refused to undertake a purge of reformist sympathisers: on the other, he cracked down upon doctrinal innovation through legislation during 1541 which re-emphasised the need to honour the sacraments, the Virgin, saints, and images, thereby indicating the limits to the sort of debate he would entertain.[32]

The interlude of 1540: the politics of performance

It is into this heated and still uncertain debate that the 1540 production of Lindsay's satire must be situated. In this form it was a play which clearly reflected the circumstances of its performance in the household of James V. Indeed, it seems to have been so constructed as to be applicable only to performance at the court of a monarch like James, under the peculiar political conditions prevailing in early 1540. It assumed a royal audience, and worked explicitly towards that audience. Moreover, it assumed a royal audience open to persuasion. If James V had been the inveterate catholic which some writers have claimed, there would have been no room for such a play at his court. If he were a convinced evangelical, there would have been no need for it. The very existence of the play suggests a court very like that of Henry VIII in the 1530s, where debate was possible, and where ideas might be explored in the subtle medium which household drama offered. Thus Lindsay might use his commission to try to push James further in the direction of reform, safe in the knowledge that, provided he kept within certain limits, he might raise issues which remained intensely controversial. In this early version one sees a play, typical of household drama, consciously crafted to focus the debate upon the person of the monarch. Unlike its

---

[31] George Buchanan, *The History of Scotland from the Earliest Period to the Regency of the Earl of Moray*, ed. and trans. J. Aikman (6 vols., Glasgow, 1845), II, p. 59. According to English sources, the Scottish clergy were also trying to distract James from ecclesiastical reform by encouraging a more bellicose foreign policy. As the Duke of Norfolk informed Thomas Cromwell during 1539, 'By divers other waies I am advertised that the clergie of Scotlande be in such feare that their king shold do theire as the Kinges highnes hath done in this realme, that they do their best to bring their master to the warr; and by many waies I am advertised that a great part of the temporalitie their wold their king shold followe our insample, which I pray God geve hym grace to come unto' (*State Papers Henry VIII*, v (iv), p. 154).

[32] Thomson and Innes, eds., *Acts of the Parliament of Scotland*, II, pp. 358–71.

later incarnation, the interlude of 1540 was clearly a vehicle for persuasion of the king.

The play (from what we know of it from Eure's correspondence) offered a panegyric of James V, and of kingship in general, but a panegyric in the classical mould, which sought to educate and persuade even as it praised. By presenting the model of an ideal, reforming monarch, it issued a clear challenge to James to live up to that ideal. The king of the 1540 satire seems to have been an imposing and impressive patriarch. His involvement in the action was limited, but decisive. Indeed, as we shall see when contrasting this version to the text of the 1550s, it was decisive in no small part *because* it was limited. As Eure's anonymous witness described, the king entered in silence once the audience had been quietened for his arrival, passed to the throne, and had,

noe speche to thende of the playe / and then to ratefyie and approve as in playne parliament all thinges doon by the reste of the players whiche represented the Thre est[at]es.[33]

This silence, followed by a final, authoritative utterance evidently impressed our witness, and its effects reinforced the notion of the sovereign as the single, decisive voice in political debate.[34] Unlike Rex Humanitas (and even Divyne Correctioun) in the later version, the king in the interlude remained enthroned, aloof from the action of the play. When he spoke it was from this magisterial position, uncompromised by what had gone on before (the contrast with Rex is, as we shall see, glaring). The tacit allusion in all this to James V's position above the religious debate was made explicit by the Poor Man, who subordinated the player-king's authority to that of the two true kings: God and James, the latter portrayed as both the magisterial suppresser of misrule throughout Scotland and, crucially, the prince whose magnificence would be complete if only he would grasp the final remaining nettle in the Scottish garden through thoroughgoing ecclesiastical reform:

And after he [Poor Man] spered [i.e. asked or looked] for the king / And whene he was showed to the man that was king in the playe / he aunsuered and said he was noe king / ffor ther is but one king / whiche made all and governethe / all / whoe is eternall / to whome he and all erthely kinges ar but officers / of the

---

[33] BL MS Royal 7, Cxvi, f. 138 (Hamer, *Works*, ii, pp. 4–6).

[34] A similar strategy is pursued in the English morality play *The Castle of Perseverance*, where God's divine authority is reinforced by having him speak only at the close of the play. See M. Eccles, ed., *The Macro Plays*, EETS, o.s. 262 (London, 1969).

whiche thay muste make recknyng / and so furthe muche moor to that effecte /
And thene he loked to the king and saide he was not the king of scotlande for
ther was an other king in scotlande that hanged John Armestrang with his
fellowes / and Sym the larde and many other moe [i.e. James himself] / which
had pacified the countrey / and stanched thifte / but he had lefte one thing
undon / whiche perteyned aswell to his charge as th[other] / And whene he
was asked what that was he made a long narracion / of the oppression of the
poor by the taking of the corse presaunte beistes [mortuary fees] / and of the
heryng of poor men / by concistorye lawe / and of many other abussions of the
spritual[itie] and churche / withe many long stories and auctorities.[35]

Throughout the interlude, however, this call for reform was carefully
couched in the Erasmian moral and financial terms most likely to appeal
to James. As Bellenden reported it, the interlude concerned itself with
'the *noughtines* in Religion'; the *presumption* of the Spiritual courts, and the
misusing of the priests, not with any of the more radical doctrinal issues
which plays such as John Bale's *King Johan* and *The Three Laws* were
beginning to voice south of the border.[36] Each of these points could
conceal a doctrinal agenda, but the play, as Bellenden reported it,
seemed actively to avoid drawing out such implications, offering instead
a consensual approach to the questions best suited to unite the king and
his more radical counsellors in approval. The more detailed account
provided by the 'nootes' confirms Bellenden's reading. It was the temporal power of the clergy and their moral inadequacy to exercise it
which Poor Man protested at, not the alleged errors in their doctrine:
'the taking of the corse presaunte beistes', 'the heryng of poor men / by
concistorye lawe', 'the greate abusion of busshoppes / Prelettes /
Abbotes / reving menes wifes and doughters', 'thair over bying of lordes
and barons eldeste sones / to thair doughters', and 'the greate superflu-

---

[35] Hamer, ed., *Works*, II, p. 5. The emphatic refocusing of the audience's attention from the
player-king to James V on the dais would have gained added impact from the particular
architectural features of the great hall at Linlithgow, which made the dais itself the focus of the
hall: 'a large window . . . was cut through the east wall to light the dais at the south end of the hall.
To give emphasis to that dais a magnificent three-bay fireplace was constructed, the lintel of
which was carried on small piers with foliate capitals, while above the lintel were corbels for
statues in front of the sloping chimney breast. The dais was eventually afforded additional
emphasis by a section of semi-circular barrel vaulting immediately above it. Although the main
function of this vault was that of carrying part of the upper floor (and in this it could be a later
insertion) it also acted as a canopy of honour, since the rest of the hall was covered by a timber
roof at a higher level' (R. Fawcett, *Scottish Architecture from the Accession of the Stewarts to the
Reformation, 1371–1560* (Edinburgh, 1994), pp. 305–6).

[36] Although Bale himself, mindful of the pragmatics of reformation politics, was not averse to
tempering his own polemics to the more conservative tastes of Henry VIII. See Walker, *Plays of
Persuasion*, pp. 169–221. For the suggestion that Lindsay was careful to avoid doctrinal comment,
see Graf, 'Theatre and Politics', pp. 153–4.

ous rentes that perteyned to the churche / by reason of over muche temporall landes given to thaym'. This last was most obviously tailored to encourage James to take action, for it was confirmed by the temporal estates 'that the kinge might take [these lands] boothe by canon lawe / and civile lawe'. Even where a doctrinal point seemed implicit, as in the attacks upon the regular clergy, it was again avoided in favour of moral criticism of 'the greate abomynable vices that reiagne in clostures / and of the Common Bordelles / that was keped in closturs of nunnes'. Similarly, the only mention of heresy (guardedly alluded to in the Busshop's attempt to bring Poor Man 'to suffer Dethe . . . by thair lawe') was made in the context of a patent ruse to manipulate the law to protect clerical property.[37] The possibility of doctrinal debate was again stifled in favour of an attack upon clerical wealth and power, issues on which all temporal estates could find common cause.

The play as described here, then, employed a relatively subtle persuasive strategy with regard to its royal audience, a strategy wholly in keeping with the political dynamics of household drama in general. The interlude provided James V with a dramatic analogue, a player king whose authority was both built up within the play and subsequently denied in favour of James' own royal power beyond it, leaving the spectator-king in a position of both moral and rhetorical advantage from which to castigate the Bishop of Glasgow and demand action. The play made a seemingly unanswerable case for reform of the church, offering James the ideal cue to turn its force directly against the leading clerics in the audience. In this sense it suited the purpose of its royal patron to the letter. But, where it seems to have exceeded its commission was in the way it firmly committed the king, even as it praised him, to a definition of necessary reform in some ways clearly more radical than he would otherwise have wished to accept. Certainly the measures adopted by the Estates appear to have been a logical response to demonstrable social and moral abuses, and, as we have seen, they steered clear of openly tackling contentious doctrinal issues. But the modest presentation conceals a more assertive programme: to reform all the abuses catalogued in the play would have involved Scotland in a reformation every bit as radical as that currently overseen by Henry VIII in England.

Although the reform of the nunneries and the other regular clergy was presented as a question simply of sexual morality, it tacitly involved an attack upon – or at best a downgrading of – the doctrine of Purga-

---

[37] Hamer, ed., *Works*, II, p. 5.

tory, with all that this would imply for a whole range of traditional beliefs and practices, from indulgences to obits, chantries, and masses for the dead. (Notably the later 1552–4 production did not flinch from the full consequences of the reforms it called for, enacting the total dissolution of all nunneries. Nuns, the prioress admitted, 'To Christis congregation / . . . ar nocht necessair' (lines 3697–8). And, as the act of the play-Parliament stated, 'that fragill ordour feminine / Will nocht be missit in Christs religioun' (lines 3871–2).) Similarly, reforms of the consistory court, and the removal of traditional clerical dues and exactions, coupled with the most radical step of all, the seizure of its temporal lands, would have left the church critically impoverished and less able effectively to pursue the struggle against heresy. None of this was stated openly, no doubt as to have done so would have instantly alienated James V. But in endorsing the reforms put forward piecemeal in the interlude, the king would have been brought a considerable distance during the course of the play from the conservative position of demanding simply reform from within.

THE OPEN-AIR DRAMA OF 1552 AND 1554

The plot

The play as performed in Cupar in 1552 and Edinburgh in 1554, and as it survives in manuscript and printed texts, falls into two distinct but closely related halves, separated by a brief 'Interlude'. The first section takes place in and around the royal court and forms a recognisable morality drama focusing upon the fall and rise of a young king, Rex Humanitas. The second takes place in Parliament and represents a meeting of the Three Estates of Scotland, called to reform the abuses identified during the first half.

Briefly summarised, the action commences with the introduction of Rex, who begins the play as an innocent, but is soon compromised by the temptations offered by the courtly vices Wantonnes, Placebo, and Solace. Having succumbed to these lesser vices, he is lured into the court of Dame Sensuality and his slide into corruption begins in earnest. The court degenerates further when it is infiltrated by Flatterie, Falset, and Dissait who, in true morality fashion find service under the aliases Devotioun, Sapience, and Discretioun. Under their influence Gude Counsall is banished and Verity, representative of the evangelical Word of God (newly arrived from over the sea) is imprisoned in the stocks by

Spirituality and the catholic clergy. Chastity is given similar treatment when she is banished from the court by Sensuality, who now dominates the king's bedchamber. Only the arrival of Divyne Correctioun begins the rectification of the situation. He releases the virtues from the stocks and, in company with Gude Counsall, purges the court of the more pernicious vices. The courtly vices, symbolic of the 'innocent' recreations permissible for a young king, are allowed to remain, but only after assuring Correctioun of their intention to lead Rex into more responsible pastimes in future. The action of this section ends with the summoning of the three Estates to reform the corruption which is the legacy of decades of misgovernment.

There then follows the curious 'Interlude', which exemplifies (through the complaints of the tenant farmer Pauper, deprived of his livestock by an avaricious clergy, and the stock antics of Robert Rome-Raker, the corrupt Pardoner) many of the social and spiritual problems which the Estates will have to address in the coming Parliament. The Parliament itself, which takes up the whole of the second 'Act' of the play, begins with a powerful symbol of corruption as the Estates, Spirituality, Temporality, and Marchand, enter the place walking backwards, each one led by his characteristic vice. Having thus graphically established its central premise that the world has gone awry, and each of the pillars of the commonweal has connived in its decline, the play proceeds to purge each of them in turn through a series of harsh new laws demanded by Pauper and John the Common-Weill and enacted by Correctioun and Rex. Gradually the two lay Estates realign themselves with the reformers and reconcile themselves to virtue, leaving only Spirituality to bear the brunt of the increasingly vicious anti-clerical satire that dominates the rest of the play. Once the church is thoroughly humbled, its lands appropriated for secular purposes, its powers pruned, and its alleged reliance on pluralism, nepotism, and rampant sensuality checked, the meeting is closed with a further powerful symbol of magisterial correction as the vices Falset, Dissait, and Common Thift are hanged on the Playfield. The play closes somewhat incongruously with the arrival of a new character, Foly who, after much comic business, preaches a sermon on the theme '*stultorum numerus infinitis*'.

The 1552–4 play: the politics of performance

In its structure and content the 1540 interlude, so far as it can be reconstructed, concentrated very much upon royal power and responsibility. James V and the player-king sat enthroned and silent at either end of the great hall at Linlithgow throughout the action. Twin nodes of power, they provided the political points of reference within which the dramatic debate was enacted, powerfully symbolising the pivotal importance of the sovereign to the play which was already tacitly declared by the geography of the hall. In the very different circumstances of the early 1550s, the play took on a markedly different form and strategy. It became an outdoor production, removed from the politically and culturally significant geography of palace, household, and courtly great hall.[38] It now occurred in a neutral space, or rather a space fulfilling and contested by many different functions, economic, social, and political.[39] But the changes in the nature of the play seem to reflect a great deal more than merely the physical dimensions of its new location. The political topography had changed profoundly too, by the time of the 1552 production. The later satire was, as we have seen, (re)written during a minority, a period without a single, unchallenged sovereign authority. Each of these changes seems reflected in the resulting dramatic text.

[38] The text of the play in its 1552–4 incarnation exists in two forms, as a series of excerpted sections copied into the Bannatyne Manuscript (National Library of Scotland, Edinburgh, MS Adv., 19. I.I., ff. 164–210), and as a much longer, continuous text, printed by Robert Charteris in Edinburgh in 1602. In the Bannatyne MS mention is made of a performance 'maid in the Grensyd besyd Edinburcht'. But the text also contains a 'Proclamatioun made in Cowpar of Fyffe', advertising a performance on 'Whitsunday upon the Castell Hill': 'Our purpose is, on the sevint day of June, / Gif weddir serve, and se haif rest and pece, / We sall be sene in till our playing place, / In gude array abowtthe hour of sevin' (lines 11–14). As there was only one year between 1541 and 1555 (the year of Lindsay's death) in which Whitsunday fell on the 7 June, that year, 1552 can reasonably confidently be taken as the date of the Cupar performance. Moreover, numerous references to the Cupar region and its inhabitants can be found in the surviving text(s) to confirm that this was indeed the version of the play performed there (or at least something very like it). The Edinburgh production is described in Henrie Charteris' 1568 edition of Lindsay's *Warkis*, which (although it does not contain a text of the play) mentions a 'play [of Lindsay's], playit besyde Edinburgh, in presence of the Quene Regent and ane greit part of the Nobilitie, with ane exceding greit nowmer of pepill, lestand fra ix houris afoir none, till vi houris at even' (Hamer, ed., *Works*, IV, p. 139). This description seems clearly to refer to *The Thrie Estaitis*. And, as Hamer argues, this seems to have been the play which the City of Edinburgh was preparing and paying for from August to October 1554, for which twelve minstrels were paid for leading the players to the Greenside, and money was paid out 'forthe making of the Quenis grace hous on the play-field, besyde the convoy hous, the jebbettis [i.e. gibbets] and skaffauld about the samyn' (Hamer, ed., *Works*, IV, pp. 141–2).

[39] Granted to the burgesses of Edinburgh by James II in 1456, the Greenside was initially intended as a site for martial displays, tournaments, and other outdoor sports, but it quickly gained a range of other recreational, ceremonial, and judicial functions. By the mid-sixteenth century it provided a location for a leper hospital and a site for the burning of heretics. The Royal Commission on the Ancient and Historical Monuments of Scotland, *An Inventory of the Ancient and Historical Monuments of the City of Edinburgh, with the Thirteenth Report of the Commission* (Edinburgh, 1951), pp. xlv and xlvi; D. Daiches, *Edinburgh* (London, 1978), p. 38.

Whereas in the interlude the pattern of authority was hierarchical, focused, and, ultimately unitary, in the later play it is diffuse, unfocused, and ultimately diverse. Physically the acting space is now more obviously differentiated. In the interlude the action took place before and between the thrones of the king and player-king, as the latter took counsel and judged the merits of the arguments presented. In the outdoor drama there are different sites and foci for the audience's attention. There is still a throne, this time upon a high scaffold, but there is also the rival scaffold and 'court' of Sensuality, creating a bi-polar focus, a moral tension in the drama. There are other foci too, other points of power from which authoritative statements and judgements are made. There is the pulpit, from which first the Doctor then Foly preach, to markedly different effect. There are also the stocks, which become alternative pulpits from which the oppressed virtues complain with the prophetic authority of martyrs. Additionally, the action takes place by and across the stream, at the bar, and at other locations on the Playfield. Finally, beyond all these there is the great beyond, the vague space 'utwith' the playing space (and, by implication, outwith Scotland too), from which all the major characters claim to have arrived (symbolised by the 'Palyoun', which acted as a tiring house), the source of their capacities either for virtue or for vice.

Moreover, within the royal court (and more obviously in the Parliament) of the play itself, *authority* is fragmented. If Professor Mill's suggestion of a full 'place and scaffold' setting for the play, with separate scaffolds for each of the various estates is correct,[40] then this fragmentation would also have had an obvious visual correlative in the layout of the court itself. Whereas the Estates of the interlude shared a scaffold with their king, sitting on a tier beneath his throne, reinforcing his sovereign status, here the Estates sit apart from (and opposed to) the royal scaffold, offering rival points of reference. And, more abstractly – but no less crucially – as we shall see, the reformation which the play offers is itself fragmentary, imperfect, and finally indefinitely postponed. Expectations of a conclusive, magisterial pronouncement of the sort which concluded the 1540 interlude are continually frustrated and deferred. Among other problems, there are just too many kings in this play.

As in the classic New Historicist formulation, power is everywhere and nowhere in the state of the play. Acts of power (proclamations,

---

[40] Mill, 'Representations', pp. 646–51.

judicial sentences, the passing of statutes, and public executions) dominate – indeed constitute – the dramatic plot. But that power is never fixed in an identifiable (and unproblematically *present*) authority. The (many) kings of the play are always imminent, promising like Rex Humanitas 'among you to compeir / with ane [triumphant], awfull ordinance, / with crown and sword and scepter in . . . hand' (lines 20–2), but they are never present in their full majesty. The kings *on stage* are either compromised, imperfect surrogates, or flawed in title or morality: shadow-kings like John the Common-Weill or Pauper, endlessly prophesying what they would do if they were in control; or proto-kings like Gude Counsall and Divyne Correctioun, exercising regal or semi-regal powers in the name of absent, ideal sovereigns. At no point in the play is an individual sovereign authority unequivocally in command. And the absence of this royal leadership manifests itself in many ways, only the most obvious of which is the moment when, during the 'Interlude', Pauper briefly usurps the place of Rex Humanitas on the elevated throne. The overall impression created is of a realm characterised by disorder, a view emphasised by Diligence's rebuke to the Provost and Bailies over Pauper's forced entry into the place:

> God wait gif heir be ane weill keipit place,
> Quhen sic ane wilde begger carle may get entres.   (lines 1940–1)

The pattern of the play throughout is one in which reformation is continually frustrated. First abuses and disorder are identified and lamented, then, in a powerful dramatic gesture their reform is promised, only for that promise to be immediately compromised and expectations of improvement thwarted. As a result, the sense of disorder and abuse is heightened and intensified. The figure of Rex Humanitas provides the most obvious, but far from the only manifestation of this pattern at work.

It has been argued that Rex presents Lindsay's model of an ideal king,[41] but this hardly seems likely of the curiously feckless figure the text presents. As the play opens, Diligence offers the audience a vision of a realm in turmoil. But the remedy for all the nation's woes is allegedly at hand.

> For I am sent to yow as messingeir
> From ane nobill and rycht redoubtit roy,
> The quhilk hes bene absent this monie yeir.   (lines 15–17)

It is this royal absence that has allowed vice and disorder to flourish.

---

[41] See, for example, Graf, 'Theatre and Politics', p. 148.

> Howbeit that he lang tyme hes bene sleipand,
> Quhairthrow misreull hes rung thir monie yeiris.   (lines 24–5)

Thus the return of the king is posited as the answer to the prayers of the nation. As Diligence confidently promises,

> Be now assurit of reformatioun.   (line 29)

But, in a manner which will become characteristic of the play as a whole, the boldness of this claim is immediately undercut by Diligence's next statement. For his first act on behalf of this triumphant reforming king is to seek the tolerance and forgiveness of the audience for what we are told will be his fall into sin and error. Even before Rex enters, then, his moral authority and political authority are called into question.

> Thocht he, ane quhyll into his flouris,
> Be governit be vylde trompouris
> And sumtyme lufe his paramouris,
> Hauld ye him excusit.   (lines 38–41)

The intention here may well be to neutralise criticism of the king in advance, and so reinforce his authority by reassuring the audience of his eventual triumph over sin. But the immediate practical effect is to nullify the powerful assertion of his dignity and authority just delivered, replacing it as the action develops with the reality of an innocent boy-king powerless to help himself and prey to external forces who govern his passions and direct his decisions.[42]

As Diligence promises, so the play proceeds. First we see the courtly vices enter and encourage Rex into an affair with Sensuality, then the more directly evil moral and political vices gain access to his court and complete his corruption. Only the arrival of Divyne Correctioun and the rallying of the virtues enables the court to be reformed and the vices expelled. As Diligence's opening summary predicts, it is to be external forces, indeed external *authorities*, that will bring about both the fall and the reformation of the king. The audience should, Diligence begs, hold Rex excused,

> For quhen he meittis with Correctioun,
> With Veritie and Discretioun,
> Thay will be banisched aff the toun
> Quhilk hes him abusit.   (lines 42–5)[43]

---

[42] Rex is, as he says himself, '*Tanquam tabula rasa*; / That is als mekill as to say, / Redie for gude and ill' (lines 224–6).

[43] The point is reasserted later in the same speech, when it is promised that: 'Chastitie will mak narratioun / How sho can get na ludging in this land, / Till that the heavinlie King Correctioun, / Meit with the king and commoun, hand to hand' (lines 66–9).

Of course the 'psychomachian' externalisation of the forces operating upon the protagonist is the central commonplace of morality drama, and need cause no difficulty for audiences on the level of plot motivation. But there is a tension here between Lindsay's morality form and his political content. There is a crucial difference between enacting the moral reformation of an Everyman figure through the symbolic action of externalised psychological forces, and enacting the political rehabilitation of a reforming king. Whilst on a theological level the externalising device adds to the effectiveness of a morality plot, suggesting the need for the sinner to obtain help from outside himself (chiefly the grace of God) in order to reform, on a political level it is more troublesome. Having been told that Rex is to be the source of the reforming authority which will redeem the fallen political world of the play, it is disconcerting in the extreme to discover almost immediately that this authority will only be activated once other figures have redeemed the fallen king. 'Who reforms the reformer?' is a powerfully unsettling question to pose at the outset of so highly charged a political drama. Similarly the externalising device has a crucial impact upon the symbolic level to the political action. While the king we are asked to *imagine* may well be a reforming patriarch, the king we *see* appears to be the plaything of faction, swayed first one way by the vices and then the other by the virtues. Again, form and content seem curiously at odds if the intention is to present a strong and unproblematically admirable personal monarch.

The differences between the king of the 1540 interlude and that of the 1552–4 text are too many and too significant to be merely accidental, and suggest that a very different analysis of royal power and authority is being undertaken in the later play. Such differences are both general and particular. Dramatic devices, for example, which had one effect in the interlude, have quite another in the later production. We are told that the Poor Man 'spered [that is looked or inquired] for the king' in the 1540 text and had to be shown where he sat. Similarly, in the 1552–4 text a number of popular figures, notably John the Common-Weil and Foly, also fail to recognise Rex on first entering the place and have to be directed towards him. But the impacts of these respective acts of misrecognition are very different. In the interlude the Poor Man's inability to recognise the king was part of a wider strategy of focusing the drama upon James V. The Poor Man subsequently, as we have seen, denied that the player-king *was* a true king, reserving that title for God and, beneath him, for James himself. Thus the diminution of the player-king's authority (implicit in his inability to appear recognisably regal) had the effect of incrementing royal authority elsewhere within the closed economy of household performance. The slur upon the player-king rebounded as praise of the true sovereign in the audience.

In the productions of the 1550s, however, there is no such compensatory strategy at work. The diminishment of the authority of Rex is more marked (he is dismissed, belittlingly, as a 'new [maid] king' (line 2433) and 'yon . . . with the goldin hat' (line 4347)), and it is not recouped elsewhere. The play makes no explicit gestures towards the powerful spectators in Mary of Guise's entourage, thus the loss of royal authority is not contained by the context of the performance. Nor is it redirected elsewhere within the play. Correctioun, the other major regal figure, is also misidentified, and has to be pointed out, with scarcely less loss of dignity, as 'yon with the wings' (line 4361). The authority lost by Rex is thus lost for good.

The crucial difference between the play of 1552–4 and the interlude of 1540 in this respect, however, is the active participation of the king of the play in the antics of the vices. In 1540 the latter were able to perform their comic routines and thereby suggest the fallen state of the kingdom, without involving the king. He, as we have seen, sat in dignified silence throughout the play. In the 1552–4 text Rex speaks freely, and his dignity lasts only so long as he is alone in the place, as the direction at this point makes clear ('Heir sall the King pass to royall sait and sit with ane grave countenance *till Wantones cum.*' (after line 101; my italics)). As John J. McGavin has shown, his very speech patterns demonstrate the speed and extent of his fall, as the characteristic, regal long-lined stanzas of his opening prayer quickly degenerate into the short-lined triplets favoured by the court vices.[44] Indeed, rarely does Rex open his mouth in this play without compromising either his dignity or his authority: a trait as evident in the 'reformed' king as it is in the earlier ingenue. For, even after his meeting with Correctioun and the purging of the court, Rex is not averse to indulging in the inverted topsy-turvy discourse associated with Foly, Falset, and Dissait, offering Diligence as a reward for his services 'the teind mussellis of the [Fernie] myre' (line 1813), a nonsensical privilege as the latter's response makes clear.

[44] John J. McGavin, 'The Dramatic Prosody of Sir David Lindsay', in R. D. S. Jack and K. McGinley, eds., *Of Lion and Unicorn: Essays on Anglo-Scottish Literary Relations in Honour of Professor John MacQueen* (Edinburgh, 1993), pp. 39–66.

> I will get riches throw that rent
>> Efter the day of Dume,
> Quhen, in the colpots of Tranent,
>> Butter will grow on brume!   (lines 1815–18)

For Rex to enter into such knockabout badinage while under the influence of the vices would be entirely compatible with the morality 'fall and rise' pattern, and so need not effect the restorative impact of his final rehabilitation. For him to do so while under the influence of Correctioun and Gude Counsall, and in the very act of summoning the parliament intended to right the wrongs besetting Scotland, casts doubt upon the full success of his recovery. Unlike the eponymous protagonist of John Skelton's political morality *Magnyfycence*, Rex never seems wholly convincing in the role of reformed and reforming sovereign.[45] But then, as we shall see, the whole notion of a fully successful reformation becomes an uncertain one in the second half of the *Thrie Estaitis*.

If Rex is too closely linked to folly and moral weakness fully to convince in the first half of the play, Gude Counsall and Correctioun are hardly less compromised as ideal reformers, albeit for rather different reasons. Again the pattern of promise and frustration established in Diligence's opening speech seems to dominate their presentation. Gude Counsall, for example, also enters with a bold declaration of his own ability to right wrongs, and of his indispensability to a well-ordered realm, reassuring the audience that

> Yit in this realme I wald mak sum repair,
> Gif I beleifit my name suld nocht forfair;
> For, wald this king be guydit yit with ressoun,
> And on misdoars mak punitioun,
> Howbeit [that] 1 haif lang tyme bene exyllit
> I traist in God my name sall yit be styllit.   (lines 594–9)

Yet he is almost immediately 'exyllit' again – denied access to the court by the moral and political vices, leaving him to roam impotently around the margins of the place, a potent symbol of the failings of counsel where the sovereign will not, or cannot listen. But the likelihood of his failure had already been suggested by the very context in which he had uttered his opening remarks. For, no sooner had he finished speaking than another newcomer had entered the place: Flatterie, his antithesis, whose exultant declaration that he too has ended a long exile 'And am cum

---

[45] See Walker, *Plays of Persuasion*, pp. 72–6. For the contrary assertion, that Rex is 'the typical morality character growing from inexperience to wisdom', see Graf, 'Theatre and Politics', p. 148.

heir now at the last' (line 608) to bring corruption and misrule, effectively shatters the optimism of Gude Counsall's earlier announcement.
Similarly, Flatterie's wild running about the place (line 602) and
scatological anecdotes (lines 624–7) banish the decorum attending
Counsall's sober speech. Just as the audience is promised that things will
get better, so they immediately get very much worse, as each of the
moral and political vices comes tumbling in, in Flatterie's wake.

The same pattern is repeated, with variations with Verity and Divyne
Correctioun. Both enter claiming the most powerful mandate of all, the
will of God, to reform the abuses of Scotland, but both prove rather less
impressive in practice than their rhetoric promises. Verity is almost
immediately locked in the stocks by the corrupt church leadership, and,
albeit Correctioun achieves the scattering of the vices from the court,
the realm is ultimately little better off as a consequence as they simply
flee to the other estates, initiating a process of the dispersal and general-
isation of vice which is to dominate the remainder of the play. Veritas'
desperate plea to God, adding him to the list of negligent, sleeping
monarchs which the play chastises, is perhaps the best index of the
increasingly parlous state of affairs which develops in the first half of the
play.

> Get up, thow sleipis all too lang, O Lord,
> And mak sum ressonabill reformatioun
> On them that dois tramp doun Thy gracious word.   (lines 1168–70)

All of this would, of course, be manageable within the strict confines of a
political morality plot, if the final reformation the play offered could be
seen to redeem all that had gone before. Just as the protagonist's final
moral reformation could cancel all debts incurred previously, so the
political reformation of Scotland might, as in the 1540 production, offer
a genuinely optimistic conclusion to the play. But this is hardly what
occurs. The reformation enacted by Rex, Correctioun, and the Three
Estates is no sooner declared in the ringing tones of Diligence's proclamation, than it is called into question and frustrated.

The sheer number of acts of power and punishment packed into the
last third of *The Thrie Estaitis* is startling. There is not only the reading of
the Acts of Parliament, but also three lengthy on-stage executions with
their accompanying moralistic confessions, and two sermons. But the
net effect of all this heavy-handed enforcement of reform is hardly a
sense that justice has been done. The fact that Flatterie (in his guise as a
friar, the chief instigator of clerical corruption and root of the clergy's

temporal power) is allowed to escape punishment immediately casts doubt upon the completeness of the reformation and the probity of the reformers. That it is he of all people who is made hangman to execute his former allies means that Correctioun's purge of society is inevitably compromised from the outset. As Flatterie's final speech before his escape from the place makes clear, he at least has outwitted the entire reforming process.

> Have I nocht chaipit the widdie [kept the gallows] weill?
> Ye, that I have, be sweit sanct Geill!
>   For I had nocht bene wrangit,
> Becaus I servit [i.e. deserved], be Alhallows,
> Till have bene merchellit amang my fallowis,
>   And heich above them hangit!
> I maid for ma falts nor my maits:
> I begylde all the Thrie Estaitis
>   With my hypocrisie.
> Quhen I had on my freirs hude
> All men beleifit that I was gude:
>   Now judge ye gif I be!   (lines 4272–83)

And those who have been hanged in his stead, although clearly vicious, hardly represent the worst of the enemies of civil society: not least as the first to be executed, Common Thift, is simply a scapegoat for a greater villain, his master Oppressioun, who has earlier duped him into taking his place in the stocks. Again, what could have been a powerful symbol of justice in action is reduced to a piece of flawed political pragmatism, partial in every sense of the word.[46]

It is clear that these executions will not end the miseries of contemporary Scotland. As each of the vices calls out to what he claims are his allies beyond the play, he merely reinforces the sense that vice and criminality are everywhere. Although these speeches are ostensibly warnings of impending punishment to the hosts of wrongdoers beyond the playing space, their effect is far from reassuring. The sheer weight of names and places listed in Thift's speech of farewell suggests a problem beyond the powers of any king or parliament to correct.

> Adew, my brethren common theifis,
> That helpit me in my mischeifis:

---

[46] For an indication of the seriousness with which 'masterful oppression' was viewed by contemporaries, see A. I. Cameron, ed., *The Scottish Correspondence of Mary of Lorraine*, Scottish History Society (Edinburgh, 1927), pp. 380, 386–8, 389–90.

Adew Grosars, Nicksons and Bellis,
Oft have we run out-thoart the fellis;
Adew, Robsonis, [Hawis] and Pyilis,
That in our craft hes mony wylis;
Lytils, Trumbels and Armestrangs.
Adew, all theifis that me belangs,
Tailyeours, [Erewynis] and Elwands,
Speidie of fut and wicht of hands;
The Scotts of Ewisdaill and the Graimis,
I have na tyme to tell your namis.   (lines 4028–39)

To this list Dissait adds, with his catalogue of fraudulent merchants and
their tricks, the names of many who may well have been in the audience,
whether at Cupar or Edinburgh.

Adew, the greit Clan Jamesone,
The blude royal of [Couper toun] –
  I was ay to yow trew:
Baith Andersone and Patersone,
Above them all Thome Williamsone,
  My absence ye will rew . . .

Ye young merchants may cry 'allace!'
[Lucklaw, Welandis, Carruders, Dowglace]
  Yon curst king ye may ban.   (lines 4094–9, 4106–8)

Finally, Falset dies listing the corrupt craftsmen that he has aided, the
webbers, walkers, and butchers; the tailors of Angus and Fife; 'my gude
maister Andro Fortoun' (line 4154); 'Tailyeour Baberage, my sone and
air' (line 4157); 'The barfit deacon, Jamie Ralfe' (line 4160); Willie
Cadyeoch and his wife (lines 4163–4); 'the brousters of Couper toun'
(line 4166); 'the sowtar Geordie [Selly]' (line 4184); all the bakers, wrights
and masons, blacksmiths, Lorimers, goldsmiths, and even the shepherds
of Scotland. Again the ostensible intention may be to warn these corrupt
tradesmen to mend their 'ways, but the result is a litany of corrupt
individuals and crafts that seems to take in almost all of contemporary
society.[47] As Falset concludes,

---

[47] References to the corruption of craftsmen and the potential of the trades to foment disorder
would have had an immediate and harsh relevance to the citizens of Edinburgh in 1554. The past
three years had seen increasing tension between the burgh council and a number of crafts, in
response to council attempts to keep prices down in a time of acute crisis. Such tensions
provoked a riot inspired by the baxters in 1551, and a number of members of the Fleshers guild
were put to an assize in 1553. M. Lynch, *Edinburgh and the Reformation* (Edinburgh, 1981), p. 70.

> Amang crafts-men it is ane wonder
> To find ten leill amang ane hunder:
>   The treuth I to yow tell.   (lines 4214–16)

As the probity and skill of these same craftsmen – represented by the Sowtar and Taylour – had been used earlier in the play as a yardstick against which to judge the inadequacies of Spirituality and the Clergy (lines 3140–73), providing a key argument for their reform, this revelation of wholesale corruption among the trades is doubly unsettling. Suddenly a whole new range of abuses not considered by the Estates is opened up as the play concludes. Simultaneously, the fixed point of reference provided by the honest lay craftsmen is spectacularly removed. Again the success of the reformation enacted by Rex and Correctioun is called into question, and the integrity of the reformers compromised. All of this is merely preparatory, however, to the final and most powerful blow to the credibility of the reformers provided by the arrival of Foly, who bursts into the place immediately upon Flatterie's triumphant exit and destroys the last bastion of the reformer's credibility, the earnestness of the reforming enterprise itself.

Foly's initial quest to obtain justice from the king(s) over a dispute with a sow is in itself a mockery of the sober enactments of justice which had preceded his arrival. But this is soon forgotten in favour of still more obviously knockabout repartee (not, however, before we see worrying signs that Rex might well have been willing to entertain the suit). The collapse into scatology (and a gleeful obsession with what Bakhtin's translators have immortalised as 'the lower bodily stratum'[48]) which had begun with the dragging of the incontinent vices to the gallows is thus completed by Foly's comic routine. First, the court is held up by the shaggy dog story of his wife and her projectile illness ('Scho blubert, bockit and braikit still, / Hir arsse gaid evin lyke ane wind-mill' (lines 4386–87)), then, having blatantly ignored and defied the king (symbolically uncrowning him as 'yon . . . with the goldin hat' (line 4347)), Foly turns upon the audience with an uproariously disruptive piece of phallic business.

> Me think my pillok [penis] will nocht ly doun –
> Hald doun your head, ye lurdon loun!
> Yon fair las with the sating goun
>   Gars yow thus bek and bend.
> Take thair ane neidull for your cace;

---

[48] M. Bakhtin, *Rabelais and His World*, ed. and trans. H. Iswolsky (Bloomington, IND, 1984), p. 23 *et passim*.

> Now for all the hiding of your face,
> Had I yow in ane quyet place,
>   Ye wald nocht waine to flend!   (lines 4438–45)

In this incident, we see Foly's role in the text and his effect upon the action wonderfully encapsulated. Like his flamboyant penis, he is himself uncontrollable and uninhibited, with no sense of either shame or decorum: an irrepressible natural and physical force, incompatible with civil society, stable government, or dramatic high seriousness alike. All three collapse in the face of his irrepressible and disruptive energy. From this moment on it is Foly who controls the place, not Rex (who readily offers him the use of the pulpit, disingenuously calling him 'brother' in the process), and not Correctioun, who is effectively silenced for the rest of the play. Foly's sermon confirms the impressions created by the other vices. His text, '*stultorum numerus infinitis*', is itself an acknowledgement of the omnipresence and unreformability of worldly vice and folly. The portfolio of fools he uncovers both widens the definition of the vicious to include the reformers themselves (he lists among his friends 'Earles, duiks, kings and empriours' (line 4514)) and brings it irrefutably into the here-and-now of the audience's own experience. With the most contemporary of the topical allusions in the play, he draws into his definition of folly the government which had mismanaged the war with England (lines 4599–602), the European powers preparing for further conflict among themselves (lines 4603–20), and the friars of St Andrews and their debates over the proper recipient of the Pater Noster (lines 4636–41). Thus the play, which had begun with the confident assurances of lasting reform offered by Diligence, ends with a powerful and unanswered assertion of the futility of all reforming measures in a world governed by folly and corruption. As Diligence confesses upon hearing Foly's nonsensical 'Prophesie of Marling',

> Marie, that is ane il-savorit [mess]!   (line 4635)

In such a world, no sovereign, even one with the impeccable reforming credentials of Divyne Correctioun, can make a lasting impact.

What had happened between 1540 and 1552 to prompt such a fundamental alteration to Lindsay's play? It is tempting to see many of the changes made to the mechanics of the plot as a conscious and carefully crafted response to the altered political priorities of minority rule, and no doubt there is some truth in this, particularly with regard to the wholly different conception of the power and authority of the king.

Whereas under an adult monarch authority was undisputed and a reformer knew that the most effective (and indeed perhaps the only) way to advance his cause was to negotiate with that authority in the person of the sovereign, under a regency administration authority was neither unitary nor undisputed. The prospect of a more assertive role for counsellors thus existed. Indeed, it became practical not merely to bolster royal authority, to encourage the regent in one direction and hope to ride to success on his or her coat-tails, but to restrict that authority and to hedge it about with advisors of one's own stamp, thereby seizing the political initiative. Hence, perhaps, the crucial role given in the 1552–4 play to Gude Counsall as a *promoter* of events rather than simply an adviser, and Correctioun's powerful declaration of the need to widen the circle of government and open up authority to outside counsel:

> I will do nocht without the conveining
> Ane Parleament of the Estat[i]s all . . .
>
> Thair may no prince do act[i] honorabill
> Bot gif his counsall thairto will assist:
> How may he knaw the thing maist profitabil,
> To follow vertew, and vycis to resist,
> Without he be instructit and solist?
> And quhen the King stands at his Counsell sound,
> Then welth sall wax and plentie as he list,
> And policie sall in his realms abound.   (lines 1585–6, 1589–96)

In its later form, the play offers the prospect of a powerful council and a parliament as the solution to religious abuses. The interlude of 1540 had advocated increased *royal* authority as the means to that end. In this alteration it surely reflects the changes in political circumstances be-tween the two performances. Under a minority, the reformers were able to take greater initiative in affairs. Indeed, they may even have thought themselves sufficiently strong to push openly for change through the formal instrument of Parliament, taking the regent with them by weight of both argument and numbers, and this change in their position is reflected in the persuasive strategy which the later play adopts.

If this reading is correct, the 1554 text remains a persuasive document, albeit a markedly more assertive one. The play reappeared at court during another period of compromise and debate. After Beaton's death the church was once again seeking to accommodate some of the more moderate reforming positions, a tendency evident in the drafting of

Hamilton's Catechism, endorsed by the provincial council of 1552. Mary of Guise herself, like James V, was perceived to be open to persuasion. Like all regents she had to compromise, to temporise, in order to maintain her shaky authority. But she was also, it seems clear, someone with whom the reformers thought they could work, not least as her own power struggles with Arran might well be served by attacks upon the clerical power base of his half-brother, Archbishop Hamilton.[49] Although the balance of power had shifted away from the person of the ruler and towards those who provide her with counsel, the play remains a negotiative text – an attempt at political persuasion not incompatible with the sort of household play from which it was developed.

This analysis fails, however, to take account of the wider, structural and tonal alterations made to the play, and what they may suggest about the role it was expected to play in the political process. Here it is tempting to see the sense of frustration and disorder which permeates the concluding episodes of *The Thrie Estaitis* as evidence of a more fundamental unease. The sense of folly and vice run riot throughout Scotland which closes the play is suggestive of a wider disaffection with political activity; a disaffection which may stem, not simply from the general political imperatives of regency government, but from Lindsay's own position as a courtier and Lyon King in a realm which had, for the previous ten years, been without an adult monarch. Clearly the experience of a decade of minority rule *could* have led the author to idealise the nature of royal power and authority, and laud its return sincerely as the solution to all difficulties, as he had done in *The Dreme* (1528),[50] and as he implied at the start of *The Thrie Estaitis*. But (on the evidence of the play as a whole) it seems to have bred the reverse, a profound despair at the possibilities of personal rule in the context of contemporary Scotland, and a sense that things had gone so badly wrong that no king could be expected to put them right by a simple act of political will. In part this may have been a pragmatic response to the dwindling prospect of substantial reform in a realm faced with many more years of minority, and thereafter the likelihood of Queen Mary returning from France with a catholic husband. Yet the temptation to see more personal, perhaps even subconscious, reasons at work is strong. For Lindsay, who

---

[49] Hence Knox could approach her as late as 1556 in an attempt to win her approval. See Wormald, *Court, Kirk and Community*, p. 110; Lynch, *Edinburgh and the Reformation*, pp. 72–3; Cameron, *Scottish Correspondence*, pp. 404–6; and Graf, 'Theatre and Politics', pp. 153–4.

[50] *The Dreme*, lines 1003–8.

for so long had seen persuasion of the king as the chief route to political reform, the absence of a king to counsel may well have seemed an insurmountable barrier to reform itself. This despair at the prospects for political action may well be reflected in a play in which reform is continually stifled by the lack of a central authority to force it through. Rather than attempting to negotiate with authority, as he had done for the greater part of his career, Lindsay may have finally abandoned the project and been reduced merely to reflecting upon its impotence.

'The Thrie Estaitis' and the politics of social reform

If Lindsay was markedly more sceptical of the notion of a reforming monarchy in 1552–54 than he had been in 1540, did that alter his attitude towards reform itself? In particular, how does *The Thrie Estaitis* treat the social reforms which he had called for throughout his poetic career as an essential element in the resurrection of the commonweal of Scotland? How had the playwright's attitudes shifted in this respect between the writing of the two versions of the play? Was the Lindsay of 1552–4 still a radical social reformer, as a number of critics have claimed? And, if so, how did that reformist drive manifest itself?

In an important article, Claud Graf suggested that the 1552–4 text sought to coax rather than shock the Scottish establishment towards reform.[51] 'The worst thing for Lindsay to do', Graf argued, 'would have been to scare the rulers of Scotland; in fact he tries to reassure them'.[52] But this reading seems to overlook a number of the more awkward aspects of the drama, and in particular the unsettling effects created by Pauper's intrusion into the play. For Graf, the presence of both John the Common-Weill and Pauper, and their forceful roles in the meeting of the three Estates, contributed to the positive portrayal in the text of those elements of the Scottish commons most sympathetic to religious reform: 'the small lairds, the merchant class and their dependants'.[53] Lindsay, Graf claimed, was thus courting the support of such men by involving their dramatic surrogates fully in the drama of reform. It seems far from clear, however, that this is how these characters would have been interpreted by contemporary audiences. While the inclusion of Marchand among the Estates might well have furthered this strategy, offering a positive role model of a sober, responsible, bourgeois oligarch, the treatment of John and Pauper seems less clear cut.

[51] Graf, 'Theatre and Politics', p. 151.   [52] Ibid.   [53] Ibid., p. 150.

The division of the role of the Poor Man of the 1540 interlude into two separate figures in the 1552–54 drama is one of the more significant differences between the two productions. For Graf the change was simply a measure of the increased importance of the poor commons to Lindsay's thinking in the later period, and consequently 'the merchant's calling John a "poor man" may mean that they are almost interchangeable characters in Lindsay's mind, and makes clear to the audience that the "commoun weill" is one with the idea of social justice'.[54] Yet the decision to divide the role seems more pointed than this. Indeed, close reading prompts the contrary suggestion that it was effected precisely to create two characters who, while closely related, were not interchangeable, thus allowing a more complex exploration of issues of poverty, popular politics, and 'commoun weill' than was possible in the earlier interlude.

Although both John and Pauper enter the action in the same way, coming into the place from among the audience, their characters are from the outset distinctly drawn. Neither is fully analogous to the Poor Man of the original interlude. John's entrance is unthreatening, and indeed deferential towards those already in the place, and is thus fully absorbable within the business of the Estates. He takes his cue from the proclamation issued by Diligence that anyone with a grievance should 'gif in his bill' (line 2423) to the Parliament. His gratitude that someone will at last hear his complaints is palpable.

> Thankit be Christ that bair the croun of thorne,
> For I was never sa blyth sen I was borne!   (lines 2428–9)

By contrast, Pauper is wholly less amenable to accommodation. His entrance is unlooked for and unlicensed by the authorities of the court. It takes place outside the strict confines of the play proper, in the curiously marginal 'Interlude' during which the major players have vacated the place and returned to the pavilion. Symbolically, whereas John waits outside the place, only leaping over the 'stank' or stream that formed an (at least nominal) boundary to the playing space, when he is invited to 'cum over' by Diligence,[55] Pauper shows no such reticence. Consequently *his* intrusion is treated as an affront, not only to the political decorum of the play-court, but also to the decorum of the entire

---

[54] Ibid., p. 145.

[55] John is invited by Diligence to 'Cum and complaine' (line 2427), and again to 'Cum over, and I sall schaw the to His Grace', at line 2434. Indeed, so slow is he in coming forward that Diligence has to chide him to hurry up at line 2438.

dramatic enterprise itself. Diligence, the master of ceremonies of Parliament and play alike, is thrown into ill-tempered confusion.

> Quhair have wee gotten this gudly companyeoun?
> Swyith, out of the field, fals raggit loun!
> . . .
> Fals huirson raggit carle, quhat Devil is that thou rugs?
>
> (lines 1938–9, 1946)

That the otherwise courtly and composed Diligence is so unsettled by his intrusion is itself a measure of Pauper's disruptive force.

The device of having characters step out of the crowd and join the action was, of course, far from novel. The entry of vices from among the audience was, as we have seen, a common feature of morality and household drama, and Lindsay exploits it to the full elsewhere in *The Thrie Estaitis*.[56] The more explicitly metatheatrical device of having what appeared to be members of the audience themselves enter the action had also been pioneered, in an English context, by Henry Medwall, who created the illusion that two household servants of his patron, Cardinal Morton, had walked into his interlude *Fulgens and Lucrece*, in the 1490s.[57] But Lindsay takes the device a step further here, using it to create, not a pleasantly unsettling comic effect (as in *Fulgens*) but a fundamentally unsettling political one. Again the contrast between the treatment of John and that of Pauper is illuminating.

Whereas it is clear, even as he steps forward from the audience, that John is an unproblematically dramatic figure, a representative of the poor commons *within the play*, Pauper resists so easy a definition. His status is more properly liminal, neither fully within the play, nor (obviously) truly outside it. Thus Diligence treats him in a way which it does not occur to him to treat John, turning upon him, as we have seen, as an invader, not of the court, but of the playing space itself. He appeals for his removal, not to the royal guards in the play-court, but to the civic authorities in the audience and the stewards responsible for controlling the crowd, accusing them of negligence.

> God wait gif heir be ane will keipit place,
> Quhen sic ane wilde begger carle may get entres;
> Fy on yow officiars, that mends nocht thir failyes!

---

[56] Solace enters from among the audience, complaining 'Now quha saw ever sic ane thrang?' (line 141), while both Flattery ('Mak roume, sirs, hoaw! that I may rin! / Lo, se quhair I am new cum [in]' (lines 602–03)) and Dissait ('Stand by the gait, that I may stier!' (line 658)) give classic examples of the 'Make Room!' formulation.

[57] A. H. Nelson, ed., *The Plays of Henry Medwall* (Woodbridge, 1980).

> I gif yow all till the Devill, baith Provost and Bailyes!
> Without ye cum and chase this carle away,
> The Devill a word ye'is get mair of our play! (lines 1940–5)

The threat that Pauper supposedly poses to the performance of the play is again stressed by Diligence twenty lines further on, as he once again turns upon the intruder in exasperation.

> Swyith begger bogill, haist the away!
> Thou art over pert to spill our play (lines 1962–3)

One effect of this disruption of dramatic decorum is, of course, para-doxically, to afford the action even greater verisimilitude. Here at last, it seems, is a representative of the real Scottish commons, bringing a harsh note of realism into the drama, and demanding justice for real social abuses, not fictional ones. Pauper issues a direct challenge to the audi-ence in the idea that the conventional dramatic solutions offered within the play can only be a spur to the political action in the real world necessary to restore the commonweal to its proper state.[58] Moreover, in using Pauper in this way, Lindsay is also able to question more funda-mentally the whole enterprise of political drama – of treating so urgent an issue as popular poverty 'in game' at all, however earnestly the endeavour was intended. For Pauper's reply to Diligence's shrill con-cern over the fate of the drama draws out the inherent incompatibility of true poverty and dramatic play, and the irrelevance of the latter to the concerns of the real poor.

> I wil not gif for all your play worth an sowis fart,
> For thair is richt litill play at my hungrie hart. (lines 1964–5)

Thus far, then, Lindsay's use of Pauper, far from supporting the idea of him as appealing to the rural gentry and merchants, is compatible with the idea that he is a radical social commentator, willing to ally himself with the poor commons in bringing their case to the government, and willing even to suggest the inadequacies of his own dramatic response to their plight as a means of underscoring its urgency. This is the aspect of *The Thrie Estaitis* which has commended itself most readily to many modern commentators, who have seen in the play much of the energy and commitment to social reform driving the politically engaged drama of modern materialist theatre. It would be unwise to leave our consider-ation of Pauper's role in the play here, however, for it is far from clear that in the context of a performance in the early 1550s, he would have

---

[58] See Lyall, ed., *Thrie Estaitis*, p. xxxix.

been seen as quite so unequivocally sympathetic a voice as has sometimes been suggested.[59]

Pauper's metatheatricality cuts both ways. It is to his role within the
drama that we must turn now for a clearer view of the effects of his
actions. Here, too, he is no less unsettling to convention and decorum,
not least as the first thing that he does after leaping uninvited into the
place is climb into the royal throne until recently occupied by Rex
Humanitas ('*Heir sall the Carle clim up and sit in the king's tchyre*' (direction
following line 1946)). That our response to this intrusion is supposed to
be at best ambivalent rather than approving, seems confirmed by the
fact that he uses the opportunity of occupying the seat of judgement to
drain a 'stoup' of beer, an action unequivocally associated with the vices
in the play to this point.[60]

It is hard to see here Graf's idea of a play which seeks only to reassure
its elite audience. For, whatever their view of the validity of Pauper's
case, it would be hard to see in his defiance of all constituted authority
(whether within or beyond the play-world) anything but a calculated
threat to their own position. From his entrance onward, Pauper represents an uncontrollable force, whose accommodation to the powers of
civil government is at best partial, and whose character is always
volatile. A recognition of this fact seems to lie behind Diligence's order,
on encountering the Pardoner and Pauper fighting at the end of the
'Interlude', that *both* should be imprisoned and subject to the ultimate
penalty:

> Quhat kind of daffing is this al day?
> Swyith, smaiks, out of the field, away!
> Into ane presoun put them sone,
> Syne hang them quhen the play is done.   (lines 2297–300)

Diligence has heard, and seemingly sympathised with, Pauper's tale of
hardship and deprivation. And Robert Rome-Raker, the 'perfite, publike pardoner' (line 2051), with his portmanteau of false relics, is as
unmistakable and conventional a figure of the clerical corruption which
has brought about the downfall of the poor as could be imagined. Yet
Diligence draws no distinction between them. In order to re-establish
the order necessary for the continuation of the play, *both* must be
identified as figures of disorder and eliminated.

---

[59] As previous note.
[60] In a play full of symbolic usurpations and uncrownings, the disruption to established authority
represented by this seizure of the throne is made all the clearer by the fact that Diligence, for all
his righteous indignation, is unable to remove him.

The association between Pauper, crime, and punishment is, then, a powerful one. As Roderick Lyall has pointed out, under the terms of the 1535 act for the 'stanching of beggaris', destitutes were confined to their parish of origin. Thus Pauper is 'manifestly a criminal', when he enters the play begging 'Of your almis, gude folkis, for Gods luife of heavin' (line 1935), having travelled from his home in 'Lawthiane, ane myle fra Tranent' (line 1969).[61] Now he is condemned afresh and confined by Diligence, only to burst back into the action later in the play, to support John the Common-Weill's testimony to Parliament with his own anecdotal evidence.

While John and Pauper share many similarities, then, they remain fundamentally different figures. Each represents the abused and downtrodden commons, certainly. And each wears the unsettling marks of their poverty in their physical appearance.[62] They each come into the action, as we have seen, from beyond the pale, crossing the symbolic divide between the 'real world' of the audience and the play-world of the actors with energetic leaps. But this is where the similarity ends. As their respective entrances demonstrate, Pauper is a far less conformable figure than John, and this distinction becomes more and more evident as the play progresses. Both offer Utopian scenarios during the proceedings, suggesting how they would use the ultimate authority to reform society, but, where John is careful to couch his proposals in the conditional, 'War I ane king, my lord' (line 2592), Pauper forgets himself, asserting the startlingly presumptive, 'Quhen I am Paip' (line 2802).

Their respective responses to the procedures of the Estates are similarly instructive in this respect. John readily proves himself capable of following set process, quickly adopting the protocol and rhetoric of parliamentary business ('On that, Sir Scribe, I tak ane instrument', he says at line 2821). Pauper remains an alienated figure, throwing in his remarks from the margins with no regard to cues or propriety. This distinction is marked in signal fashion at the conclusion of the debate, when John is formally absorbed into the reforming establishment, given a 'gay garmoun' (line 3794), and invested as a new member of the Estates. Correctioun initiates the process:

---

[61] Lyall, ed., *Thrie Estaitis*, p. ix.
[62] Pauper is a 'fals raggit loun' (line 1939), and a 'huirsun raggit carl' (line 1946), who appears to Diligence to be 'a begger bogill' (line 1962). John is similarly 'cruikit' in shape (line 2446); without clothes (line 2445), 'baith cauld, naikit and disgysit' (line 3798); and showing evident and disturbing signs of having 'bene amang his fais' (line 2444).

> Sergeants, gif Johne ane new abuilyement,
> Of sating, damais or of the velvot fyne,
> And gif him place in our Parliament syne.
> *Heir sall thay claith Johne the Common-weill gorgeouslie and set him doun among them in*
> *Parliament.* (lines 3800–2 and following)[63]

Consequently our last sight of John is of his being silently added to the ranks of the governors of the land.

Characteristically, no such accommodation is possible with Pauper, and his dissenting voice is not silenced. Despite his general approval of the reforms enacted by the Estates, his last utterance is a robust statement of only conditional satisfaction with their proceedings and a warning of the dangers ahead. That which has been concluded, he argues, must now be enforced, and more yet needs to be done, if Scotland is truly to be reformed.

> I gif yow my braid bennesoun
> That hes givin Common-weill a goun:
> I wald nocht for ane pair of plackis
> Ye had nocht maid thir nobill Actis.
> I pray to God and sweit sanct Geill
> To gif yow grace to use them weill:
> Wer thay weill keipit, I understand,
> It war great honour to Scotland.
> [But] It had bene als gude ye had sleipit
> As to mak acts and be nocht keipit:
> Bot I beseik yow, for Alhallows,
> To heid Dissait and hang his [fallowis],
> And banish Flatterie aff the thoun,
> For thair was never sic ane loun.
> That beand done, I hauld it best,
> That everie man ga to his rest! (lines 3982–97)

In this hope Pauper is destined to be frustrated. Although Correctioun promises to take on all these tasks, the final reformation the play offers is, as we have seen, far from convincing. Thus Pauper remains a marginal figure, not fully absorbed within the parliamentary process, and left at least partially unsatisfied at the end of the play.

In this crucial difference in the treatment of the two commons figures lies one of the most distinctive and interesting features of the play's

---

[63] That this readjustment of the political classes is achieved without demur or disruption is made clear by Correctioun's further declaration that 'All vertuous peopill may be rejoisit. / Sen common-weill hes gotten ane gay garmoun' (lines 3803–4).

political content. By splitting the figure of the Poor Man of the interlude into two parts, Lindsay was able to treat the call for social justice in a nuanced way, which may well have reflected an ambivalence in his own attitude towards popular protest and the grievances of the commons. Both figures point towards the same social injustices as the root cause of their deprivation, but each reacts to them in a different way. Neither is the *vox populi* which is also *vox Dei* that one saw in the Poor Man of the interlude. In John we see something akin to a representative of the 'deserving poor' of Victorian fiction: a figure of sober, deferential complaint, willing to wait for his cues, and finally able to be co-opted into the establishment with little difficulty (not least as his own attitudes and values are essentially those of his masters anyway[64]): in short, a figure very similar to those representatives of the commons for whom Lindsay was accustomed to speak in Parliament in his role as Lyon King. In Pauper we see a more assertive and troublesome figure, a man who was once an honest labourer, but who has now been induced by injustice to take matters into his own hands. When not overawed by weight of numbers, he is quite prepared to climb onto the throne or attack the clergy with his bare hands. In a play much concerned with the need for stability and sound, civil, administration,[65] his is among the most disruptive and disputatious of voices, less amenable to socialisation than those of the court vices in the first half of the play.

Lindsay's commitment to social justice, then, seems less unequivocal than some accounts suggest. Writing for an essentially courtly elite, and as a member of that elite, his portrayal of the issue seems clearly circumscribed by what it seems legitimate to call class interests. In representing the poor commons of Scotland as both John and Pauper, he offers his audience both an opportunity and a warning. He uses John to make the case for essential reforms in as sympathetic a way as possible, tying social improvement to religious reform in a way which would seem well-suited to the interests of the governors, gentry, and burgesses so important to the future of reform. Yet he uses Pauper to unsettle that same audience, to shock rather than reassure them, with a vision of a far more troublesome form of popular protest which might result if either the modest demands of John are not met, or the appeal to

---

[64] See, for example, his attack upon vagrancy and idlers, his advocacy of a strong law and order policy in the borders, and a firm line in foreign policy against the English at ll. 2587–619.

[65] Note Gude Counsall's somewhat naive plea: 'I yow requyre, my lords, be patient. / We came nocht heir for disputatiouns, / We came to make gude reformatiouns' (lines 2805–7). As the play makes plain, however, reformation is inevitably a contentious and disputatious business.

popularity is taken too far. In Pauper's attacks upon the Pardoner (and later upon Spirituality), we see a vision of popular anti-clericalism wholly alien to the civil, non-disputatious, 'gude reformations' advocated by Gude Counsall and Correctioun. And in his occupation of the vacant throne, the consequences of an untrammelled popular politics are equally startlingly presented. The apocalyptic overtones evident in the powerful and unsettling confessions of the vices are thus reflected in the social convulsions threatened by Pauper's presence in the play. In this context at least, Lindsay's appeal for reform may be rather more urgent in tone, but perhaps rather less fundamental and radical in implication, than is often suggested.

CHAPTER 5

Dramatic justice at the Marian court: Nicholas Udall's 'Respublica'

THE AUTHOR

Born in Southampton in 1504, Nicholas Udall attended Winchester College from 1517 and went up to Corpus Christi College, Oxford in 1520. After a period as a Fellow of Corpus and university lecturer in Logic, he left Oxford in 1529 and made a living as a writer and freelance scholar before being appointed headmaster of Eton in 1534.[1] While at Eton, Udall seems to have developed a reputation for the zealous administration of corporal punishment. A former pupil was later to protest about his treatment at the headmaster's hands in doggerel verse.

> From Paul's I went, to Eton sent,
> To learn straightways the Latin phrase;
> Where fifty-three stripes given to me at once I had
> For fault but small, or none at all.
> See, Udall, see, the mercy of thee, to me, poor lad.[2]

But it was his departure from Eton, rather than the disciplinary regime he oversaw there, which has aroused the most anxious scholarly comment.

On 12 March 1541, one John Hoorde, late scholar of Eton, was examined by the Privy Council in connection with a robbery he had committed at the college in company with another former pupil.[3] On the following day the second scholar, Thomas Cheyney, was also questioned and, like Hoorde, confessed his involvement in the crime.[4] William Ember, a London goldsmith who evidently acted as a fence for

---

[1] W. L. Edgerton, *Nicholas Udall* (New York, 1965), pp. 9–10. Udall's *Floures for Latine Speakynge* (1534) dates from this period of semi-independent scholarly activity.

[2] Thomas Tusser, *Five Hundreth Points of Good Husbandry, United to as many of Good Huswifery, Nowe Lately Augmented* (1573), *RSTC* 24375, II, sig., 27v.

[3] This was John Hoorde, eldest son of Richard Hoorde of Bridgnorth in Shropshire and Elizabeth née Matthew. Sir Wasey Sterry, *Eton College Register, 1441–1698* (Eton, 1943), p. 179.

[4] Thomas Cheyney was the second son of Sir Robert Cheyney of Chesham Bois, Buckinghamshire, and Mary Cheyney, née Sylsham. Ibid., p. 76.

the boys, was also committed to custody 'for the buying of certain images of silver and other plate which was stolen from the college of Eton'.[5] It was on the following day that Udall became involved in the affair. Having evidently been implicated in the crime by the boys' confessions, the headmaster was 'sent for as suspect to be of councail of a robbery lately committed at Eton by Thomas Cheyney, John Hoorde, scolers of the sayd scole, and . . . Gregory, servant to the said scolemaster'. Once summoned before the Council, Udall had 'certain interrogatoryes ministred unto hym, toching the sayd fact and other felonious trespasses, wherof he was suspected'. What emerged from this interrogation resulted in Udall's imprisonment in the Marshalsea and his dismissal from Eton and has blighted his literary reputation ever since. Scholars have been remarkably coy about this aspect of the affair, being unwilling to admit – or even to name – the nature of his offences.[6] But, what seems abundantly clear is that Udall confessed, not only to a role in the robbery, but to having a homosexual relationship with one of his co-conspirators and former pupils. When questioned, he 'did confesse that he did commit buggery with the said Cheyney. sundry times heretofore, and of late the vjth day of this present moneth in the present yere at London'. That Udall was an acknowledged homosexual itself troubled previous generations of scholars. That he admitted committing sodomy with a former pupil proves too much for even most modern commentators to accept. Hence, William Edgerton ingeniously attempted to absolve the playwright of the whole business, attributing the reference to 'buggery' to a scribal error on the part of William Paget, Clerk of the Council; suggesting that the word intended was 'burglary', and speculating, increasingly unconvincingly, that the offence and the allusion to the event having been committed 'at sundry times' and once at least in London, might be accounted for by a moment's inebriated weakness on Udall's part.

The robberies at Eton may have consisted in the drunken headmaster's breaking open the chests containing the church ornaments and of giving them

[5] H. Nicholas, *Proceedings and Ordinances of the Privy Council of England* (London, 1834–7), VII, 152–3, 155, 157. Edgerton, *Udall*, p. 37.

[6] Marie Axton talks simply of 'misconduct' (Marie Axton, *Three Tudor Classical Interludes* (Woodbridge, 1982), p. 3), Scheurweghs, printing the relevant documents, passes over the confession of buggery without comment, noting simply that the sources do not confirm Udall's involvement in the robbery (G. Scheurweghs, *Nicholas Udall's 'Roister Doister'*, in H. De Vocht, ed., *Materials for the Study of Old English*, XVI (1939), pp. xxiv–xxv). The latter does, however, chastise the author for his failure to pay his debts, concluding that 'truth obliges us to record, not only his successes as a scholar, but also his failings as a man' (p. 108).

to the boys to sell to the goldsmith. If that is so, Udall might have in this case extended their operations to London.[7]

This, Edgerton argued, was a far less serious offence than buggery – indeed, at a time of Reformation iconoclasm it need not be considered an offence at all. 'Too many people', he argued, 'had misappropriated church property at that time to make it seem the heinous crime it appears to us.'

Thus through the assumption of a careless piece of book-keeping, Udall is turned from a paedophile schoolmaster to an endearing mixture of Raffles and Robin Hood, throwing open the college coffers for his pupils' benefit. This enthusiastic attempt to exonerate Udall is engaging in its naiveté, but tells us rather more about the prejudices of its author than the events surrounding Udall's dismissal.[8] What the sources suggest, however unpalatable it might be to some critics, is that Udall was indeed guilty of sodomy with a pupil who, while adult by modern standards, was still young enough to be considered a minor at the time.[9]

If Udall suffered a period of disgrace as a result of his misdemeanours, however, it was short-lived. In September 1542 Richard Grafton published his *Apophthegmes*, an annotated translation of part of Erasmus' *Apophthegemata*, and by 1543 he was once more enjoying patronage at court, editing and translating *The Paraphrases of Erasmus* at Catherine Parr's instigation.[10] He was also able to continue his teaching career, for in 1549 he was appointed tutor to Edward Courtney, the royal prisoner in the Tower of London, and was to gain the headmastership of Westminster School on 16 December 1555, almost exactly a year before his death on 23 December 1556. He continued to enjoy support in high places during his final years, being appointed a canon of Windsor in 1551 and rector of Cranborne in 1553, and having work performed in or around the court, including his celebrated pseudo-Terencian interlude *Ralph Roister Doister* (first produced *c.* 1552, possibly before Edward VI),

---

[7] Edgerton, *Udall*, pp. 39–40.

[8] Mercifully, such speculative scholarship has not caught on, although it is tempting to apply similar palaeographic generosity to redress other potential injustices: revisionist articles beckon on Herod and the moussaka of the Innocents.

[9] The fathers of both Cheyney and Hoorde had to attend the Council with them and stand surety for further hearings. Hoorde, having been born *c.* 1522, was about nineteen years of age at the time of Udall's confession (Sterry, *Register*, p. 179). Perhaps as the result of lobbying on his behalf by influential allies, Udall seems to have escaped prosecution for an offence which, since the Buggery Act of 1534, carried the death penalty. A. Luders, *et al.*, eds., *Statutes of The Realm* (11 vols., London, 1810–28), II, pp. 441, 455, 725, and 749. [10] Edgerton, *Udall*, pp. 10–11.

an earlier interlude, *Thersites* (*c.* 1537), and perhaps also *Jack Juggler* and *Jacob and Esau*, now frequently ascribed to his authorship.[11]

Udall's religious position

From his early years as a student, Udall was, it seems, a committed religious reformer. As early as 1528, while a Fellow of Corpus, he had been disciplined with others for reading the works of Luther and Tyndale's English translation of the New Testament. [12]In 1533 he was collaborating with another Oxford man, John Leland, the future anti-quarian, in the production of pageants for Anne Boleyn's coronation. During the 1530s and early 1540s he was mixing in reformist circles and translating protestant works. In 1538 he produced an unknown play (perhaps his biblical drama *Ezechias*) in the household of Thomas Crom-well. By 1543, as we have seen, he was working on the translation of Erasmus' *Paraphrase of the New Testament*, under the patronage of Queen Catherine Parr, and in 1546 he gained from the queen a portion of the living of Hartyng, Sussex, a reward he shared with Richard Moryson, the protestant propagandist. In 1550 he translated the *Tractatie de Sacra-mente* of Peter Martyr and dedicated it to the queen, and in 1551 he contributed verses to two volumes of *encomia*, one dedicated to Martin Bucer, the other in memory of the two sons of the patroness of re-formers, the Duchess of Suffolk.

Such credentials would not have disgraced a protestant exile, thus it is unsurprising that Udall was to lose out materially on the accession of Queen Mary. The canonry at Windsor, granted in 1551, was taken from him in 1554 and given to one of the new queen's chaplains, and he was also deprived of the lucrative rectory of Colborne on the Isle of Wight. But, beyond these setbacks, Udall suffered little evident loss of favour at court. He continued to produce dramatic works in the royal household, was singled out for special praise by the queen and offered what amounted to an ongoing commission to provide plays for the court in the second year of the reign.[13] Evidently he was not considered a dangerous radical by the new regime. Even the arch-conservative

---

[11] Axton, *Classical Interludes*, pp. 1–2. William Hunnis has also been suggested as the author of *Jacob and Esau* (P. W. White, *Theatre and Reformation: Protestantism, Patronage, and Playing in Tudor England* (Cambridge, 1993), p. 118).

[12] John Foxe, *Acts and Monuments*, eds., S. R. Cattley and G. Townsend (8 vols., London, 1837–41), v, pp. 421–9 and appendix. For the following, see W. R. Streitberger, *Court Revels, 1485–1559* (Toronto, 1994), p. 148, Edgerton, *Udall, passim*, and Scheurweghs, '*Roister Doister*', pp. xi–l.

[13] See below, pp. 168–72.

Bishop Stephen Gardiner was to leave him forty marks on his death in 1555. But, as we shall see, Udall was to prove himself adept at advancing a radical case in the guise of apparently conformist counsel.

RESPUBLICA: THE PLOT

The play is a political morality in the style of Skelton's *Magnyfycence* or Lindsay's *Thrie Estaitis*. The eponymous central figure differs, however, from Magnyfycence or Rex Humanitas both in being representative of the state as a whole rather than of the prince in particular, and in being female. Her condition also differs in small but significant respects from those earlier figures. She begins the play already destitute, for example, a 'poor wydowe' in need of the wise, male ministers who will restore her estate. Her subsequent fate is, however, sadly familiar. Instead of wise counsellors, she accepts the blandishments of Avarice, disguised as Policy, who convinces her that he should take over the running of the estate. He in turn calls in his fellow vices, Insolence, Oppression, and Adulation (or Flattery), listed in the *dramatis personae* as 'gallants', who, in traditional morality fashion, adopt alter egos, here Authority, Reformation, and Honesty. Once installed in office, the vices exploit the resources of the realm for their own benefit, prompting People, an honest rustic, to protest at the ruinous lot of the common folk. The vices connive to remove People from court, however, and keep Respublica in ignorance of the true state of the nation until they have gleaned all the pickings to be gained from office. Only with the arrival of the four daughters of God, Misericordia, Veritas, Justicia, and Pax, is the true state of affairs revealed and the vices are confronted. Finally, the goddess Nemesis, specifically (the 'Prologue' informs us) a figure for Mary Tudor, enters to judge the vices.[14] Avarice is handed over to People to be pressed like a sponge until all his ill-gotten gains are returned to their rightful owners. Oppression and Insolence are imprisoned awaiting trial. Only Adulation, who offers a frank confession, is

---

[14] The 'Prologue' informs the audience that, like the 'yong babes with tholde folke' who cried out upon Christ's entry into Jerusalem, 'Soo for goode Englande sake this presente howre and daie / In hope of hir restoring from hir late decaye, / We children to youe olde folke, both with harte and voyce / Maie joyne all together to thanke god and Rejoyce / That he hath sent Marye our soveraigne and Quene / To reforme thabuses which hithertoo hath been, / And that yls whiche long tyme have reigned uncorrecte / Shall nowe forever bee redressed with effecte. / She is oure most wise and most worthie Nemesis / Of whome our plaie meneth tamende that is amysse' (lines 45–54). W. W. Greg, ed., *'Respublica': An Interlude for Christmas 1553*, EETS o.s. 226 (London, 1952 for 1946); all references to the text are to this edition.

released and permitted to use his talents hereafter in the service of the state.

Auspices

The only surviving manuscript text of the play, once owned by Sir Henry Spelman (?1564–1641) and subsequently part of the drama collection of the Reverend Cox Macro (1683–1767), describes it as 'A merye entrelude entitled Respublica made in the yeare of oure Lorde .1553. and the first yeare of the moost prosperous Reigne of our most gracious Soveraigne Quene Marye the first'.[15] That the text as we have it was performed at Christmas – or at least written with such a performance in mind – is made clear by the wish in the 'Prologue' that the audience enjoy 'helth and successe with many agoode newe yeare' (line 1) and his description of the play as 'some Christmas devise' (line 6). The 'Prologue' also indicates that the text was written for children, asking rhetorically 'But shall boyes (saith some nowe) of suche highe mattiers plaie[?]' (line 39) and referring to the production as offered by 'We children to youe olde folke' (line 47). Beyond this there is little that is certain about the play. The ascription to Udall has been convincingly made by W. W. Greg and others on stylistic grounds.[16] And there is other circumstantial evidence to link the play to Udall and to a performance at court during the Christmas season of 1553/4.

The text certainly reads as if a court performance was intended. The references to Queen Mary, the prayers for her and her council, and the bringing in of a clear surrogate figure for her in the form of Nemesis in the final act, all make most sense if a production at court was intended. Furthermore, there is clear evidence that Udall did write and produce plays for Mary during the first year of her reign. A warrant of 13 December 1554 granting 'our welbelovid Nicholas Udall' free use of the costumes and properties held by the Revels Office makes clear that he had already 'at sondry seasons convenient hertofore shewid and myndeth herafter to shewe his diligence in setting forthe of dialogues and Entreludes before us for our Regall disport and recreacion'.[17] What these productions may have involved is not clear from the surviving

[15] Ibid., p. 1.
[16] Ibid., pp. x–xviii; L. Bradner, 'A Test for Udall's Authorship', *Modern Language Notes*, 42 (1927), pp. 378–80. William Edgerton, however, takes a more sceptical line on Udall's authorship, *Nicholas Udall*, p. 65.
[17] A. Feuillerat, *Documents Relating to the Revels at Court in the Time of King Edward VI and Queen Mary* (Louvain, 1914), p. 159; Greg, ed., *'Respublica'*, p. viii.

accounts. A play had been prepared for performance at the coronation in September 1553, but seems to have been postponed until Christmas at short notice two days before the event itself.[18] The possibility that this play may have been *Respublica* has been mooted, but seems to be refuted by a further document, a warrant to the Master of the Great Wardrobe issued on the last day of September, commanding him to provide the bearer with costumes and properties for a play to be performed by the Gentlemen of the Chapel 'for the feastes of our coronacion'. The warrant lists the *dramatis personae* of this play as Genus Humanum, five virgins, Verity, Plenty, Self-Love, Care, Deceit, Sickness, Feebleness, Deformity, a Good and a Bad Angel, and the Epilogue.[19] Clearly this list does not tally even remotely with the cast or action of *Respublica*. Scholars have dealt with this evidence in a number of ways. Feuillerat, persuaded by the absence of any direct references to other plays in the Revels accounts, concluded that only one play was performed before the queen between 26 September 1553 and 6 January 1553/4, the one played at Christmas 1553, which was the same play postponed from the feast of the Coronation, i.e. *Genus Humanum* or *Self-Love*.[20] Greg, on the other hand, argued that two plays were performed, one *Genus Humanum/Self-Love* at the Coronation and another, *Respublica* at Christmas, and that *Respublica* had indeed been postponed from September/October until Christmas precisely to make way for the performance of *Genus Humanum/Self-Love* at the earlier date.[21] Neither explanation seems fully to account for the apparent contradictions in the evidence.

From the Revels accounts it seems clear that a play was prepared for the Coronation but then cancelled at short notice – a fact which seems to have left those involved less than happy, hence the somewhat tetchy remarks about the amount of work begun 'but then left off again' which

---

[18] There is an entry in the Revels Accounts for 'Newe makinge, translatinge, allteringe, garnysshinge, and fynisshinge of dyvers and sondry garmentes, aparrell, vestures, and properties for one playe or enterlude by the gentillmen of the chappell to be shewen and played before the quenes majestie at her highnes coronacion, the preparacion therfore begoon and wrowght upon aswell ageanste that tyme by vertue of a warraunte sygned with her Majesties oune handes and upon newe determynacion surseased and lefte of[f] as ageane wrowghte upon fynysshed and served att the Christemas next ensuinge' (Feuillerat, *Documents*, p. 149). The relevant accounts cover work done between 22 September and 28 September, 'wen as the same (by reason of a newe determynacion of appoyntement the play to serve att christmas nexte foloing) surseased and were left of[f] unfynysshed' (ibid., p. 150).

[19] Ibid., p. 289. The appearance of 'Self-Love' among the *dramatis personae* raises the possibility that this was a production of the otherwise unknown 'Play of Self-love', which was also performed by the King's Players for Sir Thomas Chaloner at Hoxton, Middlesex, at some point between 1551 and 1556. I. Lancashire, *Dramatic Texts and Records of Britain: A Chronological Topography to 1558* (Cambridge, 1984), p. 156.   [20] Feuillerat, *Documents*, p. 290.   [21] Greg, *Respublica*, p. x.

recur in the accounts. No references to a new play to replace this postponed production exist. Only the dating of the warrant to the Great Wardrobe, apparently sealed two days after the work in the Revels Office was left off, suggests that anything further was done to provide a dramatic entertainment for the Coronation feast. A more plausible explanation of these documents might be that no play was performed during the Coronation celebrations. An elaborately costumed and casted production of *Genus Humanum/Self-Love* was prepared, but was left off at the last moment, and the play was subsequently produced at Christmas. A warrant for the costumes for this production was prepared, and may have been post-dated to 30 September, or sealed in error on that date, but only after the decision to postpone the production had already been made, thus making it already redundant at the moment it was dated. The alternative possibility, that the Revels Office and the Great Wardrobe had been preparing for a production of *Respublica*, requiring equally elaborate costumes and properties to those listed for *Genus Humanum/Self-Love*, but had been ordered to stop two or three days before the play was due to be performed, and then began preparing for an entirely different production (a play for which the Great Wardrobe was asked to provide 19 costumes, utilising 21 yards of damask, 3 yards of kersey, and 128 yards of satin, at a maximum of three days notice) seems highly unlikely.[22]

But, if this is accepted, where does this leave *Respublica*? If one accepts Feuillerat's interpretation of the documents, it could not have been played at court over the Christmas period, 1553/4, as we have already accounted for the only play performed there during this period. But this conclusion does not seem necessary. The idea that only one play was offered at Yuletide is based upon the absence of clear reference in the Revels accounts to any productions other than that postponed from the Coronation feast. But what we know of Christmas revels in other years suggests that a number of productions were usually offered. Had there really been only one play performed this year it is highly likely that this would have attracted adverse comment

[22] Feuillerat, *Documents*, p. 289. The production of *Genus Humanum/Self-Love* called for a purple gown requiring 5 yards of satin, five white satin cassocks at 7 yards each, three purple cassocks at 7 yards each, a cassock of red and one of green satin (7 yards each), three long gowns of tawny, ash-coloured, and black satin respectively (8 yards each), a cassock of black damask and a long gown of purple damask (16 yards the pair), a short gown of red damask (6 yards), three short gowns of purple satin (six yards each), three yards of kersey each for the Good and Bad Angel's costumes, plus wings, three 'thrombde' hats and ten-dozen counters. If one accepts the dating of the warrant as precisely accurate, the Great Wardrobe would have had at best twenty four hours to provide the lot.

from other sources.[23] Arguing from silence is always a hazardous undertaking, and in this case seems to fly in the face of the other known facts. Mary's warrant to Udall, referring to his dialogues and interludes played in the royal presence at 'sondry seasons convenient', suggests a number of performances of which the surviving accounts show no trace. Furthermore, in the following year the Revels accounts themselves mention the cost of preparing materials and properties for

divers and sondry maskes both for men and wemen as plaies set forth by Udall and other pastimes prepared, furnyshed, and set forthe owte of the revelles this yeare to be shewed and done in the Kinge and quene their majesties presence from tyme to tyme as the same was commaunded and called for.[24]

The ensuing accounts themselves refer only to the masques, however. Udall's plays and the other unspecified pastimes leave no other trace in the records.

That there are no references to named plays in the surviving records need, then, not be as conclusive as Feuillerat claimed. Indeed, the evidence would seem to point in the other direction, for the Revels accounts do contain one generalised reference to other plays. A list of charges for the period 22 September 1553 to 6 January 1554 talks of the expenses required 'to furnysshe owte certen playes sett foorth by the gentilmen of the chapell'. Feuillerat's suggestion that 'playes' here must be an error for 'playe' seems unconvincing. Had the text read simply 'playes', this might be a possibility, but the phrase 'certen playes' suggests that the writer had the plural form in mind as he wrote. And, as he was accounting for entertainments for which his own office was responsible, his testimony commands respect, not least as the separate accounts from which this overall record of charges was derived also allow room for more than one play to have been supported.[25]

What, then, seems most likely is that *Respublica* was indeed performed at court over Christmas 1553/4. A number of plays were produced there by the Gentlemen and Children of the Chapel Royal during the first year of Mary's reign. *Respublica* is a Christmas play, written for children,

---

[23] When, for example, the Christmas revels of 1525/6 were particularly barren of entertainment, owing to an outbreak of plague, the chronicler Edward Hall felt it necessary to note the fact. Hall, p. 707.   [24] Feuillerat, *Documents*, p. 159.

[25] In addition to 'The charges of fynysshinge thafforseide' (i.e. *Genus Humanum/Self-Love*), they specify the cost of 'putting in redine[ss] soche thinges as in thoffice of the Revells were most behovable and lykely to be called upon at Christmas with thattendaunce of the officers and other ministers gyving theyre awayet therfore at the Courte', a description which might include the preparation of any number of properties and materials for other productions. Feuillerat, *Documents*, pp. 152 and 290.

by an author who is known to have had a number of plays performed at
court during that year. The weight of probability that *Respublica* was one
such play seems compelling. Moreover, as we shall see, it does address
directly a number of issues which were of immediate concern to the
court and the government at this time.

Complaint and satire: the political context of 'Respublica'

Critics have generally assumed that *Respublica*'s political agenda is neither pointedly critical nor particularly concrete in its assertions. It is
described as a 'gently satirical play', a text which 'eschews the violence
of religious controversy', an exercise in 'great tact' which represents not
the particular details of the recent past 'but rather the abstracted
meaning of those events'. The activities of its vices are said to be
indicative only of 'a timeless pattern of worldliness' rather than of
specific contemporary evils: 'their only distinction from earlier practitioners of such villainy is their specious cry of reform'.[26] But such
readings underestimate the wealth of particular detail which underpins
the text's political and moral strategies, and the passion with which it
engages with both contemporary events and issues *and* their 'abstracted
meaning'.

The Christmas season of 1553/4, far from being a period of 'happy'
tranquillity in which the Sovereign and her court might relax, safe in the
knowledge that they had secured a sound and lasting political and
religious settlement, was a time of profound political unease.[27] The
Marian regime was newly set on potentially precarious foundations.
Less that six months earlier the queen had been a fugitive, declared a
bastard in the Duke of Northumberland's desperate last gamble to
secure a protestant succession, and pursued into Norfolk by the duke at
the head of an army 3,000 strong. Only the loyalty of the 'backwoods'
gentry and nobility in East Anglia, Oxfordshire, Buckinghamshire, and
the Thames Valley had forced the Council in London to reverse its
earlier decision to declare in favour of Northumberland's protégé, Lady

---

[26] See R. Potter, *The English Morality Play* (London, 1975), pp. 94 and 189; P. Happé, ed., *Tudor Interludes* (Harmondsworth, 1972), p. 27; David Bevington, *Tudor Drama and Politics: A Critical Approach to Topical Meaning* (Cambridge, MA, 1968), pp. 115 and 118.

[27] For the contrary suggestion, see Potter, *English Morality Play*, p. 94: 'Thus, with prayers for Queen Mary and the commonwealth, this gently satirical play about the recent past concludes in the happy present, in the first Christmas of Mary's reign, with the Reformation seemingly banished forever from the Catholic commonwealth of England'.

Jane Grey, thereby bringing about the collapse of the duke's putative coup.[28] On 19 July, Mary was formally proclaimed Queen in London, but it was not until 3 August that she entered her capital, formalised the punishment of Northumberland and his closest supporters, and effected a reconciliation with the professional politicians who had initially connived in the duke's manoeuvres.

Mary inherited, not a thriving commonwealth, but a realm in social and economic crisis. The royal finances, virtually bankrupted by the French and Scottish campaigns of Henry VIII's final years, had been further depleted by a deteriorating economy, costly social projects, and ill-judged financial ventures under Edward VI. The grain harvest had failed spectacularly in 1545, 1549, and 1551, prompting prices to rise and causing significant hardship and social dislocation in town and country alike. In 1550 and 1551 outbreaks of plague and the sweating sickness had exacerbated the problems. The widespread sense of ruin and decay was reflected in a burgeoning literature of social complaint and increasingly shrill economic analysis. Pamphlets like Sir Thomas Smith's *A Discourse of the Common Weal of this Realm of England* (1549) and the anonymous *Policies to Reduce this Realm of England Unto a Prosperous Wealth and Estate* (1551?) sought both to offer remedies for the nation's economic decline and to locate its origins in a general failure of public and private morality.[29] To assume that a play like *Respublica* could not be directly political as it focused only upon moral shortcomings thus misunderstands contemporary perceptions of economic and political questions. Contemporaries saw economics and politics as themselves moral issues – or reflections of them – and spoke about them in those terms. Mid-Tudor analysis of the state of the nation was conducted in great part as a moral debate. Thus John Caius, in a work prompted by the 1551 outbreak of sweating sickness, saw the epidemic as divine punishment for 'that insatiable serpent of covetousness wherewith most men are so infected that it seemeth each one would devour another without charity or any godly respect to the poor, to their neighbour, or to their

[28] Jennifer Loach, *Parliament and the Crown in the Reign of Mary Tudor* (Oxford, 1988), pp. 1–10; Dale Hoak, 'Two Revolutions in Tudor Government: The Formation and Organisation of Mary I's Privy Chamber', in C. Coleman and D. Starkey, eds., *Revolution Reassessed: Revisions in the History of Tudor Government and Administration* (Oxford, 1986), pp. 87–115, pp. 96–107.

[29] Sir Thomas Smith, *A Discourse of the Common Weal of this Realm of England*, ed. E. Lamond (Cambridge, 1954). For the growth of analytical and hortatory literature of this sort, see Joan Thirsk, *Economic Policy and Projects: The Development of a Consumer Society in Early Modern England* (Oxford, 1988), pp. 12–43.

commonwealth'.[30] Moreover, *Respublica* itself, far from being a purely moral drama, is not short on detailed economic analysis.

Performed at court in the middle of this period of national moral and political self-examination, Udall's play drew its lessons from recent history and its inspiration from current events. Although purporting to lament the 'Ruin and decaye' that comes to all realms where Insolence and Avarice are allowed to flourish, the play is actually more particular in its targets, a fact which Respublica herself makes clear in the final act. With telling specificity she laments, 'O lorde howe have I bee[n] used these five yeres past' (5.9.1775–76), identifying a period which would cover the most fraught years of the Edwardian minority.[31] Nor is the Henrician regime spared from the criticism. The action of the play is clearly intended to cover the Edwardian period, but the state is presented as already on the brink of collapse when the interlude begins. As Avarice observes in act 1, Respublica,

> now latelye is left almoost desolate.
> Hir welthe ys decayed hir comforte cleane a goe
> And she att hir wittes endes what for to saie or doe   (1.1.239–42)

The implication is that the Edwardian regime had itself inherited from its predecessors a realm already in a parlous condition. This ruinous situation is, of course, only worsened as the vices gain access to the management of the state and begin to exploit it for their own ends.

The depiction of the ensuing hardship is remarkably specific in its detail. On accepting Avarice into her service, Respublica hands over to him control of 'metall, graine, cataill, treasure, goodes, and landes' (2.2.500), and it is his control of these commodities that provides the Vice with much of his pilfered income. When he is granted an audience, People complains about the prices of precisely those commodities which Avarice exploits. He knows that the realm produces sufficient to go around, but somehow this produce does not find its way to the markets at prices the commons can afford.

> ther falleth of corne and cattall
> Wull, shepe, woode, leade, tynne, Iron and other metall,

---

[30] John Caius, *A Boke or Counseill Against the Disease Commonly Called the Sweate or Sweatyng Sickness*, *RSTC* 4343. See E. S. Roberts, ed., *The Works of John Caius* (Cambridge, 1912), pp. 18–19, and P. Slack, 'Social Policy and the Constraints of Government, 1547–58', in J. Loach and R. Tittler, eds., *The Mid-Tudor Polity, c. 1540–1560* (London, 1980), pp. 94–115.

[31] The play's contemporary relevance is confirmed by the prologue's insistence that the play is intended 'for goode Englande sake this present howre and daie / In hope of hir restoring from hir late decaye' (lines 45–6).

And of all [th]ynges, enoughe vor goode and badde
and as commediens [i.e. commodious] vor us, as er we hadde.
And yet the price of everye thing is zo dere
As though the grounde dyd bring vorth no suche thing no
    where. (3.3.666–71)

It is the management of the economy rather than its essential productiv-
ity which is to blame. 'Ill ordring 'tis', People tells Respublica, 'hath
made both youe and wee threde bare' (3.3.675). The nature of that ill
ordering is made clear when Avarice confesses to the audience the
secrets of his profiteering. Among his scams he lists 'beguiling the king of
his custome' (3.6.873), and the profits from 'tallowe, Butter, cheese, /
Corne, Rawclothes, [and] lether by stelth sent beyond seas' (lines
875–6), and 'grayne, bell meatall, tynne and lead, / Conveighd owte by
crekes when Respublica was in bed' (lines 877–8). In the England of
1553, this litany of materials would have had a striking resonance. The
consequences of harvest failure coupled with a period of marked inflation were precisely the price rises and apparent scarcities complained of
by People. Unsuccessful attempts to regulate the supply and prices of
basic commodities characterised the Edwardian period. On 9 August
1549, a Proclamation recognised 'that of late time the prices of all
manner of victual necessary for man's sustenance be so heightened and
raised above the accustomed and reasonable values that thereby (except
speedy remedy be provided) very great loss and damage must needs
chance to his majesty's loving subjects'. Consequently the crown attempted to fix the prices of animals at market for the coming months.[32]
Further attempts to limit the cost of victuals were made on 20 October
1550 and 11 September 1551, with equal lack of long-term success.[33]

A second strand to government policy involved the attempt to limit
the exportation of materials. Avarice's nocturnal attempts to smuggle

---

[32] P. L. Hughes and J. F. Larkin, eds., *Tudor Royal Proclamations*, I (New Haven, 1964), pp. 464–9. See also W. K. Jordan, *Edward VI: The Threshold of Power* (London, 1970), pp. 471–82.

[33] Hughes and Larkin, eds., *Proclamations*, I, pp. 504–9 and 530–3. A further contributory factor in the inflationary economy was seen to be the enclosure of common lands without licence. This, too, is reflected in the play. People complains of the destruction of trees throughout the realm and the consequent dearth of windfall pickings of firewood from common woodlands (4.4.1093–6). Oppression, the spokesman for the enclosers, is typically unsympathetic, telling him to burn turf or his bed-straw in lieu of firewood (5.8.1625–6). People's further complaint that the price of beef has been forced intolerably high by the aristocratic monopoly on grazing land (4.4.1097–8) gets similarly short shrift (5.8.1627–8). Such hardship as these exchanges reflect had prompted the Edwardian regime into action. An Enclosure Commission was established in 1549 and a Tillage Act was passed in 1552, following up proclamations in 1548 and 1549 aimed at reducing the 'marvellous desolation' caused to the countryside. Slack, 'Social Policy', p. 102, Hughes and Larkin, eds., *Proclamations*, pp. 427–9, 451–3, 461–4, 471–3.

foodstuffs and bellmetal out of the realm through hidden creeks were specifically prohibited in a number of proclamations. On 27 July 1547, the new minority government addressed in the king's name 'our customers, comptrollers, and searchers, and other our officers and ministers within our port of London, and in all creeks and places to the said port belonging', ordering them to prevent the export of 'any manner of bell metal, butter, cheese, tallow or candles . . . out of the said port or any creeks or places to the said port' unless the traders carried Letters Patent under the Great Seal permitting them to do so.[34] On 7 December a further proclamation limited grain exportation without license, citing increased domestic prices as justification. On 30 March 1548 this ban was rescinded, but it was replaced later in the same year, along with prohibitions on the export of butter, cheese, bacon, tallow, and bell metal.[35] Further embargoes upon exportation without license were imposed in the following months on 'any manner of grain, butter, cheese, tallow or any kind of victuals' on 8 October 1548, on wheat, malt, oats, barley, butter, cheese, bacon, beef, cask, or tallow on 18 January 1549, on these commodities and veal calves, lambs, muttons, pork, wood, wood coal, ale, beer, and hides on 7 May 1550, on a comprehensive list of victuals and also bell metal, wood, and coal on 3 July and 24 September 1550, and on similar commodities on 20 October of the same year.[36]

The export of wool and rawcloth, another of Avarice's scams, was also a contentious issue at this time. In 1551 the Antwerp cloth market crashed, causing a 15 per cent reduction in trade in the following twelve months and a further 20 per cent in the next year. The net result was hardship for cloth merchants, unemployment for cloth workers, and a substantial loss of customs revenues for the crown. In response the Edwardian regime adopted measures to limit the profits passing to overseas traders. In 1552 the government risked diplomatic difficulties by banning merchants of the Hanseatic League from buying cloth in England. The domestic crisis was, however, to continue into the next reign. The loss of customs earnings was also addressed by proposals to issue a new Book of Rates, fixing the charges to be levied on imported and exported goods at a higher rate, taking into account the effects of inflation, but this proposal was not carried out until 1558, when the Marian regime was finally to grasp the nettle.

Another of People's objections concerns the hardship brought about by the devaluation and debasement of the coinage. His rent, he claims,

---

[34] Hughes and Larkin, eds., *Proclamations*, p. 391.   [35] Ibid., pp. 409–24.
[36] Ibid., pp. 435–6, 439, 490–1, 495–6, 499–503, 504–9.

now amounts to almost twice the sum that he is able to make at market for his produce.

> Vor one peece iche tooke, chawas vaine to paie him twaie
> One woulde thinke twer brasse, and zorowe have I els,
> But ichwin mooste parte ont was made of our olde bells
> . . .
> Isrecke not an twer zilver as twas avor   (4.4.1082–4, 1088)

It is a complaint for which Insolence upbraids him later when the vices gang up to drive him from court.

> Ye muste have silver money must ye jentilman?
> Youe cannot be content with suche coigne as wee can. (5.8.1623–4)

Again, this is not simply a timeless commonplace of economic complaint, but a specific allusion to contemporary events. First Henry VIII in 1544, then Protector Somerset in 1547 and 1549, debased the coinage, mixing brass with the silver, as People suspected. The net result, after a short-term profit for the crown, was to fuel inflation and reduce confidence in the currency, as the majority of the population took the same line as People and calculated prices on a coin's actual silver content rather than on its nominal value. Hostility to the new coinage was widespread and even reached the court when Bishop Latimer preached against its introduction before the king. The government was thus forced to take action to limit the consequences of its own actions. On 24 July 1551 a proclamation was issued ordering punishment for anyone caught spreading rumours of any further debasements. In 1552 the Usury Act attempted to limit the monetary speculation which the debasements had prompted.[37] The result of these measures was only to exacerbate a perception of poverty and social decay which had been endemic throughout the Edwardian period.

When Avarice protests at the multitude of beggars thronging the streets 'nowe of daies' (5.5.1432) he identifies a problem which exercised the government from the beginning of the reign. In 1547 the Vagrancy Act had attempted to apply drastic solutions to what was perceived as the crisis in vagabondage and the proliferation of masterless men. Public begging was banned, and attempts were made to establish a weekly levy – what would later become the Poor Rate – to alleviate the distress of the truly impotent poor. By contrast the undeserving poor, the, so called, sturdy beggars, were to be forced from the streets through a term of

---

[37] Ibid., pp. 440–1, 449–51, 528–9; Slack, 'Social Policy', p. 97; C. E. Challis, 'Presidential Address', *British Numismatic Journal*, 68 (1993), pp. 172–7; C. E. Challis, *The Tudor Coinage* (Manchester, 1978), pp. 96–112, 175–86.

virtual slave labour, whereby employers might take on those found to be able-bodied but without work, without wages for a period of two years.[38] The scheme was both too draconian and too unwieldy to solve the vagabondage problem at the first attempt and the act was repealed in 1550, but it marked a new determination to address the problems of unemployment and poverty at governmental level. More conventional methods of social control were also employed. On 7 May 1550 a proclamation ordered all beggars and those without work to leave London. On 28 April 1551 a further proclamation enforced existing legislation against wandering vagabonds and other masterless itinerants (a class among whom professional acting troupes were grouped), while in 1552 an Act of Parliament banned begging once more and established a weekly collection for the relief of the needy in each parish.[39]

This interest in social justice was, however, not entirely egalitarian. The obverse of the government's concern for the poor and rootless was a predictable anxiety about the threat posed to social order by the aggrieved poor and disaffected vagabonds. As Dale Hoak has observed, 'perhaps no Tudor government ever stood in greater fear of a rebellious commons than did that of the Duke of Northumberland in the period 1550–53'.[40] When People stands up before Respublica and complains about the lot of the nation's poor, then, he not only voices a righteous cry for justice, but also presents a dire warning of the consequences of further mismanagement and abuse. The vices treat his protest as pre- cisely the sort of popular rising of which the government lived in fear.

> AVARICE: And howe dyd all frame with our mounsire
> Authorytee?
> OPPRESSION: Att length he wonne the full superiorytee
> ADULATION: But the rude grosse people at hym repyneth sore,
>   And against us all fowre with a wyde throte dothe he
>   rore.   (3.5.821–4)

Far from shying away from the specifics of social satire, then, *Respublica* addresses social concerns with remarkable particularity. It is a play constructed out of the poverty and social distress of the mid-Tudor

---

[38] It may well be to this legislation specifically that People refers when he complains of the vices that 'sometime they face us, and call us peason knaves / And zwareth goddes bones thei will make is all slaves' (3.3.701–2).

[39] Slack, 'Social Policy', p. 102; P. Slack, *Poverty and Policy in Tudor and Stuart England* (Harlow, 1988), pp. 122–3; Hughes and Larkin, eds., *Proclamations*, I, pp. 489–90, 514–18. For other attempts to address economic problems at this time, see Thirsk, *Economic Policy*, pp. 43ff.

[40] Dale Hoak, 'Rehabilitating the Duke of Northumberland: Politics and Political Control, 1549– 53', in Loach and Tittler, eds., *Mid-Tudor Polity*, pp. 29–51, p. 30.

period. What it is important to note, however, is the way in which that distress is shaped into a satirical strategy. The text does not simply reflect social conditions, it interprets them in a moral and political framework. The failures of government and administration which it claims have led to the present crisis are presented as the result, not simply of incompetence, but of moral culpability. Where the ministers of the Edwardian period are pilloried, it is for seeking, literally to cash in on the realm's misfortune, profiteering under the guise of attempts to restore the economy to order. The crisis in which Respublica finds herself at the start of the play, symbolic of the Henrician legacy, simply provides the long-awaited opportunity for Avarice and his fellows to 'feather [their] . . . neste[s]' (1.1.88).[41] Avarice's exploitation of the commonweal will be piecemeal but comprehensive, involving the gathering up of all

> The glenynges, the casualties, the blynde excheates,
> The forginge of forfayctes, the scope of extraictes,
> The xcesse, the waste, the spoile, the superfluites,
> The windefalles, the shriddinges, the flycynges / The petie fees.
> With a thowsaunde thinges mo which she maye right well lacke
> [I] woulde fyll all these same purses that hange att my bakke (1.1.99–104)

Each of the 'gallants' aims likewise 'to gett store of money' (1.1.287); and become a lord of high estate at Respublica's expense during the brief 'tyme of hey making' (line 901) before Time makes known their abuses through his daughter Veritas.[42] The methods by which this is achieved are the subject of lengthy (and, as we have already partially seen, pointedly specific) elaboration. Avarice lists thirteen sources of his ill-gotten gains, each filling one of the bags he carries concealed under his coat. He identifies 'leasses encroched and foorthwith solde againe' (3.6.856); 'intresse of thys yeares userie' (line 857); 'mattiers bolstred upp with perjurie' (line 858); 'bribes above my stipende in offecis' (line 859); 'the selling of benefices' (line 860); 'my rentes that my clerkes yearelye render me / To bee and contynue in offyce under me' (lines 861–2); 'my sectourshipp [i.e. executorship] of my Mother' (863) and 'other sectour-shipps whole / Whiche the madde knaves woulde have scattered by

---

[41] As Avarice admits, Respublica's plight creates 'A tyme that I have wayted for a greate longe space' (1.1.89).

[42] As Oppression observes to Respublica with sly irony, the 'reforms' enacted by the vices have been entirely for their own profit. 'For my parte I will sware the gospell booke uppon / That if the Lawes I have made shoulde everye one / Redowne to myne owne singuler comodytee / They coulde not be frendelier framed then thei be' (4.4.1131–4).

penie dole' (lines 865–6); 'churche goodes scraped upp withoute alawe' (line 867); 'beguil[ing] the king of his custome' (line 873); 'selling counterfaicte wares' (line 874); the profits from 'tallowe, Butter, cheese, / Corne, Raweclothes, lether by stelth sent beyond seas' (lines 875–6); 'grayne, bell meatall, tynne and leade, / Conveighd owte by crekes when Respublica was in bed' (lines 877–8); and finally 'facing owte of dawes [i.e. fools], / Bothe from landes and goodes by pretence of the lawes' (lines 879–80). Taken together, this list provides a comprehensive portfolio of malpractice and corruption. In many cases the crimes mentioned are timeless abuses, but they also have, as we have seen, a precise contemporary relevance.

A major theme of the satire is the means by which the vices gain lands and incomes at the expense of the commonweal. In the first act, Insolence declares his intention to become a lord of high estate (1.3.291). Oppression insists that he have a share too,

> When ye come to the encrochinge of landes
> . . .
> I will looke to have parte of goodes landes and plate.(1.3.293 and 295)

Each aims to obtain 'goode mannour places twoo or three' (line 301), and Insolence goes still further, declaring

> I muste have castels and Townes in everye shier
> . . .
> pastures and townships and woods
> . . .
> chaunge of Farmes and pastures for shepe,
> With dailie revenues my lustye porte for to kepe.   (1.3.301–10)

Where these estates will come from is made clear by Avarice and Oppression. Bullying of leaseholders out of their rights is one of the abuses practised by Avarice and condemned by the play (3.6.856 and 879–80), but the main thrust of the satirical attack is against the acquisition of episcopal lands and estates by enforced exchange. The theme is introduced in act 3 scene 5 when Oppression boasts,

> Faith if I luste I maie were myters fowre or fyve
> I have so manye haulfe bisshoprikes at the leaste.   (lines 780–1)

Adulation indeed complains that he has managed to obtain only £300 per annum and one manor place (line 784) because Oppression has 'flytched the bisshoprikes alreadie' (line 792). The latter elaborates his methods when he advises Adulation to grasp what estates remain, suggesting that even the most audaciously unjust exchanges can be achieved ('geve a fether for a gooce' (line 796)) if he moves quickly enough. 'Didst thowe with anie one of them [i.e. the bishops] make suche exchaunge[?]', asks Adulation,

> OPPRESSION: Yea, I almooste leaft them never a ferm nor
>   graunge.
> I told them Respublica at their wealth dyd grutche
> And the fyfte pennie thaye had was for them to[o] muche
> So Authoritie and I did with theim soo choppe
> That we lefte the best of them a thred bare bisshop.
> To some we lefte one howse, to some we left none,
> The beste had but his see place, that he might kepe home.
> We enfourmed them, and we defourmed theym,
> We confourmed them, and we refourmed theym.
> ADULATION: And what gave ye theim in your permutacions?
> OPPRESSION: Bare parsonages of appropriacions,
> Bowght from Respublica and firste emprowed
> Than at the highcste extente to bisshops allowed,
> Leate owte to theire handes for fowrescore and ny[netee]n
>   yeare   (3.5.797–810)

There are, however, still some pickings remaining for Adulation.

> OPPRESSION: there is yet enoughe left, for a better plucke
> For some of them were aged and yet would not dye,
> And some woulde in no wyse to owre desyres applye.
> But we have Roddes in pysse for tham everye chone.
> That they shalbe flyced yf we reign, one by one.   (3.5.816–20)

Again, these lines have specific contemporary relevance. In the later years of the reign of Henry VIII and during the Edwardian minority the episcopal estates were subject to a series of aggressive, asset-stripping exchanges with the crown. In return the bishops were offered rectory estates acquired from monastic houses during the dissolutions of the late 1530s. The overall beneficiaries were generally favoured courtiers and administrators who were subsequently granted the lands and rents outright as rewards for service, or were able to buy them up at often very favourable prices when the crown had to realise its assets to finance its wars and pay off its short term debts.

The bishopric of Exeter was the subject of a series of enforced exchanges in the years following the Dissolution. Bishop Veysey saw over two-thirds of the estates of his see lost to the crown in the period from 1539 to 1550. In 1548 he had to give up his London residence and the valuable manor of Crediton in Devon. In 1550 Bishop's Tawton and

Bishop's Clyst were transferred to John Russell, Earl of Bedford. By 1551 the see was so 'much diminished' in income that the crown allowed the new bishop, Miles Coverdale to revalue his estate for tax purposes at only £500 per annum.[43] Other episcopal estates suffered similar losses. In 1535 the crown took twenty-two manors from the bishopric of Norwich, gaining an estimated £920 worth of annual income in return for approximately £752 worth of ex-monastic rectories. Among the beneficiaries of royal success were Thomas Cromwell and the king's physician, William Butts.[44] The archbishopric of Canterbury was also a victim, losing through exchanges approximately £277 of annual income between 1536 and 1546.[45] From 1539 onwards the bishopric of Bath and Wells also suffered. Dr William Petre gained an annuity of £40 from the Dean and Chapter in that year and subsequently confiscated jewels and plate for the king's use. In the same year the bishop's London house was granted to William Fitzwilliam, Earl of Southampton, and by 1547 the manor of Dogmersfield in Hampshire had passed to Thomas Wriothesley, the earl's successor. The Duke of Somerset also profited substantially from the wealth of the see, claiming manors, including Wells itself, during his period as Lord Protector. In all some 55 per cent of the gross income of the see was probably lost in the years 1539–60. The bishopric of Lincoln suffered if anything a still more dramatic depredation, being reduced from a net income of £1,963 per annum to one of £828 per annum in the seven years of Edward VI's reign.[46]

A list of the chief beneficiaries of this despoliation of episcopal lands reads like a *Who's Who* of the Edwardian establishment: the Russell family, the Dudleys, the Herberts, and the Darcys, Lord Paget, and William Paulet all gained substantially. One estate, Southwell in Nottinghamshire, a property of the archbishopric of York, passed from the crown in gift in 1550 to the Earl of Warwick, the future Duke of Northumberland, who in turn sold it a year later to the Master of the Rolls, John Beaumont. When Beaumont was convicted of corruption, the manor, along with all his lands and goods, passed back to the crown, from whose hands it was finally restored to the archbishopric by Queen Mary in 1557.[47] It is no wonder that one of the chief tasks that Sir William Petre identified when he drew up a list of the most pressing

---

[43] W. G. Hoskins, *The Age of Plunder: The England of Henry VIII, 1500–1547* (Harlow, 1976), pp. 125–6, 141–2; W. J. Sheils, 'Profit, Patronage, or Pastoral Care?: The Rectory Estates of the Archbishopric of York, 1540–1640', in R. O'Day and F. Heal, eds., *Princes and Paupers in the English Church, 1500–1800* (Leicester, 1981).   [44] Hoskins, *Age of Plunder*, pp. 138–9.

[45] Ibid., pp. 140–1.   [46] Ibid., pp. 141–3.

[47] Ibid., pp. 144–5; W. K. Jordan, *Edward VI*, pp. 456–7.

problems facing the new government in August 1553 was the condition of the episcopal estates and the financial state of the church as a whole.[48]

The assumption that *Respublica* was performed before a court audience readily receptive of its satirical message is thus an oversimplification. The Yuletide entertainments of 1553/4 did not witness a new regime complacently congratulating itself upon its triumph over the previous corrupt administration. The majority of the courtiers and civil servants who gathered to celebrate the first Christmas of the Marian reign had themselves been members of the Edwardian government at whose demise the play rejoiced, and had profited substantially as a result.

The limited number of experienced and able individuals available to serve in the central administration, coupled with an obvious desire on the queen's part not to alienate members of the political community upon whom she had to rely, meant that there was no major purge of government officers on her accession. Although the royal household saw a significant alteration in its personnel, the vast majority of Edward's counsellors and ministers were retained to serve his successor, often in the same roles. Almost the entire Privy Council remained in post. The chief architects of the Edwardian financial policies so vilified by *Respublica*, the Lord Treasurer, William Paulet, Marquis of Winchester, and Sir Thomas Gresham continued in the same roles in the Marian government. Winchester also retained his office as Master of the Court of Wards until 1 May 1554. John Russell, Earl of Bedford remained as Lord Keeper of the Privy Seal, a post he had held since 1542, and both Sir William Petre, and William, Lord Paget, central figures in the minority administration, retained their positions of influence.[49] The play's sustained focus upon the failures of policy and abuses of power allegedly perpetrated by Edward's courtiers and ministers would thus have made acutely uncomfortable viewing for many among its initial audience.

It has been suggested that the play carefully avoids reference to specific individuals in its condemnation of abuses.[50] This observation catches the spirit of the play, but may not be absolutely true. When Avarice tells Respublica of the wonders he would have performed if she

---

[48] Loach, *Parliament and the Crown*, p. 74.
[49] E. B. Fryde, D. E. Greenway, S. Porter, and I. Roy, eds., *Handbook of British Chronology* (3rd edn, London, 1986), pp. 107, 112; Penry Williams, *The Tudor Regime* (Oxford, 1979), pp. 87–9; Hoak 'Two Revolutions', pp. 104–7; J. A. Guy, *Tudor England* (Oxford, 1988), pp. 228–9.
[50] Bevington, *Tudor Drama and Politics*, p. 116.

had not fallen 'to checking and blamyng' (5.6.1542) and prevented him, he launches into a series of curious topographic allusions.

> I woulde have browght haulfe Kent into Northumberlande
> And Somersett shiere should have raught to Cumberlande,
> Than woulde I have stretche[d] the countie of Warwicke
> Uppon tainter hookes, and made ytt reache to Barwicke.
> A pece of the Bishopric shoulde have come southwarde –
> Tut, tut, I tell yowe, I had wonderous feates towarde. (5.6.1547–52)

On one level this is just the sort of nonsensical litany in which vices traditionally indulge in the moral interludes. But, as with many another example, it does contain some pointed observations. The reference to the expansion of the counties of Northumberland and Somerset that would have occurred if Avarice had been given free reign would not have passed unnoticed in December 1553. It is hard to avoid the inference that the play is here aiming a specific swipe at the Dukes of Somerset and Northumberland, suggesting that they above all others were motivated by avarice in their dealings during their periods of office.[51] That the noble title of one of the leaders of the minority regime might be mentioned without specific intention is just possible, that both should be cited in the space of two lines invites a satirical interpretation, not least as the following line describes how Warwick, Northumberland's previous title, would be similarly enlarged. That Insolence might at some points be a figure for Northumberland himself is also possible. In the final scene he is accused of having committed 'Lucifer's owne faulte t'aspire to the highest seate' (5.10.1913): an ambition which he does not display in the play itself, but which might reflect the duke's attempts to interfere with the succession in favour of Lady Jane Grey.

Such personalised allusions are, however, only peripheral to the satirical thrust of the play. It is the condemnation of avarice and self-interest among the Edwardian administrators generally, and the call for moral and social reformation which carry forward the main burden of the play's agenda.

---

[51] H. B. Norland, *Drama in Early Tudor Britain, 1485–1558* (Lincoln, NE, 1995), pp. 203–4. That the reference to a piece of the bishopric coming southward may also have a topical relevance is equally possible. The bishopric of Durham had been dismembered by Northumberland and its London residence, Durham Place, had been taken from it (thereby appropriating a 'piece of the Bishopric' in the south). In December 1553, Mary's first Parliament debated the restoration of the see to its former state and the return of Durham Place to the bishop's use. A bill was passed by the Lords to this effect, but was rejected by the Commons on 5 December. Loach, *Parliament and the Crown*, pp. 80–1.

The religious politics of 'Respublica'

Critics largely concur over the nature and tone of *Respublica*'s religious message. For Peter Happé, it is a play which remains essentially silent on the pressing confessional issues of the period. 'The play eschews the violence of religious controversy, there being no hint of the theological or ecclesiastical changes which Mary may have been contemplating in 1553.' For David Bevington the play consciously avoided such questions, concentrating upon court politics rather than theology or ritual, and avoiding any outright attack on protestant beliefs *per se*.[52]

In fact the play is shot through with detailed references to ecclesiastical issues and policies. The concentration is primarily upon material rather than spiritual questions, but at a time when the future government, endowment, and status of the church was at issue such things could hardly be divided.

The nature of clerical office and the role of the priesthood are addressed directly in a brief debate between Respublica, Oppression, and People.

> OPPRESSION: Firste youre priestes and bisshops have not as thei
> have had.
> RESPUBLICA: [When they] had theire lyvinges men were bothe
> fedde and cladde
> OPPRESSION: Yea, but they ought not by scripture to be calde
> lordes.
> RESPUBLICA: That thei rewle the churche with scripture well
> accordes.
> OPPRESSION: Thei were prowde and covetous/ and tooke muche
> uppon theim.
> PEOPLE: But they were not covetous that toke all from
> theym[?]   (4.4.1069–74)

As we have seen, the exploitation of episcopal estates is a central theme of the attack upon the vices. The criticism of corruption in church affairs goes rather further than this, however. The wholesale sequestration of church ornaments and goods at the time of the Reformation is singled out for detailed condemnation. Avarice identifies the contents of his eighth bag of coins as the profits from

---

[52] Happé, ed., *Tudor Interludes*, p. 27; Bevington, *Tudor Drama and Politics*, p. 115. See also Norland, *Drama in Early Tudor Britain*, p. 207: 'No mention is made of the organisation or doctrine of the church. The author deals only with principles largely of an economic nature: he presents no programme of social or religious change.'

> church goodes scraped upp withoute alawe,
> For which was as quicke scambling as ever I sawe,
> Of their plate, their jewels, and copes, we made them lowtes,
> Stopping peoples barking with lynnen rags and clowtes.
> Thei had thalter clothes, thalbes, and amices
> With the sindons in which wer wrapte the chalices   (3.6.867–72)

When the exploitation of church wealth has implications for the condition of the church itself and the quality of the spiritual support which it can provide, material questions and spiritual ones coincide. Consequently the play stresses the intellectual and spiritual poverty of the vices at the same time as it draws attention to their rapacious acquisition of wealth. Oppression's inability to follow a simple Latin phrase prompts Avarice to mock his pretensions to determine the livings and conditions of the higher clergy.

> Loe herc a fyne felowe to have a bisshoprike
> A verse of latynne he cannot understande,
> Yet dareth he presume boldelye to take in hande,
> Into a deanerie or archdeaconrye to choppe,
> And to have the liveloode awaie from a bisshopp.   (3.6.920–4)

Similarly, lower down the ecclesiastical structure, when Avarice decides to put ill-educated men into the parish livings at his disposal in order to maximise his financial returns, he does so at the expense of the parishioners who must suffer the ministrations of an inept incumbent.

> I have a good benefyce of an hunderd markes
> Yt is smale policie to give suche to greate clerkes
> They will take no benefice but thei muste have all,
> A bare clerke canne bee content with a lyving smale.
> Therefore sir John Lack Latten my frende shall have myne
> And of hym maie I ferme yt for eyght powndes or nyne
> The reste maie I reserve to myselfe for myne owne share
>   (3.6.955–61)

The suggestion that *Respublica* does not touch upon ecclesiastical or theological issues is thus mistaken. The play does address the central ecclesiastical questions of the moment, and addresses them directly. Nor does it stop short of offering solutions to them. On the crucial question of the restoration or otherwise of former episcopal estates and rectories, the play makes a clear statement in favour of a full restoration.[53]

---

[53] Bevington, *Tudor Drama and Politics*, p. 120. For the contrary suggestion that 'Nothing is said . . . in

Avarice, as we have seen, is handed over by Nemesis to People in the final scene,

> That he maie bee pressed, as men doo presse a spounge
> That he maie droppe ought teverye man hys lotte
> To the utmooste ferthing that he hath falslie gotte.　(5.10.1903–5)

People confirms that he will 'squease hym as drie as a kyxe [a dry stalk]' (line 1906). As the bulk of the profits mentioned by Avarice and the other vices has come from ecclesiastical sources, this conclusion can only allude to a substantial restoration of church wealth.

It was surely this interest in the spoliation of church lands and their possible restoration which commended the play manuscript to its first recorded owner, Sir Henry Spelman. For Spelman had a lifelong interest, amounting almost to a professional obsession, in the material wealth of the Church of England and its depredation at the time of the Reformation. His antiquarianism was no idle curiosity in relics of the past, but an earnest scholarly project aimed at providing the materials for a comprehensive account of the history and condition of the church in England, its liberties and property.[54] A series of polemical tracts published both during his lifetime and after his death by his son Clement and others, sought to identify the consequences of ecclesiastical spoliation and denounce the motives and characters of those responsible. In *De Non Temerandis Ecclesiis* (1613) Spelman argued that church property was created for and dedicated to the service of God, and could not therefore be appropriated for secular profit. Any attempt to do so amounted to an act of sacrilege. In his preface to the posthumous 1646 edition of the same text, Clement Spelman developed this contention historically, asserting that the 'sacrilegious' Dissolution of the Monasteries in the 1530s and the attendant royal sequestration of church wealth had drawn down God's wrath upon Henry VIII, blighting the Tudor succession. On Henry, the younger Spelman issued a terse and damning judgement: 'His family is extinct, and like Herostratus, his name not mentioned, but with his crimes.'[55] In *The History and Fate of Sacrilege* (published in 1698, but thought too vitriolic and controversial for inclusion in the folio edition of Spelman's *Works* published by Edmund Gibson in the same year), the condemnation of the guilty was extended into an account of the misfortunes befalling all those families who had

---

the play about restoring church lands', see Norland, *Drama in Early Tudor Britain*, p. 205.
[54] G. Parry, *The Trophies of Time: English Antiquarians of the Seventeenth Century* (Oxford, 1995), pp. 157–64.　[55] Ibid., p. 162.

profited from the sale of church property after the Dissolution, fitting them into a heavily moralised narrative of transgression and punishment.

That it was Spelman, rather than another antiquarian, who took the trouble to have *Respublica* copied into his manuscript collection provides further evidence to support the view that it was considered by contemporaries to be a highly political play, and one which addressed contentious ecclesiastical issues directly. For a reader such as Spelman, *Respublica* would have provided a congenial satirical attack upon the very people who had done well out of the Reformation. Its presentation of the Dissolution and spoliation of the episcopal estates as the products of unfettered avarice, insolence, and oppression, was merely a succinct dramatic summary of the theme which Spelman was exhaustively to chronicle in his prose tracts.

Dramatic damage limitation: Nemesis, Queen Mary, and the cure of Respublica's ills

The solution which Nemesis imposes on the play in act 5, scene 10, would have accorded well with both Spelman's sense of justice and a Tudor monarch's conception of the royal prerogative. When faced with a choice between severity and generosity, the goddess opts for a judicious mixture of the two, but, like Jupiter in Heywood's *Play of The Weather*, she keeps her subjects in doubt as to the precise details of her judgements. Misericordia had counselled the queen to proceed with softness.

> nowe have yee occasion
> and matier to shewe youre commiseracion
> [It] is m[uche m]ore glorie and standith with more skyll,
> Lo[st]e shepe to recover, than the scabye to spill.   (5.10.1856–9)

Justicia, predictably, had erred on the side of rigour, arguing that 'straight justice' was needed to redress great enormities, and 'severitee muste putt men in feare to transgresse' (line 1863). Nemesis' response is a model of equanimity, as befits a goddess lauded by Veritas as 'cleare of conscience and voyde of affeccion' (line 1783).

> Ladies we have harde all your descrete advises
> And eche one shall have some part of youre devises.
> Neither all nor none, shall taste of severitee
> But as theye are nowe knowen through ladie Veritee

> So shall theye receyve our mercie or our Ire,
> As the wealthe of Respublica shall best require. (lines 1872–7)

This stress on the material wealth and well-being of the realm as the final arbiter of action reflects the focus of the play's satire and the author's own political strategy. In presenting the excesses of the Edwardian regime as financially motivated rather than the product of religious zeal (significantly it is Avarice who governs the vices and presents himself as Policy, not a character associated with a more obviously confessional agenda) Udall is able to present their redress in similar terms. He steers the last acts of the play toward reform of the economy and the financial structure of the church, rather than toward any alteration to its doctrinal base. Hence it is episcopal lands and parish livings that are explicitly referred to when Avarice is apprehended and squeezed of his ill-gotten gains, not the former monastic lands or the wealth of the newly suppressed chantries (he tries to shift the blame to Oppression for dispossessing 'Bishops, deanes [and] provestes' and 'lands with churche and chapple' (lines 1848–9)). The doctrinal questions concerning the existence of Purgatory and the value of prayers and masses for the dead associated with the monastic and chantry dissolutions can, therefore, be left untouched. Udall is quite prepared to argue for a church restored to much of its former wealth, but it is the reformed church of the Edwardian settlement which he wants to strengthen, not the full-blown catholic institution with its monks, friars, and chantry priests.

The play treads carefully but determinedly through the thickets of religious policy in a way characteristic of the other household dramas studied in previous chapters. Udall adopts the rhetoric of restoration and renewal associated with the new Marian regime, and addresses the real social hardships created by Edwardian and later Henrician policies squarely and resolutely. But he does so for his own purposes. Like Heywood in *The Spider and The Flie*, a work of genuine catholic celebration at Mary's accession, Udall lauds the queen as the new broom who will sweep away the abuses and divisions of the recent past in favour of a virtuous and harmonious new order.[56] Like Heywood, Udall also calls for moderation in the punishment of those responsible for the previous regime. Avarice and Oppression are disciplined severely at the close of the play, but the third member of the corrupt triumvirate, Adulation,

---

[56] In John Heywood's text, Mary is presented, literally, as the housemaid whose broom sweeps the cobwebs from the window-pane, thus ending the dispute between the combative insects. See J. S. Farmer, ed., *The Spider and The Fly . . . by John Heywood* (London, 1907).

symbolic of proper respect for royal authority and service to the crown as well as flattery, is allowed to continue in office once suitably chastised.

Both Heywood's narrative poem and Udall's drama acknowledge the Marian regime's need to reconcile to it the leaders of the political nation.[57] Both texts present this necessary compromise as a triumph of queenly moderation and good government. This is not to say that either is soft on those responsible for what has gone before. Udall, as we have seen, does not flinch from specifying the problems. Like Adulation, the bulk of the old Edwardian administration and the majority of the court had to sit through a play which characterised the alleged abuses of their governance with at times excoriating severity, but which ultimately allowed them to emerge from it chastened and purified.

Unlike Heywood, however, Udall employed the appeal for magnanimity in victory to call for a settlement which protects what reformers would have seen as the doctrinal gains of the Edwardian years. Concessionary in areas which did not touch upon the fundamentals of faith, he channelled his play's reforming emphases away from the restoration of catholicism *per se* and into a renewal of the commonwealth and bolstering of the position of the bishops and the parish clergy. He offered his royal audience a model of reformation to which she could respond sympathetically, and presented himself as the kind of moderate and loyal counsellor who might be retained and listened to for sound advice in troubled times.[58] But, in so doing he defined the kinds of reformation most obviously required in ways which suited him.

Such a stance has exposed Udall to charges of time-serving. How, it has been asked, could someone who had advocated further reformation under Edward now celebrate the accession of a catholic monarch and condemn the policies of the previous regime?[59] As we have seen, there need be no contradiction if *Respublica* is read carefully and in context. Faced with the *fait accomplis* of a conservative sovereign, Udall used the opportunities available to him as a household dramatist to defend

---

[57] Mindful of the need to win over the political nation, Mary pointedly asked for no subsidies from either of her first two Parliaments (those of 1553 and 1554), even remitting any outstanding payments from that granted by the last Parliament of Edward VI. P. Williams, *The Tudor Regime* (Oxford, 1979).

[58] Udall wisely eschewed the hysterical reaction to Mary's accession of those zealous reformers who sought to intimidate and provoke the new queen into concessions. In the same month as the play was performed, December 1553, opponents of ecclesiastical reaction had thrown a dog, shaven above the ears to represent a tonsured priest, into Mary's Presence Chamber, a symbol of their hostility to popish priestly power. *CSPSp*, xi, p. 418; Loach, *Parliament and The Crown*, p. 83.

[59] For a discussion of this issue, see W. Perry, 'Udall as Time-server', *Notes and Queries*, 194 (1950), p. 120; White, *Theatre and Reformation*, p. 129, and Norland, *Drama in Early Tudor Britain*, p. 207.

reform in the most effective way he could. He may have jumped aboard the bandwagon of catholic reaction, but he did so in the hope of slowing its progress and directing it along less dangerous paths.

Respublica provides a valuable example, then, of the dynamics of household drama and the opportunities it provided for the expression of dissenting opinions at court. It shows just how severe a dramatist could be in criticising the perceived failings of his audience, not simply in moral terms, but in matters of high policy. Udall could castigate the courtiers and ministers among his spectators for economic mismanagement, oppressive policies, and outright theft and corruption, safe in the knowledge that the culture of the royal household and the license of good counsel which it fostered allowed him to do so. He could do this partly, of course, because his sovereign favoured it. Criticism of Edwardian policy, if voiced in a controlled environment, was valuable ammunition to Queen Mary during the first six months of her reign. Like James V of Scotland addressing the moral of the 1540 interlude of *The Thrie Estaitis* to the Bishop of Glasgow, she could turn to her ministers and ask with psychological and political advantage how they intended to right the wrongs they had seen dramatised before them. But the play also shows how far such a 'loyalist' gesture could be used to advance less acceptable causes and direct the sovereign's attention away from areas of particular sensitivity to the author. As with Heywood's interludes and Lindsay's satire, one must be alive in reading *Respublica*, not only to what the dramatist says, but also to how he says it, and – often more importantly – to what he leaves unsaid.

The play thus has much to tell us about the conventions and procedures that characterise drama throughout the Tudor period. But, if on one level it is commonplace, one example among many of household drama, *Respublica* is also unique in being the first extant dramatic product of the court of a queen regnant. How it responds to the new imperatives of female rule is also revealing. David Bevington in a perceptive account of the play, has argued that it offers an extreme example of royal absolutism, rejecting the whole notion of conciliar government in favour of a direct relationship between divinely sanctioned ruler and obedient subject. 'The queen figure in Act V', he argues, 'is no umpire, who listens to all estates impartially . . . Nemesis . . . listens only to the voice of divine guidance'.[60] This, I think, underestimates the importance ascribed to counsel, both in the play and

---

[60] Bevington, *Tudor Drama and Politics*, pp. 118–19.

in the concluding prayers which refocus attention from the play world to the real problems and anxieties of the audience. Here it is significant that Mary's Council gains equal billing with the queen in the petition for long life and health, and her councillors are instructed not only to serve their mistress, but also themselves to maintain the commonwealth (5.10.1936–8).[61] Far from being marginalised, the role of the Council as a governing body is thus placed in the most rhetorically powerful position in the play. Bevington's reading also in my view underplays the genuine difficulties created for the playwright by the novel fact that the sovereign in whom he sought to invest absolute reforming power was a woman.

If one focuses exclusively on the figure of Nemesis, the notion that the play experiences no difficulty with the idea of female sovereignty might be sustainable. But Nemesis is only one of Udall's female characters, and a relatively minor one, who occupies the playing space only during the final scenes. For the bulk of the drama attention is focused on a far less authoritative woman, Respublica herself. And she, as we shall see, presents a wholly different conception of female involvement in politics.

The state's two bodies: gender and Respublica's political anatomy

The idea that the realm might be imagined as a human body is a commonplace of Tudor political thinking. In one image it combines the idealised notion of a commonweal of many members all interdependent and contributing harmoniously to a single goal, with the hierarchical dictum that obedience to a single authority – the Head of State – was necessary for a realm to function effectively. What the reconceptualisation of this anthropomorphic model as a specifically female body involves is a marked increase in the physicality of that imaginary conception of the state. What had been merely an ideal when it was conceived as a largely asexual male anatomy, became increasingly corporeal when conceived of as female. The implications of the prevailing conception of the female body: frail, sensual, and manifestly carnal, are carried over into the sphere of political discourse. The language of statecraft becomes eroticised by the language of courtship, seduction, and sexual and domestic mastery. The political imperatives of the domestic sphere thus become entangled with those of public debate. In this way Respublica's status as a female embodiment of the realm is a crucial determi-

---

[61] Such prayers for the Council had not been used in the plays addressed to Henry VIII, but in those written for Mary and her female successor, Elizabeth I, they were to become commonplace.

nant of the language and political discourse of the play. Just as the male establishment was awkwardly coming to terms with the new cultural and political demands of operating under a queen regnant, so the play itself manifests those awkwardnesses by figuring the state as a woman.[62]

Respublica is introduced in the *dramatis personae* as 'a wydowe', and the play considers her in those terms. On one level she is an abstraction: the realm of England, lacking her proper spouse, a sovereign king. But on another, more obvious level she is a woman of authority, who moves, speaks, and expresses emotions in the acting place. The stage has no time for abstractions, as soon as an actor takes on a role it becomes a person with human shape and attributes. In this way Respublica quickly blurs the distinction between state and sovereign, becoming a figure inextricably associated with the new queen herself, as she negotiates with her counsellors, consults her subjects, and seeks to address the problems facing her realm. It is thus with a figure very like a queen that Avarice and the gallants practise their deceptive trade.

Unlike the counsellors and ministers of *Magnyfycence* or *The Thrie Estaitis*, *Respublica*'s vices are specifically 'gallants', their on-stage personae stressing their courtly, seductive appearance rather than their ministerial capabilities. Their presence – like the threat they pose – is immediate and carnal rather than theoretical and spiritual. Unlike Magnyfycence, Respublica is inherently handicapped. She needs male advisors to help her to govern herself. She laments the absence of 'a perfecte staigh' to secure her (2.1.457). When Avarice poses as Policy, she tells him 'Well I fele the lacke of your helping hande by the Roode' (2.2.493). When she prays for rescue it is tellingly for male assistance that she calls: 'Is there no good manne that on me wyll have mercy?' (line 477). When faced with a crisis she is 'att hir wittes endes for what for to saie or do' (1.3.240).

As a vulnerable, unmarried woman, Respublica is the subject of physical handling of a sort not represented in any of the political moralities created during a male reign. She is a female body to be guided, directed, pulled, and pushed by the hands of men. The vices will 'clawe hir elbowe' to remind her of their service (line 269). Her complete submission to Avarice is as much physical as it is metaphorical, as the imagery makes clear.

---

[62] It might be objected that the play deliberately forestalls identification of Respublica and Mary by making the former representative of the state rather than a prince, and by overtly identifying the queen with Nemesis. But, as the following paragraphs will suggest, these distinctions quickly break down under the dramatic imperatives of performance.

RESPUBLICA: I will putt miselfe whollye into your handes
. . .
AVARICE: I thanke youe ladye
And I trust ere long to ease all [y]oure maladie.
Will ye putte yourselfe nowe wholye into my handes?
RESPUBLICA: Ordre me as youe wyll. (2.2.499, 505–8)

And the manner in which the vices attempt to win her support is constructed in their minds as a thinly veiled seduction. Avarice suggests that she

Fayne wolde . . . have succoure and easemente of hir griefe
And highly advaunce them that wolde promise reliefe . . .(1.3.241–2)

The 'service' which they offer is both ministerial and sexual. Avarice promises to 'bring hir in suche a paradise / That hir selfe shall sue me to have my service' (lines 253–4). The metaphor of the ship of state in need of a captain becomes conflated with the physical presence of a woman to be groped and manhandled. Avarice tells Insolence to 'Bee not . . . skeymishe to take in hand the stern' (line 278), and he promises 'I will bourde hir, and I trowe so wynne hir favoure / That she sh[a]ll hire me / and paie well for my laboure' (lines 331–2). The vices attempt to outdo each other in bawdy bravado over how well each will 'serve' the state.

ADULATION: I will doe hir double servis to another.
AVARICE: Ye double knave youe, will ye never be other?
ADULATION: She shall have triple service of me honestye.
AVARICE: Ye quadrible knave, will ye ner use modestie?
Thowe drunken whoresone, doest thoue not see nor perceive
Where Respublica standes readie us to receyve? (2.3.534–9)

When Respublica tries to dismiss Avarice, rejoicing that she shall be rid of him at last, she lays herself open to his bawdy misunderstanding of 'ridding' for 'riding'.

AVARICE: Naie by this crosse ye shall never be rydde for me.
RESPUBLICA: And of thy compares
AVARICE: Well leate them doo as thei luste.
I will ryde upon Jyll myne owne mare that is juste
Other waies I shall doe yowe service of the beste.
RESPUBLICA: Thowe wicked wretche dareste thowe with me to
jeste? (5.6.1503–8)

Once conceived as a woman the state thus becomes liable to be treated as one, its problems being dismissed as the product of fickle or weak-willed female inadequacy. Avarice rejects Respublica's fears of misrule as the product of her 'false heart' (4.4.1102). When she finally throws him out, he interprets her regeneration as an act of shrewishness: 'My ladie is waxte froward' (5.8.1639). Even the female virtues treat her with a tetchiness which is rarely seen in the treatment of male protagonists.

> MISERICORDIA: What saie ye to me? What, wooman, can ye not speake?
> I am come downe, all youre sorowes at ons to breake
> Speake, wooman . . .   (4.4.1227–9)

Respublica is, then, doubly subject to the actions of others. As a personification of the state, she is abused by the ministers upon whom she has to rely for her government. As a woman, she is manhandled by both the vices who falsely claim to protect her and the virtuous female characters who treat her as a malleable figure of womanly frailty.

Elsewhere in the play, in Nemesis and the four Daughters of God, Udall is able to offer uncompromising images of power in female form, largely because the frame of reference he draws upon is explicitly inhuman. As abstractions, they play out the limited and conventional roles inherent in their names: Misericordia speaks always for forgiveness, Justicia for stern judgement. No such shorthand was possible with Respublica, as her role in the text is too complex and her sphere of operation too earthly. Thus Udall had to look elsewhere for inspiration and, as no familiar and readily acceptable model of worldly female sovereignty was available to him, he necessarily fell back upon assumptions based upon experience, in which women were necessarily inferior to men, regardless of their status. Hence the state becomes 'a wydowe', an incomplete equation identified only by her lack of a husband. In such a frame of reference, the only readily acceptable path was for her to find a reliable male guardian and governor. Like her dramatic counterpart, Queen Mary was, of course, to take this course at the first opportunity, albeit arousing anxieties of a still more direct kind by choosing the catholic Philip II of Spain as her husband. But the problems of unmarried female sovereignty were to recur with even greater urgency in the reign of Mary's longer-lived and resolutely virgin successor, Elizabeth I, as the following chapter will explore.

CHAPTER 6

Strategies of courtship: the marital politics of 'Gorboduc'

While Queen Mary readily conformed to male expectations, taking a husband and tempering her sovereignty in the political arena with wifely subservience in the domestic sphere, Elizabeth I resolutely did not. Her refusal to marry superseded all other issues to become the most pressing political problem of the first three decades of her reign.[1] Ministers, courtiers, and noblemen, foreign diplomats and their princely masters, all sought consistently to tempt, cajole, or frighten her into accepting a husband or naming an heir. They did so with formal petitions from Parliament, through elaborate courtships – conducted either in person or through proxies – through the carefully coded allegories of poets, and, as what follows will make clear, through plays.

The first of the plays deliberately to intervene in this ongoing debate about the queen's marriage plans and the future of the realm is the subject of this chapter. It provides a valuable example of the lengths to which authors would go to persuade Elizabeth into a marriage in what they portrayed as the national interest, and of the means by which they sought to do so. It also offers, thanks to the fortuitous survival of an account of the play in performance, an opportunity to analyse the impact of a household play on a Tudor audience.

THE CREATION OF *GORBODUC*

The occasion

During the Christmas period 1561/2, Thomas Sackville and Thomas Norton's tragedy *Gorboduc* was performed in the Inner Temple in Lon-

[1] I would like to thank Dr G. W. Bernard of the University of Southampton for bringing to my attention the manuscript, British Library Additional MS 48023, upon which this chapter draws heavily, and for his help and encouragement during the writing of this piece, and Dr Simon Adams of the University of Strathclyde, who very kindly read much of the material used here in draft form and offered invaluable advice. My chief debt here, however, is to my co-author of the article 'The Politics of *Gorboduc*' (*English Historical Review*, 10 (1995), pp. 109–21), Henry James, who has kindly allowed me to use the results of our collaboration in this chapter.

don as part of the Inns of Court's seasonal revels. Less than a month later, on 18 January 1562, the same play, with an accompanying masque was performed again, this time before the queen at Whitehall. Scholars have long realised that the composite entertainment offered a direct intervention in the political controversy surrounding Elizabeth I's marriage plans (or lack of them) and the uncertainty of the succession. Now the discovery of an apparently eye-witness account of *Gorboduc*'s first performance makes it possible to be more definite about the specific political context of the play, and its reception by the courtiers, administrators, and lawyers who made up its first audiences. What follows will explore that context and draw out the implications of this new source for our understanding of the play, analysing how the politics of performance differed between the two productions of the drama and its subsequent printing in 1565 and 1570.[2]

The authors

Thomas Norton and Thomas Sackville were students of the Inner Temple with a talent for literary endeavour. Both were lauded among the poets gracing the Inns by Jasper Heywood who, in his translation of Seneca's *Thyestes* (1560), commended 'Sackvyldes Sonctes sweetely saust', and remarked that 'Norton's ditties do delight'.[3] The choice of the two to furnish the Yuletide play for 1561/2 was, then, in many ways a natural one, and that they found it a congenial task is suggested by the fact that they were to collaborate again on a non-dramatic work, 'Sacvyles Olde Age' at some point between 1566 and 1574.[4] It was not only literary interests which the two men shared, however. Both also had an active interest in practical politics.

Norton, a Londoner and son of a member of the Grocers' Company, began his career in the household of Edward Seymour, duke of Somerset, acting as tutor to the former Protector's children.[5] He entered the Inner Temple in 1555, and while there wrote the poetry commended by Heywood, including a contribution to that index of who-was-who in mid-Tudor English literature, *Tottel's Miscellany*. In 1558 he was sworn

---

[2] Since the publication of 'The Politics of *Gorboduc*', a number of other studies have considered the eye-witness account in BL MS Add. 48023. See, for example, N. Jones and P. W. White, '*Gorboduc* and Royal Marriage Politics: An Elizabethan Playgoer's Report on the Premiere Performance', *English Literary Renaissance*, 26 (1996), pp. 3–16, and Susan Doran, 'Juno Versus Diana: The Treatment of Elizabeth I's Marriage in Plays and Entertainments, 1561–1581', *Historical Journal*, 38 (1995), pp. 257–74, especially pp. 262–3.   [3] *RSTC* 22226.
[4] M. A. R. Graves, *Thomas Norton: Parliament Man* (Oxford, 1994), p. 40.
[5] For this and what follows, see Graves, *Norton*, pp. 17–18, 41–8.

freeman of the Grocers' Company, and in the same year entered the last Parliament of Mary Tudor's reign as one of the two members for Gatton. Thereafter Norton's career commuted between the twin poles of the City and Parliament, which he was to serve with diligence and vigour until his death in 1584. In the two sessions of Elizabeth's second Parliament, 1563 and 1566/7, Norton became increasingly active, operating as a 'man of business' for Secretary Cecil and other members of the Council, and these connections were to serve him well in subsequent years as he performed a range of other tasks, producing polemical tracts in support of the government and opposing what he saw as the catholic threat to the realm created by the disputed succession. While he was never the incendiary puritan that historians such as J. E. Neale once portrayed him,[6] Norton was nonetheless strongly committed to the protestant cause and a protestant succession. He married Thomas Cranmer's daughter Margaret in the 1550s, and was the translator of the first English text of Calvin's *Institution of Christian Religion* (1561). When he came to collaborate in the production of *Gorboduc*, that commitment to reformed religion and a protestant succession was to find perhaps its most eloquent and effective expression.

Thomas Sackville was more moderate in his religious sympathies and closer to the centre of power. A contributor to the 1563 edition of William Baldwin's *Mirror for Magistrates*, he was entirely familiar with the political impact of literature. But his involvement in politics was to take a more conventional path. The son of a Privy Councillor, Sackville, like Norton, progressed from admission to the Inner Temple (in July 1555) to service in the 1558 Parliament (as a Knight of the Shire for Westmoreland). But he was destined to rise higher than Norton, joining the Privy Council himself in 1586 and becoming chancellor of the University of Oxford in 1591 and Lord Treasurer of England in 1599. He became Lord Buckhurst in 1567, and Earl of Dorset in 1604.[7] Despite the very different backgrounds of the two men, however, the work upon which they collaborated managed to combine their interests in a form which contributed effectively to the political debates in which both had a passionate interest. While voicing acute concern over the dynastic and religious fate of the nation, it was nonetheless welcomed at court and became a landmark in the dramatic history of the period, providing a powerful demonstration of the principles of household drama in action.

[6] J. E. Neale, *Elizabeth I and Her Parliaments* (2 vols., London, 1953 and 1957), I, pp. 182 and following.
[7] J. Swart, *Thomas Sackville: A Study in Sixteenth Century Poetry* (Groningen, 1949), pp. 5–11.

The political context

The close associations between the Inns of Court men, their drama, and contemporary politics are well known.[8] The authors, actors, and audiences of these 'in-house' entertainments were themselves current or future politicians and administrators, men who would find service with the crown, in municipal government, or in the households of the provincial nobility.[9] Schooled in the nuances of the common law, which both justified and limited conduct in the political arena, trained in the skills of forensic and analytical debate, and closely connected with central figures in the government, the lawyers were well placed to reflect upon, and intervene in, the crucial political questions of the day.

Robert, Lord Dudley was one courtier and nobleman who was keen to secure the assistance of men from the Inns of Court to further his political ambitions. In particular, having entered the Inner Temple in 1559, he became 'Good Lord' to the Inner Templars by intervening on their behalf at court in a dispute concerning certain Inns of Chancery.[10] The same contemporary witness who provides the eye-witness account of *Gorboduc*, offers a description of this affair.

Controversie was betwene the two Temples, for the Inner Temple had three Innes of Chauncery that is Clyffordes Inne, Lyons Inne and Clementes Inne where the Midell Temple had only New Inne. It was thought good by the L[ord] Ke[e]per[11] and the chief Justices which were all of the Mydell Temple that the Inner [sic. Mydell?] Temple should have Clem[ents] the rather because they had before Strand Inne w[i]ch belonged to them, and was distroyed by the Duke of Somersett. But by the suete of the L[ord] Rob[ert] to the Quene, the Inner Temple kept all three. Wheruppon in memoriall therof and of so grete a benefytt receved by the L[ord] Robert they decreed in their p[ar]liament th[a]t none of their howse should be of counsell against the Lo[rd]

[8] See, for example, Mortimer Levine, *The Early Elizabethan Succession Question* (Stanford, 1966), pp. 30–44; E. W. Talbert, 'The Political Import of the First Two Audiences of *Gorboduc*', in T. P. Harrison, A. A. Hill, E. C. Mossner, and J. Sledd, eds., *Studies in Honor of De Witt T. Starnes* (Austin, TX, 1967), pp. 89–115; Doran, 'Juno Versus Diana', pp. 257–74; Graves, *Thomas Norton*, pp. 90–103; and especially M. Axton, *The Queen's Two Bodies: Drama and the Elizabethan Succession* (London, 1977), *passim.*

[9] M. A. R. Graves, 'The Management of the Elizabethan House of Commons: The Council's "Men-of-Business"', *Parliamentary History*, 2 (1983), pp. 17–20, 32–8; Patrick Collinson, 'Puritans, Men of Business and Elizabethan Parliaments', *Parliamentary History*, 7 (1988), pp. 187–211; M. A. R. Graves, 'The Common Lawyers and the Privy Council's Men-of-Business, 1584–1601', *Parliamentary History*, 8 (1989), pp. 189–215.

[10] F. A. Inderwick, ed., *A Calendar of the Inner Temple Records* (London, 1898) I, pp. 215–19; Axton, *Queen's Two Bodies*, pp. 40–7. Whether it was Dudley or the Inner Templars who made the initial soundings is unclear.

[11] Sir Nicholas Bacon, Keeper of the Great Seal, the senior legal officer as there was no Lord Chancellor at this point.

Ro[bert] nor his heyres, that his armes should be sett upp in the hall for a perpetuall monument. [12]

In addition, the Inner Temple also honoured Dudley by electing him their Christmas Prince, the central figure in their Yuletide revels for 1561/2. And the central elements of those revels, *Gorboduc* and a masque of Beauty and Desire, carried between them, as Marie Axton has suggested, both a plea for a settlement of the succession and a message favourable to Dudley in his attempt to became husband and consort to the queen. [13]

From almost the start of her reign, Elizabeth was felt to hold Dudley paramount among her favourites. Early in 1559 it was rumoured that she might marry him when his wife, Amy Robsart, was thought to be seriously ill. Throughout 1559 and 1560 the despatches of the Spanish Ambassador, Alvaro de La Quadra, asserted the queen's love for Dudley, and recorded rumours that the latter would divorce, or even murder, his current wife to further his suit. [14] The death of Amy Robsart in 1560 hardly dampened speculation that a royal marriage was imminent.

Judging by contemporary comment it seems that the queen may well have been serious about marriage in general, and a match with Dudley in particular, in 1560/1. [15] It is unclear precisely what finally convinced her against it. It may well have been that in the end she did not want to risk arousing the opposition of prominent councillors through so controversial a match. [16] But in the Christmas period of 1561/2 the queen's true

[12] BL Add. MS 48023, f. 358v (December 1561). This supplements and amends the information offered in Axton, *Queen's Two Bodies*, p. 41, footnote 2, and M. Axton, 'Robert Dudley and the Inner Temple Revels', *Historical Journal*, 13 (1970), pp. 365–78, p. 365, where it is claimed (on the basis of Inderwick, ed., *Calendar*, I, pp. 215–20) that the dispute concerned only Lyon's Inn. The text in Inderwick in fact leaves it unclear which Inn, or Inns, were concerned. For the suggestion that this dispute is itself allegorised in *Gorboduc*, see D. S. Bland, *Three Revels From the Inns of Court* (Avebury, 1984), pp. 12–13.

[13] Axton, *Queen's Two Bodies*, pp. 40–7; Axton, 'Robert Dudley', *passim*; J. G. Nichols, ed., *The Diary of Henry Machyn*, Camden Society, o.s. 42 (London, 1848), pp. 273–4. For the masque, see J. G. Nichols, 'Gerard Legh's *Accedens of Armory*', *Herald and Genealogist*, I (1862), pp. 42–68, 97–118, 268–72, and for the revels generally, J. Nichols, *The Progresses and Public Procession of Queen Elizabeth* (3 vols., London, 1823), I, pp. 131–41.

[14] *CSPSp*, 25 (pp. 57–8), 29, 74 (p. 112), 95, and 119 (p. 175).

[15] *CSPSp*, 27, 29, 64, 74, 121, 123, 125, 133, and 150; *CSPF*, 533; *CSPF, 1562*, 438 (4); BL Add. MS 48023, f. 353v; W. MacCaffery, 'Elizabethan Politics: The First Decade, 1558–68', *Past and Present*, 24 (1963), pp. 25–42, p. 37; see also Norman. L. Jones, 'Elizabeth's First Year: The Conception and Birth of the Elizabethan Political World', in C. Haigh, ed., *The Reign of Elizabeth I* (London, 1984), pp. 27–54.

[16] *CSPSp* 69, 74, 75, 77, 119, 122, *CSPF, 1562*, 246. That William Cecil was active in stirring up opposition to the Dudley match is clear (see, for example, Conyers Read, *Mr Secretary Cecil and Queen Elizabeth* (London, 1955), pp. 199–210; Simon Adams, 'The Dudley Clientele, 1553–1563',

feelings were an unknown quantity, and Dudley clearly felt that the highest marital prize of all was there to be pursued. It is his pursuit of this goal, and the lawyers' more general discussion of the dangers to the realm attendant upon the lack of a nominated heir to the throne, which provides the political context for the performances of *Gorboduc* and the masque of Beauty and Desire in 1562.

The plot

Gorboduc is rightly considered a landmark in English literary history. As the earliest extant five-act verse tragedy in English, the earliest attempt to imitate Senecan tragic form in English, the earliest surviving English drama in blank verse, and the earliest English play to adopt the use of dumb-shows preceding each act, it offers itself as a point of departure for much of the Renaissance dramatic experimentation of the following decades. But in political terms at least, it is important to see the play as equally a thoroughly conventional piece, conforming to the tradition of the dramatic *speculum principis*, and as such very similar to the 'plays of counsel' by Heywood and others familiar at the court of the queen's father, Henry VIII.[17]

The play, an analogue of the *King Lear* story, chronicles the ruinous consequences of King Gorboduc's capricious attempt to alter the succession and overturn the rule of primogeniture. Against the advice of the wisest of his counsellors, he divides the kingdom during his lifetime between his two sons, Ferrex and Porrex, thus setting up a rivalry

in G. W. Bernard, ed., *The Tudor Nobility* (Manchester, 1992), pp. 241–65, especially pp. 256–7). Cecil had put it about that he would withdraw from the court if the marriage went ahead. It was also he, remarkably, who spread the rumours, reported by De La Quadra, that Amy Robsart was not in fact ill, but that the queen and Dudley were plotting to poison her (*CSPSp*, 27, 74, 119). But Cecil was not the only one working to spoil the match. The Earl of Arundel, himself a suitor for Elizabeth's hand in the earliest months of the reign (ibid., 6; BL Add. MS 48023, f. 357), had told the queen that even if she wished to govern the country by passion he could assure her that the nobles would not allow her to do so (*CSPSp*, 198). Arundel's opposition to Dudley was itself a constant feature of English political life in 1561/2. As Lord Steward, the most senior office holder in the royal household and a Privy Councillor, he may have been a more serious opponent than historians have allowed for. S. Haynes, *A Collection of State Papers . . . Left by William Cecil, Lord Burghley* (London, 1740) I, p. 365; BL Add. MS 35831, f. 33; *CSPSp*, 60–2, 139 and 211; Levine, *Succession Question*, pp. 17–21. For the Duke of Norfolk's opposition to the Dudley match, see *CSPSp*, 69 and 119.) See *CSPSp*, 86 and 89 (p. 131) for hostility between Arundel and Lord Clinton, a close ally of Dudley. That a Dudley marriage might see an upsurge of factionalism and the settling of old scores might have been a real fear for those former Marian counsellors who had played a part in the downfall of Lord Robert's father, the Earl of Northumberland (see Adams, 'Dudley Clientele', pp. 256–7).

17 See Greg Walker, *Plays of Persuasion: Drama and Politics at the Court of Henry VIII* (Cambridge, 1991), *passim*, and chapters 2 and 3, above.

between them based upon mutual insecurity. The younger son, Porrex, fearing an attempt upon his life and lands, consequently kills his older brother, provoking the queen, Videna, whose preference had always been for her elder child, to kill the younger in revenge. This only provokes a wider cycle of violence, however, as the commons, moved by such cruelty, rise in rebellion and kill both Gorboduc and his queen, which in turn prompts the nobles to raise bands of horsemen to put down the rising.[18] Unable to agree on the succession, the nobles fear the prospect of civil war. Into this turmoil steps an invading foreigner, Fergus, Duke of Albany, who threatens to establish his claim to the crown by force alone. The play ends with Gorboduc's wisest counsellor, his secretary Eubulus, lamenting the fact that the realm could have been spared this predicament if only the King had taken the good advice of his counsellors, shunned flatterers and, after the death of his sons, settled the succession definitively and with force of law.

> then parliament should have bene holden
> And certeine heires appointed to the crowne,
> To stay the title of established right,
> And in the people plant obedience,
> While yet the prince did live, whose name and power
> By lawfull sommons and authoritie
> Might make a parliament to be of force,
> And might have set the state in quiete stay.   (5.2.264–71)[19]

Gorboduc and the Elizabethan succession debates

By dramatising the subject of a disputed succession, Sackville and Norton were, of course, broaching perhaps the paramount political question of the moment: the future of the English crown. At a time when the English succession was itself uncertain, and the leaders of the political nation were urging their new queen to take definitive steps to resolve the issue,[20] *Gorboduc* provided its royal audience at Whitehall

---

[18] Interestingly bands of horsemen had actually been established by the Edwardian Council in 1550–52, during a period of threatening peasant rebellion, an event which perhaps provided the playwrights with their model. Dale Hoak, *The King's Council in the Reign of Edward VI* (Cambridge, 1976), pp. 199–202. The author of BL Add. MS 48023 himself noted, in the Edwardian section of his text, 'Howe bandes of horsemen were devysed, and howe they were distributed, and what was their wages. How they continued not longe, for the grete charge' (f. 351v).

[19] References to the play are to the 1570 edition, printed in facsimile by Scolar Press (*Gorboduc: The Tragedy of Ferrex and Porrex* (Menston, 1968)); the line numbering is my own addition.

[20] In the 1559 Parliament the Commons had petitioned the queen to settle the succession, preferably by marriage. In her reply, read to members by John Mason, she had held out the possibility of her naming an heir as a concession, suggesting that 'albeit it might pleas almightie

with a spur to action in the vision of a realm thrown into chaos by an unresolved succession. As the archetypal good counsellor, Eubulus, declares, the audience might see before them the consequences of Gorboduc's failure to act decisively at a similar juncture.

> Loe here the end of Brutus royall line,
> And, loe the entry to the wofull wracke,
> And utter ruine of this noble realme. (5.2.180–2)

The point is reinforced by Gwenard, one of the lords attempting to hold the realm together, who resolves rather to die than

> see the hugie heapes of these unhappes,
> That now roll downe upon the wretched land,
> Where emptie place of princely governaunce,
> No certaine stay now left of doubtlesse heire,
> Thus leave this guidelesse realme an open pray,
> To endlesse stormes and waste of civill warre. (5.2.109–14)

And, as if further corroboration was needed, Eubulus concludes the play with a nightmarish description of a realm fallen into civil dissension and lawless tyranny: all for the want of an established heir to the throne.

> Loe, Brittaine realme is left an open pray,
> A present spoyle by conquest to ensue.
> Who seeth not now how many rising mindes
> Do feede their thoughts, with hope to reach a realme?
> And who will not by force attempt to winne
> So great a gaine, that hope perswades to have?
> A simple colour shall for title serve:

God to contynew me still in this mynde to lyve out of the state of mariage, yet it is not to be feared but he will so woorke in my harte and in your wisdomes as good provision by his healpe maybe made in convenient tyme, wherby the realme shall not remayne destitute of an heire that may be a fitt governor, and peraventure more beneficiall to the realme than suche ofspring as may come of me' (BL Lansdowne MS 94, f. 29(v); T. E. Hartley, ed., *Proceedings in the Parliaments of Elizabeth I* (Leicester, 1981), i, p. 45). In 1563 the Lords were to petition the queen that she should take determined steps to ensure political stability, first by marriage and second by assuring 'that some suche certen limitacion might be made how th'imperiall crowne of this realme shuld remain if God call your highness without any heire of your body (which our lord defend) as these your lordes and nobles and other your subjectes then living might sufficiently understand to whom they shuld owe their allegiances and duties due to be don by subjectes and that they might by your majesties license and by your favour coummune, treate and conferre together this parliament time for the well doing of this' (PRO SP Dom, Eliz., 27/35; Hartley, *Proceedings*, i, pp. 58–62). During March 1563, Lord Keeper Sir Nicholas Bacon was to warn Elizabeth in her gallery at Westminster of the dangers of an uncertain succession. Using language highly reminiscent of *Gorboduc*, he was to speak of 'The fearefull slaughters, the pittifull effusion of bloude, the miserable spoyles that have so ofte happened by sufferance of non certenties of titles to crownes' (BL Harleian MS 5176, ff. 93–4; Hartley, *Proceedings*, pp. 63–5).

Who winnes the royall crowne will want no right,
Nor such as shall display by long discent
A lineall race to prove him lawfull king.
In the meane while these civil armes shall rage,
And thus a thousand mischiefes shall unfolde.   (5.2.191–202)[21]

The particular moral of the story is then made clear to the audience:

Hereto it commes when kinges will not consent
To grave advise, but followe wilful will.
This is the end, when in fonde princes hartes
Flattery prevailes, and sage rede hath no place.
. . .
And this doth growe when loe unto the prince,
Whom death or sodeine happe of life bereaves,
No certaine heire remaines, such certaine heire,
As not all onely is the rightfull heire,
But to the realme is so made knowen to be,
And trouth therby vested in subjectes hartes.
To owe fayth there where right is knowen to rest.   (5.2.234–7, 246–52)

Thus Sackville and Norton, both of whom had links with those of the queen's counsellors anxious to put an end to constitutional uncertainty, presented the case for an immediate determination of the succession.[22]

---

[21] Perhaps the most terrifying aspect of this scenario for the men of property in the audiences at Court and in the Inner Temple, however, would have been the prospect of unrestrained social mobility and economic anarchy which civil dissension threatens to open up: 'All right and lawe shall cease, and he that had / Nothing to day, to morrowe shall enjoye / Great heapes of golde, and he that flowed in wealth, / Loe he shall be bereft of life and all, / And happiest he that then possesseth least' (5.2.204–8).

[22] Sackville's father, Sir Richard, was a Privy Councillor and governor of the Inner Temple, whose members included many other courtiers and counsellors. He was also a close friend of Lord Robert Dudley (Haynes, *A Collection*, p. 365) and enjoyed connections with his family stretching back into the reign of Edward VI, when Sackville had been one of the few men of substance to take the field in support of Lady Jane Grey (Robert Wingfield of Brantham, *Vitiae Mariae Angliae Reginae*, ed. and trans. D. MacCulloch, in *Camden Miscellany*, 4.28 (1984), p. 267), although Thomas Sackville's own religious and political views do not make him a natural ally of those, like John Hales, most opposed to the Scottish claim (see Simon Adams, 'The Release of Lord Darnley and the Failure of the Amity', in M. Lynch, ed., *Mary Stewart: Queen in Three Kingdoms* (Oxford, 1988), pp. 123–53). Norton was, from the 1560s onwards, a 'business manager' for the Privy Council in Parliament, organising committees and acting as a general trouble-shooter (M. A. R. Graves, 'Thomas Norton, the Parliament Man: An Elizabethan MP, 1559–1581', *Historical Journal*, 23 (1980), pp. 17–35. But see also Collinson, 'Puritans, Men of Business', pp. 197–200; and Graves, 'The Common Lawyers', pp. 189–215). On 26 January 1563 it was Norton who read the petition of the committee on the queen's marriage and limitation of the succession to the Commons. He may well also have chaired the committee and drafted the petition himself (J. E. Neale, *Elizabeth I and Her Parliaments* (London, 1953), I, p. 105; Graves, *Thomas Norton*, pp. 103–4). In 1581 Norton spoke out against the projected Anjou marriage and ended in the Bloody Tower as a consequence (Collinson, 'Puritans, Men of Business', p. 198).

It was not, however, sufficient for her advisors that Elizabeth should merely name an heir. The decision as to whom that heir should be was clearly of central importance and fraught with complications. In 1561 the two most plausible candidates to succeed the queen were the protestant Lady Katherine Grey, and the catholic Mary, Queen of Scots, the latter of whom had the closer hereditary claim to inherit.[23] That the most likely successor to the throne was thus both Francophile and a catholic was clearly an alarming prospect for a number of Elizabeth's protestant counsellors, hence the attempt, backed by some of their number, to exclude any Scottish claimant from the succession, thereby ensuring an English, protestant, heir. This was to have been achieved either by following the will of Henry VIII (which had specifically disinherited his Scottish relatives, descendants of his sister Margaret, in favour of those of his younger sister Mary), or by a new Act of Succession, giving Elizabeth similar powers to those claimed by her father to will the crown before her death.[24]

Thus the fraught discussions of the last act of *Gorboduc*, concerning how best to determine a secure and rightful succession, had a strong and particular contemporary relevance. In a situation in which, as the play acknowledges, 'expert' opinion was divided over both the respective strengths of the rival claims and the desirability of a catholic or protestant heir presumptive,[25] all such advice was partial.

It is in this context that the play's vociferous hostility to the claims of Fergus, duke of Albany, has conventionally been read. Arostus is the chief spokesman for this xenophobic position. The native-born lords, he declares, should forbear advancing their own claims to the title,

[23] Levine, *Succession Question*, pp. 6–12. Other candidates included Lady Lennox (and her son Lord Darnley), Lady Margaret Strange, and Henry Hastings, Earl of Huntingdon.

[24] *CSPSp*, 149, 150 (p. 227), 159, 190. As Simon Adams has argued, the situation was complicated by the fact that there were strong diplomatic reasons not to alienate the Scots which persuaded the queen and her closest advisers against an open repudiation of the Stuart claim (Adams, 'Release of Lord Darnley', pp. 133–44). This may well help to explain the nuanced position on the succession seemingly advanced in *Gorboduc* (see below, pp. 214–17 and notes). It is the fear that Elizabeth might die before a legal means of determining the succession could be established that is reflected in *Gorboduc*'s insistence that a parliament be called to decide the issue during the life of the sovereign ('whose name and power / By lawfull sommons and authoritie / Might make a parliament to be of force' (5.2.268–70)). For on her death, the governmental institutions of the realm, Household, Parliament, and Privy Council, would all lapse with the body natural of the sovereign that gave them constitutional legitimacy.

[25] As Arostus laments 'of the title of discended crowne / Uncertainly the diverse mindes do thinke / Even of the learned sort, and more uncertainly / Will parcial fancie and affection deeme' (5.2.127–30).

Till first by common counsell of you all
In parliament the regall diademe
Be set in certaine place of governaunce,
In which your parliament and in your choise,
Preferre the right (my lords) [without] respect
Of strength of frendes, or what soever cause
That may set forward any others part.
For right will last, and wrong can not endure.
Right meane I his or hers, upon whose name
The people rest by meane of native line,
Or by the vertue of some former lawe,
Already made their title to advaunce.
Such one (my lords) let be your chosen king,
Such one so borne within your native land,
Such one preferre, and in no wise admitte
The heavie yoke of forreine governance,
Let forreine titles yelde to publike wealth.
And with that hart wherewith ye now prepare
Thus to withstand the proude invading foe,
With that same heart (my lords) keepe out also
Unnaturall thraldome of [a] strangers reigne,
Ne suffer you against the rules of kinde
Your mother land to serve a forreine prince.　　　　(5.2.157-79)

Here one sees the play's most direct intervention in the contemporary succession debate. As a number of critics have asserted, who else could contemporaries have thought of when confronted with the figure of the Duke of Albany ('manifestly a Scottish title: it was usually held by a Stuart'[26]) but Mary Stuart, Queen of Scots? And who else could have been intended as the 'right' choice, but the candidate of the 'native line', Katherine Grey, whose claim was demonstrably based upon the 'former law / Already made' of Henry VIII's will, empowered by Act of Parliament to determine the succession? It was surely the latter's claims, scholars have concluded, that the play was advancing when advocating that Parliament should meet and 'certaine heires [be] appointed to the crowne' (5.2.265).[27] Such identifications are suggestive, but do not tell the whole story.

Intimately related to the succession question, of course, was the issue

[26] Levine, *Succession Question*, p. 41.
[27] Ibid., pp. 30 and 38–41; Axton, 'Robert Dudley', p. 366; L. H. Courtney, 'The Tragedy of "Ferrex and Porrex" ', *Notes and Queries*, 2.10 (1860), pp. 261–3; David Bevington, *Tudor Drama and Politics: A Critical Approach to Topical Meaning* (Cambridge, MA, 1968), pp. 145–6; Mark Breitenberg, 'Reading Elizabethan Iconicity: *Gorboduc* and the Semiotics of Reform', *English Literary Renaissance*, 18 (1988), pp. 194–217, p. 200.

of the queen's marriage. In 1561–2, and indeed for most of the 1560s, contemporaries generally assumed that the queen would marry and, hopefully, have issue of that union. Marriage would thus offer a solution to the succession problem. And, as we have seen, throughout 1560–1 at least, Lord Robert Dudley remained the most likely candidate for the queen's hand: a situation which one observer thought good for the 'glorie of God' (i.e. the protestant cause) and 'the securitie of the realme'.[28] So far, however, this consideration of *Gorboduc* has not touched upon the marriage question as, on the evidence of the extant texts, the play does not seem to address it. The new evidence about the play in performance, however, prompts us to rethink that position.

As Marie Axton has argued, the masque of Beauty and Desire which the men of the Inner Temple took to Whitehall with *Gorboduc* on 18 January seems to have been a clear allegorical statement of the desirability of Robert, Lord Dudley as a royal consort. The fictional framework of the Christmas revels established Prince Pallaphilos, the nation's champion and founder of the Order of Pegasus (an allusion to Dudley's office as Master of the Horse?), as a model of sound political counsel and the defender of the temple of Pallas against (by implication ungodly, catholic) pollution. The ensuing story of Beauty and Desire offered a narrative of chivalric wooing culminating in a marriage within that 'princely' temple. As Axton argues, the advocacy of marriage contained in these narratives seems well suited to complement the account of the terrors of political division and the need for a parliamentary solution to the succession offered by *Gorboduc*.

The lawyers [in the masque] created for Elizabeth a Prince, presented him as protector of the established religion, and offered him as the solution to the marriage question . . . The tragedy, by contrast, dealt with the question of disrupted succession . . . the consequent civil war and the impossibility of choosing a legal successor under those circumstances. The contrast between the two entertainments was intended to be striking. Marriage was the approved course.[29]

What is implied, then, is a distinctly two-pronged strategy, in which the masque forwarded the Dudley match, while the play concerned itself only with the more obviously constitutional issue of the succession. And, on the evidence of the printed text this is persuasive. But the new evidence suggests, as what follows will show, that these two approaches

[28] Thomas Fitzwilliams to Sir Nicholas Throckmorton, 5 December, 1561, PRO SP 70/33 f. 7v.
[29] Axton, 'Robert Dudley', p. 374–5. See also Graves, *Thomas Norton*, pp. 96–7.

were even more closely related than Axton argues. *Gorboduc*, too, addressed the marriage issue directly, and at length, offering the prospect of a match (implicitly with Dudley) as the long-term answer to the succession question as well as a short-term solution to a diplomatic and dynastic conundrum.

It is important to note in this context that Dudley was not the only suitor for Elizabeth's hand in the winter of 1561/2. He had a rival, and a powerful one at that, in the form of Eric XIV, king of Sweden. Historians have not given sufficiently serious attention to the Swedish attempt to secure a match with Elizabeth. They have preferred to see the marriage issue, despite the existence of a number of other, minor, suitors, as effectively a question of 'Dudley or no-one' until the more glamorous French and Imperial candidates began to be considered later in the decade. But Dudley himself took the matter entirely seriously, as did his domestic enemies. On 13 September 1561 it was reported by the Spanish ambassador that those enemies, headed by Arundel and the Marchioness of Northampton, were promoting the Swedish marriage project,[30] which had been floated as early as 1559, and was recommended by the fact that the Swedish royal family was both protestant and wealthy.[31] In July 1561 wedding souvenirs had begun to circulate, somewhat prematurely, in London.[32] Then King Eric's 'Great Ambassador', Chancellor Nicholas Guildenstern, arrived during the summer to a grand official welcome. By September the king himself was 'hourly looked for'.[33] The nobility and gentry of the realm were alerted to be prepared to receive the king and to have their wives ready to come to court. Instructions were sent to noblemen to meet the king should he

---

[30] *CSPSp*, 139. Also involved were Katherine Ashley, and perhaps also her husband, John, Chief Gentleman of the queen's Privy Chamber and Master of the Jewels (see PRO SP 70/40 ff. 72–83; BL Add. MS 48023, f. 366) who had reportedly been briefly committed to his chamber and put out of court 'for dyspleasure of my L[ord] Rob[ert]' in January 1561 (BL Add. MS 48023, f. 353v). I am grateful to Simon Adams for pointing out the correct date of this incident.

[31] *CSPSp*, 24, 31, 35, 74, 117, 481, and 533. Under September 1561 the author of BL Add. MS 48023 noted the 'Grete desire of the K. of Swedens coming of the merchauntes and Londoners, because they thought he would bring grete treaure with him. And because they sawe his brother spend so much here' (f. 356v). The king's brother, Duke John of Finland, had been in London between Michaelmas 1559 and Easter 1560, furthering Eric's suit, during which time he reputedly spent '20,000 dollars' and was 'very liberall to the poore' (ibid., f. 354). For the queen's own studiedly ambiguous attitude towards the negotiations, see ibid., 88, 139, and 145.

[32] Haynes, *A Collection*, p. 368.

[33] BL MS Add. 48018, f. 284v; BL MS Add. 35830, f. 140v; *CSPF, 1561/2*, 535. See also *CSPF, 1561/2*, 272, 481 and 493; and *CSPSp*, 137 and 139. In Peebles two burgesses wagered, in the presence of magistrates, ten marks against a barrel of tar, that 'the Quene grace of Inglond suld mary the King of Swane sua scho war marrit with any man for ane year' (J. W. Buchan and H. Paton, *A History of Peeblesshire* (3 vols., Glasgow, 1925–7), II, p. 182).

land on the east coast, while at court the great office-holders, the Marquis of Winchester (Lord Treasurer), Earl of Arundel (Lord Steward), and Lord Howard of Effingham (Lord Chamberlain) made preparations for the visit. On 25 September, Sir William Cecil detailed the arrangements for the formal welcome. Lodgings, food, escorts, even the protocol for the royal banquet were set down ('when it shall please hir Majestie to have the King dyne with her, there must be two Clothes of Estate, th'one for hyr, thother for hym').[34] In October interest was maintained with the timely publication of George North's *Description of Swedland, Gotland and Finland*.[35] But in November, as the court swelled with an influx of expectant dignitaries, news came through of bad weather at sea. By early December it was clear that the king's arrival could not realistically be expected before the spring of 1562.[36] Meanwhile, the Swedish ambassador continued to press his master's suit against the counter-claim advanced by Dudley.

The latter's hostility to the Swedish marriage was to continue through January 1562. Lavish hospitality laid on for the Privy Council by Guildenstern was pointedly snubbed by Dudley, the earls of Warwick, Bedford, and Pembroke, and lords Clinton and Howard of Effingham. When the mayor and aldermen of the City of London similarly refused an invitation, it was rumoured that 'they durste not or they were otherwyse commaunded'.[37] By March 1562 the Swedish King had still not arrived. His ambassador, realising the increasing unlikelihood of his success, prepared to leave for home as 'the Queen maketh soe much of the L[ord] Rob[ert]'.[38] Finally, on 14 April, he departed. Dudley's hopes consequently increased greatly, especially when, on 24 April, in the chapter house of the Knights of the Garter, he was recommended as husband to the queen with the approval of 'the most parte of all the knightes there present'. Arundel and Northampton were reported to have 'depparted owte of the howse when they herde yt moved'.[39] The Swedish project was finally over for all practical purposes, although vain attempts by members of the queen's household to entice King Eric to England continued, and the idea retained a certain amount of residual

[34] Haynes, *A Collection*, pp. 370–2.   [35] *RSTC* 18662.
[36] PRO SP 70/32 f. 62; SP 70/33 f. 7v; BL Add. MS 48023, ff. 357v-8.
[37] BL Add. MS 48023, f. 360. See also *CSPF, 1562*, 438. Interestingly, the author of Leicester's Commonwealth, a tract highly critical of Dudley, was to cite his opposition to the Swedish proposal among his 'offences', noting his 'defeating of all her Majesty's most honourable offers of marriage . . . the first with the Swethen King' (D. C. Peck, ed., *Leicester's Commonwealth* (Athens, OH, 1985), pp. 79–80).   [38] BL Add. MS 48023, f. 363. See also *CSPSp*, 157.
[39] BL Add. MS 48023, f. 363.

popular support.[40] But while it lasted, the project had been a dangerous one from Dudley's viewpoint, and had drawn from him a concerted campaign to assert his own candidacy against it. It is in the light, not only of the marriage and succession issues generally, but of this campaign in particular, that we should consider the first performances of *Gorboduc*.

GORBODUC IN PERFORMANCE: THE EYE-WITNESS EVIDENCE

Among the Yelverton papers in the British Library is a collection of the papers of Robert Beale, the Elizabethan courtier and administrator. Among these are what appear to be the working notes for a chronicle,[41] concentrating in part upon matters associated with Robert Dudley. And it is here that one can find the following account of *Gorboduc* as performed in 1561/2.[42]

Ther was a Tragedie played in the Inner Temple of the two brethren Porrex and Ferrex, K[ings] of Brytayne betwene whome the father had devyded the Realme, the one slewe the other and the mother slewe the manquil[e]r [i.e. the man-queller or man-killer]. It was thus used. Firste wilde men cam[e] in and woulde have broken a whole fagott, but could not, the stickes they brake being severed.[43] Then cam[e] in a king to whome was geven a clere glasse, and a golden cupp of golde covered, full of poyson, the glasse he caste under his fote

---

[40] Ibid., ff. 364v, 366, 368; *CSPSp*, 180 and 193; *CSPF, 1562*, 344, 345, and 437 (4) and (7).

[41] The provisional, 'work in progress' nature of the text is apparent at a number of points. On the first page, for example, the author observes 'Howe Sir R. Moryson was sent Ambassador to the Emperor and Sir William Pickering to the Flemyshe King', and adds 'Loocke for eyther of their lettres' (BL Add. MS 48023, f. 350). Similarly, on folio 352, noting that Sir Ralph Sadler was sent North to negotiate with the Scots, the author reminds himself to 'Require of Mr Sadler what was don there and desire to have Mr Rayltons lettres and minites which he had being there, with Sir R. Sadeler'.

[42] Ibid., f. 359v. The Beale MS as a whole offers a partial narrative of events to 1562, focusing on incidents concerning the Dudleys, and offering at times a strongly critical account of their involvement, most notably in alleging Lord Robert's connivance in the murder of Amy Robsart and describing his subsequent show of mourning as 'greate hypocrysie' (f. 353). As Simon Adams has recently suggested in correspondence, the author is perhaps best placed in the circle of John Hales and others critical of the Stuart claims. Robert Beale was a protégé of Hales and involved in the Hales Book affair of 1563/4 (see Graves, *Thomas Norton*, pp. 101–3). That the author was not part of the Dudley circle is made clear at folio 353: 'The Tuesdaie after michelmas daye [1560] he [Lord Robert] repayreth to the Courte, at Hampton Courte. And Mr Danett and I mett him, and yt was reported to the Quene, that we in dyspyett would not do him reverence, but we putte of our cappes. And for my self I knewe him not, for I never sawe him before, ne knew not yt was he, tyll he was paste.' He may not have been a lawyer, but the depth of incidental detail in the description of *Gorboduc* (the golden cup is described as having a golden cover, and also the king is said to have crushed it under foot rather than simply broken it) coupled with the references to the dumb-show characters as 'coming in', suggests that he was present at the Inner Temple performance.   [43] The dumb-show before act 1.

and brake hyt, the poyson he drank of,[44] after cam[e] in mourners.[45] The shadowes were declared by the Chore[us] first to signyfie unytie, the 2 [i.e. second] howe that men refused the certen and toocke the uncerten, wherby was ment that yt was better for the Quene to marye with the L[ord] R[obert] knowen then with the K[ing] of Sweden. The thryde to declare that cyvill discention bredeth mo[u]rning. Many thinges were handled of mariage, and that the matter was to be debated in p[ar]liament, because yt was much banding but th[at] hit ought to be determined by the councell. Ther was also declared howe a straunge duke seying the realme at dyvysion, would have taken upon him the crowne, but the people would none of hytt. And many thinges were saied for the succession to put thinges in certenty.[46] This play was the [blank] daye of January at the courte before the Quene, where none ambassadors were present but the Spanyshe.[47]

There are clearly a number of important features to this account, which supplement and in some cases alter our perceptions of *Gorboduc*. That the king of the second dumb-show cast the proffered glass underfoot and broke it is new information, fleshing out the terser account in the 1570 printed text, which states simply that he refused it.[48] Of far greater importance is the new information in the sentence which follows, offering an exposition of that second dumb-show. The Chorus, we are told, declared the meaning of the 'shadowes' (i.e. the dumb-shows), and did so in an interesting way. The reading of the first of these 'shadowes' is entirely in keeping with the printed text as we have it. Both the printed 'Order' or description of the mime and the words of the Chorus stress that the mime of the breaking of the sticks was intended to demonstrate the importance of unity.[49] But in the second case their interpretations are very different. Far from reading it as an allegory of the respective merits of the known and the unknown, the 1570 edition interprets the mime of the glass and golden cup as a demonstration of the dangers of

[44] The dumb-show before act 2.
[45] The dumb-show before act 3. I am grateful to Professor John R. Elliot Jnr for advice on the reading of the MS at this point.   [46] Act 5, scenes 1 and 2.
[47] This last claim finds support in the letter of 22 January 1562 from De La Quadra to Francis Yaxley, which states that the ambassador had indeed recently seen a tragedy performed at court. Frustratingly, however, he claims not to have understood it. PRO typescript *Calendar of SP 46/Part One (Supplementary): General Papers to 1603* (London, 1965), p. 18. The original is PRO SP 46/2, no. 147. I am grateful to Professor Elliot and Dr Jane Everson for their help with the translation of this document.
[48] The 'grave and aged gentelman . . . offred up a cuppe unto him of wyne in a glasse, which the king refused' (sig. Cii(v)).
[49] The Order states that 'thereby was signified, that a state knit in unitie doth continue strong against all force. But being divided, is easely destroyed' (sig. A.iii). The Chorus declares: 'The strength that knit by faste accorde in one, / Against all forrein power of mightie foes, / Could of it selfe defende it selfe alone, / Disjoyned once, the former force doth lose. / The stickes, that sondred brake so soone in twaine, / In faggot bounde attempted were in vaine' (1.2.376–81).

heeding flattery. The 'Order and Signification' goes to some lengths to declare:

Hereby was signified, that as glasse by nature holdeth no poyson, but is clere and may easily be seen through, ne boweth by any art; so a faythfull counsellour holdeth no treason, but is playne and open, ne yeldeth to any undiscrete affection, but geveth holsome councell, which the yll advised Prince refuseth. The delightful gold filled with poyson betokeneth flattery, which under faire seeming of pleasant wordes beareth deadly poyson, which destroyed the Prince that receyveth it. As befell in the two brethren Ferrex and Porrex, who refusing the holsome advise of grave counsellours, credited these yong paracites and brought to them selves death and destruction therby.(sig. Cii(v))

The Chorus concurs.

> Wo to the prince, that pliant care enclynes,
> And yeldes his mind to poysonous tale, that floweth,
> From flattering mouth. And woe to wretched land
> That wastes it selfe with civil sworde in hand.
> Loe, thus it is, poyson in golde to take,
> And holsome drinke in homely cuppe forsake.   (2.2.103–8)

Where, then, can the author of the Beale manuscript have gained his very different impression of the mime? His notes are clear that 'The shadowes were declared by the Chore[us]'. Hence it must be accepted that, in the initial performance at least, the play itself offered this different exposition of the second dumb-show, stressing the benefits of the certain against the uncertain. Whether the Chorus also made clear the application of this moral to the current rivalry for the queen's hand, or whether this was a deduction which our commentator reached for himself, is less certain, the syntax being too loose for a definite judgement to be reached. But it is clear from this and from what follows that the second dumb-show in particular, and the play in general, *were* read by the audience in the specific context of Dudley's suit to marry the queen and the challenge offered to it by the Swedish mission. That this was no idiosyncratic interpretation of the play is made clearer by our witness's further comment, following the (conventional) exposition of the third dumb-show, that thereafter 'many thinges were handled of mariage, and that the matter was to be debated in parliament, because yt was much banding but that hit ought to be determined by the councell'. This claim is probably the most interesting of all the observations of our anonymous commentator. For in the surviving texts there is no reference whatsoever to royal marriage, or marriage *per se*. Indeed, there are no female characters of royal or noble blood among the *dramatis personae* (other than Queen Videna, who dies with her husband and is never in a position to become a candidate for marriage) who could conceivably give rise to a discussion of marriage.

What, then, are we to make of these remarks? It might be objected, of course, that what our witness is (mistakenly) recalling at this point is not the play itself, but the masque of Beauty and Desire which followed, and which, as we have seen, did discuss marriage at length. But this seems unlikely. The account of the play is otherwise a detailed one and, save for the points mentioned above, it is wholly in accord with the surviving printed texts. Moreover, no other reference is made to the masque. What interested our commentator seems to have been *Gorboduc* and *Gorboduc* alone. Thus it seems safe to take these comments as direct references to the play. But how and where could the discussion of marriage have been introduced? The manuscript mentions it after its account of the third dumb-show, implying that it may well have come at some point after this (and before the fifth act, which is described in some detail in the following sentences). But there is little evidence in the printed text to suggest where exactly such a discussion could have been introduced, or what it could have involved. There is a passing reference in the final act to survivors of 'the princes kinne' (5.1.11). Thus it is possible that the courtiers in act 3 considered a marriage between the two princes and other members of the royal family in order to forestall the conflict between them, or that in act 4 a marriage between Porrex and a hitherto unmentioned wife or daughter of the murdered Ferrex might have been mooted as a means of healing the divided realm. Alternatively, and with more relevance to contemporary politics, the nobles could have discussed a marriage between one of their own number and a surviving royal princess in order to strengthen a native British claim to counter Fergus' bid for the crown. But all that the manuscript account allows us to state with any certainty is that at some point in the play a discussion of marriage did take place (a discussion which was subsequently removed when the text came to be printed in 1565), and this could only have been interpreted as a further direct intervention in the contemporary political and diplomatic debate. The more general implications of this fact will be considered below. Meanwhile, it is possible to draw other, more definite, conclusions from the observations in the Beale manuscript, observations which have both particular and general consequences for a reading of the play.

It is, for example, possible to reinterpret the figure of Fergus, the northern duke, in the light of this new account, as not simply an allusion to Mary, Queen of Scots and her claim to the throne, as scholars have previously assumed, but as a composite figure. Since Fergus is recognisably Scottish, he clearly draws attention to the long-term danger of a Stuart succession. But since he is male, and coming down from the north, he also alludes clearly to the more immediate dangers of 'foreign thraldom' posed by the King of Sweden's proposal. In one figure, the play represents both threats posed to an 'English' succession from beyond the realm.[50] Similarly it is also possible now to throw more light upon the play's apparently positive references to Katherine Grey's claim to the succession. Hitherto scholars have found it somewhat baffling that Dudley should have sponsored the performance of a play which seemed to endorse the settlement of the succession upon the 'native line' represented by Lady Katherine, by Act of Parliament (Arostus had argued for the settlement of the crown upon one 'Upon whose name / The people rest by meane of native line, / Or by the vertue of some former lawe, / Already made their title to advaunce' (5.2.165–8)). Was this not rather obviously counter-productive, given his own ambitions?[51] But, given what we now know

---

[50] Fergus' claim that his 'secret friendes / By secret practise shall sollicite . . . / To seeke to wynne to me the peoples hartes' (4.1.160–2) would thus act as an attack upon both those who favoured the Stuart claim to the throne and those, like Arundel and Katherine Ashley, who were promoting the Swedish marriage.

[51] See above, footnote 20. Axton offers the suggestion that Dudley may have genuinely favoured Lady Katherine's cause, citing the fact that she went to Lord Robert's bedside in September 1561 to seek his protection during the worst of her troubles over her secret marriage to the Earl of Hertford. (Axton, *Two Bodies*, p. 46, and Axton 'Robert Dudley', pp. 376–7; Graves, *Thomas Norton*, p. 76). The logic runs that she would not have sought his help unless she knew that he was sympathetic. But such reasoning would force us to accept that Dudley also favoured the conflicting claims of Katherine's rival, Lady Margaret Lennox, and her plans to marry her son, Lord Darnley, to Mary Queen of Scots. For she too sought Dudley's aid in 1561, through her client Francis Yaxley, who 'shewetht his devyse to my Lorde Robert . . . [to] bring the matter [of the marriage] in hede' (BL MS Cotton Caligula B VIII, f. 299v). This seems unlikely. If anything the contemporary evidence suggests that Dudley would probably have favoured the claims of his brother-in-law, the Earl of Huntingdon, if the matter came to a head, while Lady Katherine was actually supported by Dudley's rival, Henry, Earl of Arundel (*CSPSp*, 139, 190, 198, and 211: for the view that Dudley did not greatly care for the Huntingdon claim either, and was more concerned to reach an acceptable accommodation with Mary, whose claim he saw as 'unstopp-able', see Adams, 'Release of Lord Darnley', p. 137). On 7 February 1563, ambassador De La Quadra reported that 'the nobles are divided on the subject of the Succession, as the enemies of the Lord Robert see that she [Elizabeth] would really condescend to appoint Lord Huntingdon her successor, and that this would be opening the door to the marriage with Robert and put the kingdom in his hands, they have most of them met with the Earl of Arundel and the majority are inclined to assist Lady Catherine' (Adams, 'Release of Lord Darnley', p. 211). Perhaps the most plausible conclusion concerning Dudley's attitude towards Lady Katherine's plight and claims is that he looked upon them with tolerant indifference, as he hoped his own marriage to the queen would make the Grey claim ultimately irrelevant (Axton, 'Robert Dudley', p. 375; Graves, *Thomas Norton*, pp. 97–9).

of the play's initial performance(s), the two claims seem readily reconcilable.

In this context it is vital to recall that *Gorboduc* was designed for performance before audiences, not all of whom shared its opinions. Both in London and at Whitehall it was played in the presence of a number of those who most opposed the idea of Parliament 'appointing' heirs to the crown. It has generally been assumed that the drama was very much 'a lawyers' play', reflecting a consensus held by the Inn which produced it. But at the Inner Temple it actually addressed a legal fraternity, many of whom maintained that Henry VIII had no right to alter the succession by will, since the crown, being a corporation, was not something which could be made or unmade by men. In this view the right of Mary Stuart to the throne, should Elizabeth die without heirs of her body, was fundamental to the nature of the monarchy itself. Hence, as early as 1537, Robert Aske, the lawyer and 'Great Captain' of the Pilgrimage of Grace, had stated that since the Norman Conquest no 'King declared his will to the crown of this realm, nor never there was known in this realm no such law'.[52] In the 1560s such views were repeated by arguably the most outstanding lawyer of the day, Edmund Plowden, who pointed out that if Henry VIII's will was followed, then the kingdom would have been 'gayned by estopell, and not by truth'.[53] More immediately, the day before the second performance of *Gorboduc*, on 17 January 1562, it was reported that William Rastell, the former printer, by this time a judge in Queen's Bench, had sensationally fled the country rather than be called to give an opinion 'on the succession to the crown, declaring as it is suspected, that there is no certain heir. All this is to exclude the Scotch queen and Lady Margaret and declare that the selection of a king devolves upon the nation itself [i.e. in Parliament].'[54] At its first performance, then, Sackville and Norton's play was not preaching to the converted, it was seeking to persuade an at least partially sceptical audience of the merits of its case.

More obviously, at Whitehall on 18 January 1562 the play was performed before a royal spectator who had cooled considerably on the question of marriage to Dudley in recent months and was far from convinced of the necessity for Parliament to endorse a nominated successor to the crown. From almost the start of her reign, Elizabeth had steadfastly refused to adjudicate on the succession debate taking place

---

[52] M. Bateson, 'The Pilgrimage of Grace and Aske's Examination', *English Historical Review*, 5 (1890), pp. 563–4.
[53] Axton, *Queen's Two Bodies*, chapters 2 and 3; BL Harley MS 849 (Plowden's treatise on the Succession), f. 34v.   [54] *CSPSp*, 149.

around her. In September 1561 she complained to the Scottish ambassador, William Maitland of Lethington, that 'so many disputes have be[e]n already tutching it in the mouthis of men', and argued that naming a successor would make her own position untenable through the creation of a reversionary interest. Drawing upon her own experiences in the reign of her sister Mary I, Elizabeth spoke of the 'Inconstancye of the people of Ingland, how thay ever mislyke the present government, and has thair eyis fixit upone that persone that is nixit to succe[e]de.'[55]

Spurred by the very real fears of Elizabeth's death following a bout of smallpox in October, attempts were made in late 1562–3 to reach a compromise. A proposal which survives in draft form in the hand of Sir William Cecil attempted to fill the likely political vacuum on the death of the queen through a new Act of Succession which would ensure,

that if the Q[ueen's] Ma[jest]y our souverain Lady should decess (which Almighty God forbid) without issue of hir body or before the time that any person shall be declared by authority of parlem[e]nt to be the lawfull heir or successor to hir Ma[jes]ty . . . then . . . all such persons, which . . . be of the privy counsell . . . shall remain and continue counsellors . . . untill the daye that by proclamation to be made by authority of parlement it shall be declared to whom of right the Imperiall crown of this Realm of England ought to belong.[56]

Evidently the idea was seriously considered, but was probably too revolutionary to win royal support.[57] Either way, in January 1562 such a proposal lay in the future. *Gorboduc* was played before a queen who had seemingly set her mind against formalising the queue of claimants for her sacred office. Hence the play as it was originally performed pursued a subtle persuasive strategy. It offered both the sceptical lawyers and the equally sceptical Elizabeth I a range of choices concerning the suc-

---

[55] J. H. Pollen, *A Letter from Mary Queen of Scots to the Duke of Guise, January 1562*, Scottish History Society, 43 (Edinburgh, 1904), p. 41. The author of the Beale MS seems to reflect this declaration when he noted under March 1562 that 'the comen brute is that the Quene myndeth to establyshe the succession to the Crowne. [But] Some say that she will not do yt because she is perswaded that yf there were any heire apparente knowne the people would be more affectionated to him than to her, because the nature of Engl[ish] men is variable, not contented with the state present, but desirous of alteracions and that the people in hearing never so lytell faulte in the prince woulde, yf the successor were knowne, exaggerate yt' (f. 362). These arguments were clearly spelled out in the Parliaments of 1563 and 1566 (Hartley, *Proceedings*, pp. 93–5, 129–53). For Elizabeth's cooling on the issue of marriage to Dudley during 1561, see Read, *Mr Secretary Cecil*, pp. 198–210.

[56] PRO SP 12/28 f. 20. See Patrick Collinson, 'The Elizabethan Exclusion Crisis and the Elizabethan Polity', *Proceedings of the British Academy*, 84 (1993), pp. 51–92, p. 66. Commenting on the smallpox scare, the author of the Beale MS notes the 'grete lamentacion made [for] no man knoweth the certenty for the succession, every man asketh what parte shall we take' (f. 369).

[57] *CSPSp*, 218, 221; Neale, *Elizabeth I and Her Parliaments*, 1, pp. 112–13.

cession. The line seems to have been that a legal settlement of the question in Parliament – however problematic – was a more attractive option than civil war, but, crucially, that the queen's immediate marriage to Dudley was more attractive still. This last would create none of the legal and constitutional precedents associated with an acceptance of Henry VIII's will and the Grey claim, and avoided the destabilising effects upon relations with Scotland that continued agitation over that claim would inevitably entail.[58] But it also offered the prospect of royal offspring and a secure succession without the political and diplomatic dangers inherent in accepting a foreign consort. Thus the play warned at length in the fifth act of the dangers of civil turmoil, and recommended a parliamentary or conciliar determination of the succession as one possible solution to the present crisis. It had, however (if I have read the Beale manuscript correctly), already considered a royal marriage earlier in the play, at a point where such a match could have forestalled all the later disruption. Aware of the contemporary relevance of the debate, and having been presented with the options in a heavily partisan fashion, the audience was clearly expected to approve accepting the (Dudley) devil they knew rather than either embracing the 'unknown' King of Sweden, or risking a constitutional and diplomatic leap in the dark.[59]

More generally, what the new account of the play proves conclusively is the close relationship between drama and politics in the period which has been the central interest of this study. It proves that *Gorboduc* was read by its first audience as a direct commentary upon, and intervention in, contemporary political debates: not just in general terms, but in the specific context of the Swedish suit for Elizabeth's hand. Drama and politics did not inhabit separate spheres of operation at this time. Contemporaries were accustomed to reading the most direct political relevance into dramatic representations, even where the subject matter did not immediately suggest it. The Beale manuscript also confirms the very precise topical nature of the political interventions which such plays were seen to offer. *Gorboduc* counselled the queen and the political nation, not simply that a royal marriage was necessary and desirable, but that such a marriage should be to a given individual, Robert

---

[58] See Adams, 'Release of Lord Darnley', pp. 139–44.

[59] It is important to note that the defence of the parliamentary solution in favour of the 'native line' is spoken by Arostus, a counsellor already compromised by his having initially approved of Gorboduc's proposal to divide the realm (1.2.77–147). As such, it lacks the dramatic weight of the conclusions offered by Eubulus, whose wisdom as a counsellor was manifest in his initial misgivings at the scheme.

Dudley, and not to another, the Swedish King. This in turn suggests a play conceived both within a strictly limited timescale (the Swedish marriage remained a live issue, as we have seen, for only a matter of months) and with very immediate issues in mind. *Gorboduc*, despite the universality of much of its moral counsel, was created for a particular purpose, a purpose which was fulfilled in two specific performances during Christmas 1561/2.

All of this provides an emphatic refutation of those critics who have argued against topical readings of Tudor plays on the grounds that these approach the plays too 'narrowly', and are too reductive to account for the plurality of meanings contained in a given text.[60] What the Beale manuscript shows is that plays such as *Gorboduc*, and the genre of courtly plays of counsel to which they belong, were precisely aimed at a given issue, and at a given audience for whom that issue had relevance. To point this out is not reductive: it is to replace the text within the political and cultural conditions which initially produced it. To argue that a play was conceived with a specific occasion and a specific political purpose in mind is, however, not to deny the range of other significances that it might possess for other audiences at other times. And here the Beale manuscript allows us to trace a valuable case study of a play in the process of changing to accommodate a new audience and a new form.

As I have argued elsewhere, it is important to consider a play as performed in its original household or courtly setting as a quite distinct entity from the 'same' play performed elsewhere, or published as a printed text. Whereas a drama might carry all sorts of particular personal and political resonances for an audience familiar with its subtext, or with the views of its creator(s) the patron for whom it was created, such references would have far less relevance for the audience in a distant market-town, or the reader who picked up the printed text perhaps years later.[61] In the case of *Gorboduc*, we now have evidence of the play both in its initial production, and in its subsequent printed state. And what the Beale manuscript demonstrates is that the printed texts differ from the performance text in several important ways.

Quite what one makes of these differences is, of course, a matter for speculation. It is possible that the different interpretation of the second

---

[60] David Bevington, although generally sympathetic to political interpretations of Tudor drama, cautions that *Gorboduc*'s treatment of the succession 'has perhaps been too narrowly interpreted' (*Tudor Drama and Politics*, p. 141). This view is also advanced, rather more forthrightly, in Swart, *Thomas Sackville*, pp. 71–2.

[61] Walker, *Plays of Persuasion*, pp. 14–15 *et passim*, and chapters 1 and 2, above.

dumb-show and the discussion of marriage which our witness records were essentially extemporisations, extra lines added by the actors (with or without the author's consent) to give the play an even greater political resonance than the formal script allowed, in a setting where they were confident of an informed reception. But the manuscript's insistence that *'many thinges* were handled of mariage' [my italics] suggests rather more than this. A few extra lines might convincingly be added to an agreed script without disrupting a performance. But the sort of prolonged debate which this description suggests looks far more like a carefully prepared and rehearsed alternative script. Thus we are faced with a situation in which the text prepared for publication (even that of the supposedly pirated edition of 1565[62]) was altered to remove a number of its more specific political allusions. The politics of performance were, in this case, clearly distinct from the politics of publication.

It is possible that the material on marriage and the Swedish suit was removed by the authors, or the printer, for what one might term purely 'artistic' or commercial reasons. Such outdated and specific allusions might have seemed unappealing in a play which had to find a new, more general, audience in its printed form. Or, conceivably, Dudley had become so disillusioned with the prospects of achieving a royal marriage by 1565 that he himself requested that the references to it be removed.[63] But it is also possible that what we see in the printed text(s) is actually a continuation of the political campaign begun in the original performances at the Inner Temple and at court.[64] Having lobbied boldly on the

[62] The claim, advanced by John Daye, the printer of the 1570 edition, that the earlier text was a corrupt pirate script ('torne . . . disfigured . . . and . . . dishonested', sig. Aii), seems very much like mischievous commercial special pleading in the light of the evidence of the Beale manuscript, which confirms that the two printed texts were, not only very similar, but were both careful to edit out the same elements of the performance text. The only significant difference between the two versions is the removal from the later text of eight lines rejecting outright the possibility of regicide ('That no cause serves wherby the subject maye / Call to accompt the doynges of his prince, / Muche less in bloode by sworde to worke revenge'). While these may have been unexceptional statements of loyalty in 1565, they might have been inconvenient in 1570, when Elizabeth's protestant counsellors were arguing for the execution of a prince, Mary, Queen of Scots. For this suggestion, see Jones and White, *'Gorboduc* and Royal Marriage Politics', p. 118.

[63] In September 1564 it was being claimed 'on good authority' that Dudley had no further chance of marrying the queen (*CSPSp*, 395). Simon Adams' suggestion (prompted by a statement made by Dudley to the French envoy in August 1566, *CSPSp*, 518) that Lord Robert may never have been that serious about his suit, as he thought Elizabeth would never marry, seems a better summary of the position of the disillusioned Dudley of the later 1560s than of the enthusiastic canvasser of 1561–2 (Adams, 'Release of Lord Darnley', p. 137 and note).

[64] The alternative possibility is that the material specific to the Swedish match and the discussion of marriage was removed, not, as has been argued here, after the court performance of January 1562, but before it. Thus the play could have been performed in two distinct versions within a month, the second eventually providing the text for the printed editions of 1565 and 1570. The

need for a Dudley marriage in 1561, the play subsequently concentrated on the more general issue of securing the succession (by one means or another) and used the second dumb-show to justify the sort of harsh counsel which the play itself was offering. In a performance behind closed doors in 1561–2 the stark advice offered to the queen and her counsellors might have been acceptable. In the open forum of the printed text it would have been less so. But for those readers who had witnessed the original performance, the removal of the specific (and clearly memorable) references to royal marriage, and their replacement by an allegorical assertion of the need for good counsel (a central characteristic of which was, as we have seen, that it was not always initially appreciated by those who received it) could only have reinforced the impact of that original advice. In a political environment in which it was increasingly unwise to advance the question of a royal marriage directly if one wished to sway the queen towards it,[65] the printed text made do with more general counsel. But the preoccupation

meagre available evidence is seemingly contradictory and ultimately inconclusive as to which version of the play was performed at court. The Beale MS witness says of the performance he saw 'This play was . . . at the courte before the Quene' (BL Add. MS 48023, f. 363). That he mentions no changes to the production implies that he knew of none. Conversely the printers of the published texts make strong claims to be offering the public the play as it was performed at court. The 1565 edition advertises itself as 'set forthe as the same was shewed before the / Quenes most excellent majestie, in her highnes / Court of Whitehall, the xviij day of January Anno Domini 1561. By the Gentlemen / of Thynner Temple in London.' The 1570 edition is even more insistent that it presents the play, 'set forth without addition or alteration but altogether as the same was shewed on stage before the Queenes Majestie, about nine yeares past', and suggests that the Inner Temple and Whitehall performances were the same. What may be inferred from this? The failure of the Beale MS to mention changes might be dismissed as the product of ignorance on the part of its author (albeit his apparently close links with Dudley's affairs and the connections with other courtiers attested in his notes ought to have provided him with a fair knowledge of events at court). The printer's claims might equally well be rejected as simply sales pitches designed to claim a vicarious seal of royal approval for a play which would otherwise appear less marketable. I favour the view that the changes were more likely to have been made after the court performance than before it, on the grounds that Dudley, Sackville, and Norton were unlikely to produce a play containing a discussion of the royal marriage question at the Inner Temple and then hastily remove that discussion for a performance before the one audience for whom it had an immediate personal and political significance: the queen herself. If the play was crafted as a vehicle for lobbying on the royal marriage (as the Beale MS makes clear that it was) then the court would seem the natural arena for its production. Moreover, the relatively tolerant attitude with which Elizabeth regarded discussions of her marriage plans in the first years of her reign (see BL Landsdowne MS 94, f. 29 (and v); Hartley, *Proceedings*, pp. 44–6) suggests that there would be no bar to taking such a play to court at this time. In subsequent years, however, her attitude was to harden.

65 In 1566 Elizabeth was to give a clear warning of her increasing impatience with the subject, telling a delegation of both Houses that 'Ther hath been some that have ere this said unto me they never required more than that they might once hear me say I would marry. Well, there was never so great a treason but might be covered under as fair a pretence' (Neale, *Elizabeth I and Her Parliaments*, I, pp. 146–8).

of the playwrights remained the same: to persuade a reluctant queen and a sceptical legal establishment of the need for radical action to settle the succession. That this was true of the printed text has long been understood. That it was also true, albeit in a rather different context, of the play as it was originally performed is now equally clear. Having been recommended by Dudley as dramatic counsel for the queen, the play took advantage of the licence that his sponsorship granted to make its case in the strongest and most direct terms its authors could devise.

Epilogue

Chapter 1 began with an admission of the limitations inherent in studying dramatic performance solely through its textual traces. These limitations have remained apparent throughout this study, re-emerging at various points with greater or lesser urgency. Barring significant developments in the search for a time machine, it will not be possible for us to see precisely how *The Thrie Estaitis*, *Gorboduc*, or any of the other plays examined here were delivered in their first productions. As a result, we have had to make do with a poor second best, using the manuscript or printed page in tandem with other, external evidence to try to investigate the impact of these first performances in the royal courts of the sixteenth century. That we have lost much in so doing is clear. The potency of the non-verbal elements in these plays, attested to by the overwhelming concentration upon the dumb-shows in our eyewitness account of *Gorboduc*, means inevitably that the version of 'the play' to which we have access through the script alone is impoverished: not simply a lightweight version of the play, but a substantially *different* one. But, even where words were spoken, and we can read them on the page, problems remain.

The fundamental unit of dramatic activity, and the ultimate source of dramatic truth is, of course, the human body. Measured against the immediate, affective impact of the actor's movements and delivery, and his or her sheer presence on-stage in the here and now of performance, even the most powerfully rhetorical script is of only secondary importance. Innocuous-looking passages of dialogue can be given a political edge through suggestions of impersonation, or pointed glances towards members of the audience. Apparently sincere speeches may be subverted, transformed, or ironised into their antithesis by a gesture or conspiratorial grin towards the audience from the actor delivering them. Not to have access to these extratextual aspects of performance therefore leaves us ultimately unsure of the precise impact of the plays we have considered in their contemporary contexts.

The proceeding chapters have, however, been able to suggest some measure of the political and cultural importance of these plays in the halls, courts, and households which produced them. They have demonstrated how the great hall plays could intervene directly in political debates, whether by contributing to a general climate, as Heywood's plays of accommodation sought to do in the 1530s, or by advocating precise courses of action which their creators wished to be taken, as *Gorboduc* attempted in 1562. More particularly we have seen in each case the crucial importance of the patron to the political equation created by the household drama. These plays were created in order to appeal to those patrons as their principal spectators, not just aesthetically, but in terms of a direct engagement with their circumstances and opinions. In the case of royal patrons, the playwrights employed their persuasive art in an attempt to influence national policy, to shift the sovereign's opinions subtly but significantly in the direction they and/or their backers desired. Where there was no adult sovereign available to act as principal spectator, or where the sovereign was in some way outside the normal experience of the playwright, forcing him to adjust his attitude towards political authority, the results were evident in the texts produced. Hence the collapse of the unitary focus of Lindsay's *The Thrie Estaitis* in its outdoor version, devised and played during a minority regime (woe indeed to the household playwright whose king was a child!). And hence the awkwardness with female sovereignty evident in Udall's *Respublica*, created in the early months of Mary Tudor's reign. By the accession of Elizabeth, playwrights had seemingly come to terms with the idea of a female monarch and could temper their dramatic strategies accordingly. But even here, perhaps as a reflection of the queen's much vaunted capacity to 'rise above' the limitations of her sex (the polite fiction whereby her rule was accommodated to the misogynistic prevailing theories of political conduct),[1] the allegories of government offered to her overwhelmingly employed male figures of sovereignty to act as her analogues and anti-types.

The plays studied here have, then, much to tell us, not only about the nature and purpose of political drama in the early modern court, but about political conduct more generally in the period. It is now something of a commonplace to suggest that the sovereign was the centre of political activity in a personal monarchy: a head of state who ruled as

---

[1] See, for example, C. Levin, *The Heart and Stomach of a King: Elizabeth I and the Politics of Sex and Power* (Philadelphia, 1994); S. Frye, *Elizabeth I: The Competition for Representation* (Oxford, 1993); P. Berry, *Of Chastity and Power: Elizabethan Literature and the Unmarried Queen* (London, 1989).

well as reigned. But a close examination of plays such as *The Thrie Estaitis*, *The Play of The Weather*, and *Gorboduc*, provides a sobering reminder of just how intensely personal such a monarchy could be. It also reveals how independent-minded political activity was possible in such a system, how articulate individuals might initiate or sustain a political debate in a culture in which the sovereign's will was paramount, without falling into the hackneyed and self-limiting postures of royalist propaganda or anti-government complaint. These plays focused upon the sovereign, his or her preoccupations and prejudices, not out of mere sycophancy or lack of imagination, but because to move the mind of the monarch was the surest way to effect political change. And the well-developed mechanisms of court culture provided the means and justification for them to do so in the idea of good counsel, so allowing for political exchange in a system which otherwise might appear to exclude it. Good counsel created opportunities for political expression which the dramatist, schooled in rhetoric and licensed to explore issues of personal and national integrity through the Morality form or Senecan tragedy of state, was ideally placed to exploit.

To study these plays of counsel is, then, to examine a form of literature which contributed directly to the politics of the Renaissance court, both in general terms, in sustaining a culture in which politics was habitually moralised and kings were open to criticism on a moral level, and in the detailed determination of policy. The tendency of political historians to ignore or marginalise such plays on the grounds that they were the work of courtly yes-men dealing with only ephemeral matters is, then, doubly unwise.[2] That the plays were performed at court made them more rather than less effective vehicles for political debate. That they staked their claim for an audience primarily on the fact that they addressed issues of personal morality and integrity ensured that they were at the centre rather than the margins of those debates, for, as the previous chapters have suggested, the language of morality was also the language of politics at the royal courts of the Renaissance.

[2] The most overt example of this tendency was provided by the doyen of Victorian historical scholarship, James Gairdner, who, in introducing the volume of 'Letters and Papers' of the reign of Henry VIII for 1540, dismissed the courtly entertainments of that year in an aside. 'On these', he observed, 'it is not necessary to enlarge . . . For serious business, of course, we must look to what was going on in Parliament.' *LP*, xv, pp. xxxv–vi.

Appendix 1

THE REGULATION AND CENSORSHIP OF PRINTED DRAMA

There has been considerable scholarly interest in political and religious censorship of literature and drama in the sixteenth century.[1] But the evidence for official intervention in the printing of playbooks is actually surprisingly limited. Although the introduction of printing may have had a considerable impact upon the availability of dramatic texts to both actors and readers, it is clear that its impact upon the perceptions of the political authorities was initially far less powerful. The reasons for this are suggestive of wider attitudes towards the role and functions of play-making in the period.

From the 1530s the crown and local officials responded to drama with increasing interest and firmness, circumscribing, directing, and – where they thought it necessary – banning it outright. But they did so to drama in performance, concerned as much by the occasion which the acting of plays provided for crowds to gather and mischief to take place as by anything in the play texts themselves. Their response to drama on the printed page was largely to ignore it, even in situations where one might expect them to have acted.

From Henry VII onwards, each Tudor sovereign acted to impose his or her authority upon the playing of drama in a process which would lead eventually to the licensing of players and the prohibition of unattached companies. Henry VIII's 'Act for the Advancement of True Religion and the Abolishment of the Contrary' of 1543 permitted the playing of moral drama provided its contents did not run counter to the

[1] See, for example, the discussion in G. Wickham, *Early English Stages* (3 vols., London, 1959–81), II, part I, pp. 54–97, and Richard Dutton, *Mastering the Revels: The Regulation and Censorship of English Renaissance Drama* (Basingstoke, 1991), passim.

tenets of established religious doctrine.² Simultaneously, action was taken on an *ad hoc* basis against those taking part in unacceptable productions through royal pressure upon the authorities in the localities, as when Henry wrote (if the letter is genuine) to the city fathers in York empowering them, in the wake of a seditious production of a play of St Thomas the Apostle, to apprehend and imprison any 'papists who shall, in performing interludes which are founded on any portion of the Old and New Testament, or say or make use of any language which may tend to excite those who are beholding to any breach of the peace'.³

On occasion the initiative was taken by the local officials themselves, as when in 1545 the authorities of the City of London proclaimed that henceforward, in order to prevent disorderly gatherings of the young and the idle, the performance of plays within the City boundaries should be limited to the houses of aristocrats or City officers, the homes of the 'sad comminers or hed parisshioners of the same Citie or in the open stretes of the said citie as in tyme past it hath bene used and accustomed or in the common halles of the companyes, fellowshipps or brother-heddes of the same citie'.⁴ But on each occasion the intent was clearly to limit and control the opportunities for unruly behaviour provided by the performance of drama through the use of existing cultural pressures, restricting it to traditional playing sites and to occasions in which social control could operate, whether through the actions of noble patrons or guild-masters, or via the more subtle influences exerted by an internalised desire to conform to conventional playing practice. Official anxieties were clearly provoked primarily by the gathering of unruly crowds in general, secondly by the thought that such crowds might be exposed to the expression of seditious ideas, and only thirdly and very infrequently by the thought that those same ideas might be spread by

---

² A. Luders, *et al.*, eds., *Statutes of the Realm* (11 vols., London, 1810–28), III, p. 894. The Act declared that 'it shalbe lawfull to all and everye persone and persones, to sette foorth songes, plaies, and enterludes, to be used and exercysed within this Realme and other the Kinges Domynions, for the rebuking and reproaching of vices and the setting foorth of vertue . . . [provided that] . . . allwaies the saide songes, playes or enterludes meddle not with the interpretacions of Scripture, contrarye to the doctryne set foorth or to be sett foorth by the Kinges Majestie'. See above, p. 20.

³ J. O. Halliwell-Phillips, ed., *The Letters of the Kings of England* (2 vols., London, 1846–8), I, p. 354. For doubts about the text, see Ian Lancashire, 'History of a Transition', in Leeds Barroll, ed., *Medieval and Renaissance Drama in England*, III (New York, 1986), pp. 277–88.

⁴ Wickham, *Early English Stages*, II, pp. 327–8. For similar local action, see the Minutes of the Court of Aldermen for 4 July and 7 November 1549, printed in E. K. Chambers, *The Elizabethan Stage* (4 vols., Oxford, 1923), IV, p. 261, and for later action in Hull, see Patricia Badir, 'Un-civil Rites and Playing Sites: Some Early Modern Entertainment Records From Kingston Upon Hull', *Records of Early English Drama Newsletter*, 20 (1995), pp. 1–11.

the unregulated circulation of play texts before or after the performance.[5] Hence the suppression of plays frequently went hand in hand
with action against other forms of public nuisance such as buckler
fighting or even the beating of clothes in windows overlooking the
street.[6] It would also be unwise to discount the fears expressed by the
City authorities that the gatherings brought about by play production
were likely to foster and spread plague and other infectious diseases.
Rather than being simply censorship dressed up as a concern for public
health, the attempts to close or regulate the performance of interludes,
such as the City precept of 12 May 1569, might better be read as genuine
attempts to counter infection.[7]

When Edward VI succeeded his father, the Privy Council acting in
his name tightened the controls upon potentially seditious playing. An
insecure minority administration with a potentially divisive religious
agenda, the Edwardian regime was unsurprisingly concerned to limit
the possibilities for the expression of dissent. On 6 August 1549 a
proclamation prohibited the performance of all plays and interludes for
the space of two months – between 9 August and All Saints' Day,
specifically closing the qualifying clauses listing acceptable venues left by
the civic proclamation of four years earlier. The Council ordered every
subject that 'They nor any of them openly or secretly play in English
tongue any kind of interlude, play, dialogue or other matter, set forth in
form of a play, in any place, public or private, within this realm.'[8] At the

[5] This point has been made most recently by Simon Shepherd and Peter Womack, who, speaking
specifically about the proclamation of 1545, illustrate a wider truth about dramatic regulation
generally. 'Whoever wrote the document thinks of a play, not as something written by a
dramatist, but as something done by a group of actors: not as a text, but as a certain kind of social
behaviour' (Simon Shepherd and P. Womack, *English Drama: A Cultural History* (Oxford, 1996), p.
3). See also Wickham, *Early English Stages*, II, part 1, pp. 66–75.
[6] Chambers, *Elizabethan Stage*, IV, p. 261 (Minutes of the Court of Aldermen, 4 July 1549, for the
former); IV, p. 267 (City precept of 12 May 1569, for the latter). Although plays were listed along
with ballads and 'books' as printed forms subject to regulation in a proclamation of 8 July 1546,
performance was the authorities' chief concern, and this remained the case throughout the
sixteenth century (P. L. Hughes and J. F. Larkin, eds., *Tudor Royal Proclamations* (3 vols., London,
1964–9), I, pp. 373–6). Under the proclamation, printers were forbidden to 'print any manner of
English book, ballad, or play, but [i.e. unless] he put in his name to the same, with the name of the
author and day of the print, and shall present the first copy to the mayor of the town where he
dwelleth, and not to suffer any of the copies to go out of his hands within the next two days
following'. Had printers followed these instructions with any regularity, charting the history of
the printed book would be a considerably easier task.
[7] Chambers, *Elizabethan Stage*, IV, pp. 267, 269, and following. See also, Leeds Barroll, *Politics, Plague,
and Shakespeare's Theatre: The Stuart Years* (Ithaca, 1991). For an analysis of these issues in the context
of recent literary critical trends, see Barbara Freedman, 'Elizabethan Protest, Plague, and Plays:
Reading the Documents of Control', *English Literary Renaissance*, 26 (1996), pp. 17–45.

same time steps were taken to police and regulate the print trade to prevent the production or spreading of seditious literature. On 13 August 1549, as the Act Book of the Privy Council noted, 'An Ordre was taken that from hensforth no prenter sholde prente or putt to vente any Englisshe booke butt suche as sholde first be examined by M[aster] Secretary Peter, M[aster] Secretary Smith, and M[aster] Cicill, or the one of them, and allowed by the same'.[9] But there was no overlap between the two legislative initiatives. At no point were printers specifically instructed not to print playbooks, no matter how copious the list of prohibited types of literature became.[10]

Not until the reign of Mary Tudor was the connection between printing and playing made again in a regulatory context, and then only

[8] Hughes and Larkin, eds., *Proclamations*, 1, pp. 478–9. Once the period of outright prohibition had lapsed, the attempt to stifle only those performances seen as potentially seditious resumed. Thus the Act of Uniformity of the same year outlined penalties for anyone playing in any interlude who attempted to 'speake anye thinge in derogacion depravinge or dyspisinge' of the Book of Common Prayer (Norman Sanders, *et al.*, eds., *The Revels History of Drama in English*, 11 (London, 1980–3), p. 126).

[9] J. R. Dasent, ed., *Acts of The Privy Council* (32 vols., London, 1890–1907), 11, pp. 311–12.

[10] Thus John Mardely was instructed not to publish or cause to be published 'any booke, ballett, or other work' (ibid.). By 1554 the list of prohibited works had expanded to 'writinges, Rimes, Ballades, Letters, Papers and Books', see p. 229, below. That drama was considered threatening only when it was played is made clearer still by the proclamation of 28 April 1551, against 'Vagabonds, Rumour Mongers, Players and Unlicensed Printers, etc.' The association between players and printers in this modern summary of the proclamation's contents is suggestive of a comprehensive attempt to include drama along with other printed works, as forms of possibly seditious literature. But in practice the text kept the two forms of activity strictly separate. Government action was necessary, it declared, because, 'diverse printers, booksellers, and players of interludes, without consideration or regard to the quiet of the realm, do print, sell, or play whatsoever any light and fantastical head listeth to invent and devise, whereby many inconveniences hath and do arise and follow among the King's loving and faithful subjects' (Hughes and Larkin, eds., *Proclamations*, 1, pp. 516–18, p. 516). In response, the crown declared that 'no printer or other person . . . [shall] print or sell within this realm . . . any matter in the English tongue, unless the same be allowed by his Majesty or his Privy Council . . . Nor that any common players or other persons upon like pains do play in the English tongue any manner interlude, play or matter without they have special license to show for the same in writing under his Majesty's sign, or signed by six of his highness Privy Council' (Hughes and Larkin, eds., *Proclamations*, 1, p. 517). Sir Edmund Chambers saw considerable significance in the fact that this legislation, as he saw it, placed the printing and playing of interludes 'on exactly the same footing' (Chambers, *Elizabethan Stage*, 111, p. 160). But this suggestion is misleading if it implies an identity of purpose in the treatment of each activity. Printers and players are linked by association in this proclamation, in that both are identified as capable of spreading dangerous ideas among the populace. But the possibility that some of the dangerous books which the printers might print and sell could be the same play texts which the players might perform does not seem to have concerned the Council. Nor, crucially, are playwrights mentioned in the proclamation. There is no attempt to identify the words played with a responsible author who might be disciplined, thus capping the problem at source, as would be attempted later in the century and in the Jacobean period. Drama is treated purely as a public event, realised spontaneously in the moment of performance. The printed book is usually assumed to belong to a different sphere of activity for regulatory purposes.

in a single piece of legislation. In the queen's first year a proclamation aimed at suppressing religious controversy addressed the various ways in which seditious ideas might be spread. It began with the activities of preachers: 'the subtlety and malice of some evil-disposed persons which take upon them without sufficient authority to preach and to interpret the Word of God after their own brain in churches and other places both public and private', but then moved on to such other activities as

playing of interludes and printing of false fond books, ballads, rhymes, and other lewd treatises in the English tongue touching the high points and mysteries of religion, which books, ballads, rhymes, and treatises are chiefly by the printers and stationers set out to sale to her grace's subjects of an evil zeal for lucre and covetousness of vile gain.[11]

So far the familiar distinction is maintained. Interludes are played: false fond books are printed. But the prohibition enacted in the proclamation takes a less discriminate line, ordering all subjects

of whatever state, condition, or degree they be, that none of them presume from henceforth to preach, or by way of reading in churches or other public or private places (except in the schools of the universities) to interpret or teach any Scripture, or any manner points of doctrine concerning religion; neither also to print any books, matter, ballad, rhyme, interlude, process, or treatise, nor to play any interlude except they have her grace's special licence for writing of the same.[12]

Here, for one brief moment, the crown considered a play, not only as a public event, a performance, but also as a text which might be circulated in the same way as other books and so might be controlled through restrictions upon the print trade in the same way as other books. But the initiative evident in this proclamation was not pursued. Subsequent legislation reverted to the old distinction between plays and books. The 1554–5 'Act Against Seditious Rumours' specified that 'dyvers and sundry evill disposed persons'

have devised, made, written, printed, publyshed, and set forthe dyvers heynous, sedicious, and sclanderous writinges, Rimes, Ballades, Letters, Papers, and Books, intending and practising therby to move and stir sedicious Discorde, Dissention, and Rebellyon within this Realm.[13]

---

[11] Hughes and Larkin, eds., *Proclamations*, ii, pp. 6–7.   [12] Ibid., ii, p. 7.
[13] Luders, *et al.*, eds., *Statutes of The Realm*, iv, part 1, pp. 240–1.

A series of fines or mutilations (loss of both ears or the right hand for the first offence, etc.) was thus laid down for

any person or persons [who] shall after the said daye . . . maliciouslie devise, write, printe, or set forthe any maner of Booke, Rime, Ballad, Letter, or Writing containing any false matter, clause, or sentence of sclander, reproche, and Dishonour of the King and Queenes Majestie.[14]

Interludes have once again disappeared from the itinerary of potentially seditious literary forms.

Subsequent legislation continued to restrict and curtail the performance of certain types of drama, culminating in the Elizabethan 'Act For the Punishment of Vagabonds, etc.' of 1572, which permitted only those acting companies enjoying the formal patronage of a nobleman to travel and ply their trade.[15] Equally, measures were taken to restrict the circulation of literature deemed seditious or subversive.[16] But only with the creation of the Stationers' Company Register and the empowering of the Lord Chamberlain with the responsibility to examine and approve play texts, was a regular, albeit relatively ineffective, system of scrutiny and licensing for dramatic scripts as literary forms put into place.[17]

The evidence does not demonstrate that the crown consciously excluded playbooks from the lists of harmful literature attached to these acts and proclamations. The frequent omission of the terms 'interlude' or 'play' from lists of literary genres covered does not necessarily mean that they were not tacitly subsumed under the catch-all terms 'books' or 'any other matter'. But what it does suggest is that whoever drafted these documents did not think of dramatic texts – unlike printed ballads,

---

[14] Ibid., IV, part 1, p. 241. Similarly, the Injunctions of 4 March 1554 ordered bishops 'to travail for the condemning and repressing of corrupt and naughty opinions, unlawful books, ballads, and other pernicious and hurtful devices, engendering hatred among the people and discord among the same' (John N. King, 'The Account Book of a Marian Bookseller, 1553–54', *British Library Journal*, 3 (1987), pp. 33–57). A proclamation against heretical books and materials of 13 June 1555 was aimed at those who 'presume to write, print, utter, sell, read, or keep, or cause to be written, printed, uttered, read, or kept, any of the said books, prayers, or writings [of a number of specified prohibited authors] or any book or books written or printed in the Latin or English tongue concerning the common service or ministration set forth in England . . . in the time of King Edward VI' (Hughes and Larkin, eds., *Proclamations*, II, p. 59).

[15] Hughes and Larkin, eds., *Proclamations*, II, p. 115. On this theme, see Chambers, *Elizabethan Stage*, IV, pp. 263–4; Dutton, *Mastering the Revels*, pp. 22–3.

[16] See, for example, Hughes and Larkin, eds., *Proclamations*, II, pp. 312–13; 341–3; 347–8; 376–9; 506–8.

[17] The Elizabethan Injunctions of 1559 placed the licensing of plays in the hands of the royal or ecclesiastical authorities, but in practice much of the day-to-day administration of the process devolved upon the Stationers. Chambers, *Elizabethan Stage*, pp. 264–5 and following.

songs and rhymes – as sufficiently important to be specifically named among these other forms: a sobering reflection, perhaps, upon the limited impact of the printed playbook as a cultural and political phenomenon in this period.[18]

Where playbooks did arouse the interest of the authorities, it tended to be as a means of checking up on performances, or preventing them from occurring at all. On 5 September 1557, for example, the Privy Council wrote to the Lord Mayor of London, ordering him to send officers to the Boar's Head tavern, where it was reported that 'a lewde playe, called a Sacke full of Newes' was going to be performed. The officers were instructed to arrest the actors 'and to take thire playe book from them and to send the same hither'.[19] A similar confiscation had clearly taken place in Kent the previous month, for a letter of 11 August to the mayor and aldermen of Canterbury was accompanied by 'the lewde playe booke sent hither by them and thexaminaccions also of the players therof'.[20] The city officials were ordered to act against the players in accordance with existing legislation.[21] In each case the text itself may well have been a manuscript prompt-book rather than a printed volume, but evidently it was the performance that took priority: the prospect that the text itself might be duplicated and circulated separately does not seem to have troubled the Council.

[18] W. W. Greg, *A Bibliography of the English Printed Drama to the Restoration* (4 vols., London, 1951–62), IV, p. clxiv. Under the Stationers' Company Ordinances, every new book produced in London or its environs had to be entered in the Company Register. In practice, however, up to one third of all new titles seem never to have been so entered.

[19] Dasent, ed., *Acts of The Privy Council*, VI, p. 168. On the following day orders were sent for the release of the players, with a warning to them and all other companies only to perform those plays specifically seen and allowed by the Bishop of London (ibid., VI, p. 169).

[20] Ibid., VI, p. 148.

[21] 'Upon understanding what the lawe was touching the said lewde playe, they shulde theruppon proceade against the players fourthwith according to the same and the qualities of their offences, which ordre they are willed to followe without delaye' (ibid.). For an attempt to subject all interludes performed in London to such scrutiny, see the Minute of the Court of Aldermen of 7 November 1549, printed in Chambers, *Elizabethan Stage*, IV, p. 261.

Appendix 2

PRINTED PLAYS AND THE GREAT HALL TRADITION, 1510–1580

In Chapter 1 it was claimed that, of the 81 surviving printed plays from the period before 1580, at least 47 shows signs of having been originally written for performance in a great hall. This is in itself a remarkable statistic, but, if one excludes those 'closet' dramas obviously printed for educational or religious purposes and not intended to be played (category A, below) and those texts which survive in too fragmentary a form for their auspices to be determined (category B), then the predominance of great hall plays (category E) becomes even more evident. Of the remaining 62 playbooks published, 9 reveal no direct evidence of auspices (category C), and only 6 show clear signs of having *not* been designed for a hall environment. The latter were all written for outdoor performance in the context of other entertainments (category D).

A 'CLOSET' PLAYS

Seneca's *Troas*, translated by Jasper Heywood (1559), *RSTC* 22221; *Thyestes*, trans. Heywood (1560), *RSTC* 22226; *Hercules Furens*, trans. Heywood (1561), *RSTC* 22223; *Agamemnon*, trans. John Studley (?1566), *RSTC* 22222; *Medea*, trans. Studley (?1566), *RSTC* 22224; and *Octavia*, trans. 'T. W.' or 'T. N.' (?1566), *RSTC* 22229; Sophocles' *The Lamentable Tragedie of Oedipus*, translated by Alexander Nevyle (1563), *RSTC* 22225, the parallel texts of Terence's *Andria*, translated by Maurice Kyffin (1588), *RSTC* 23895, and John Palsgrave's *Acolastus* (1540), *RSTC* 11470; H. N.'s *Enterlude of Myndes* (?1574), *RSTC* 18550; Arthur Golding's translation of Theodore Beza's *Tragedie of Abraham's Sacrifice* (1577), *RSTC* 2047; and Henry Cheeke's translation of Francesco Negri de Bassano's *Freewyl* (1573), *RSTC* 18419.

B   FRAGMENTS

Lewis [or 'W'] Wager, *The Cruel Debtor* (*c.* 1566), *RSTC* 24934; the anonymous *The Prodigal Son* (*c.* 1525–34), *RSTC* 20765.5; *Albion Knight* (?1565), *RSTC* 275; *Temperance and Humility* (?1528), *RSTC* 14109.5; *Good Order/ Old Christmas* (1533), *RSTC* 18793.5; *Detraction* (?1566), *RSTC* 14109.2; *Somebody, Avarice and Minister* (*c.* 1547–50), *RSTC* 14109.3.

C   PLAYS OF UNCERTAIN ORIGIN

Everyman (*c.* 1510–19), *RSTC* 10604; *St John The Evangelist* (?1550), *RSTC* 14644 (although the use of Latin tags and quotations suggests a school or college play); John Bale's biblical dramas, *John The Baptystes Preachynge* (?1547); *God's Promises* (1547), *RSTC* 1305; *The Three Lawes* (1548), *RSTC* 1287; and *The Temptation of Our Lord* (1547), *RSTC* 1279 (all perhaps initially written for household performance by Bale's company, but rewritten while the author was in exile as flexible scripts for publication and performance); the anonymous *Common Conditions* (1576), *RSTC* 5592 (which requires a 'wood' in the place with at least one climbable tree, but whose marginal directions ('Enter . . . from Phrygia') suggest revision with a reading rather than playing public in mind); John Phillip's *Patient and Meeke Grissell* (?1569), *RSTC* 19865 (although the large cast and use of music and song suggest a play for children); and *New Custom* (1573), *RSTC* 6150 (which again contains Latin tags and allusions suggesting a school or college play).

D   OUTDOOR PLAYS

Robin Hood (?1560), *RSTC* 13691 ('A newe play for to be played in Maye games'); and the private and civic entertainments for Queen Elizabeth, *The Entertainment in the City of Bristow* (1575); Gascoigne's *The Princely Pleasures at Kenelworth Castle* (1576); and *The Entertainment at Norwich* (1578); *The Entertainment in Norfolk and Suffolk* (1578); and *The Entertainment of the French Ambassadours* (1578).

E   GREAT HALL PLAYS

John Rastell, *The Nature of The Four Elements* (*c.* 1525–7), *RSTC* 20722; *Calisto and Melebea* (*c.* 1525–30), *RSTC* 20721; Henry Medwall, *Nature* (1530–4), *RSTC* 17779; *The Four Cardinal Virtues* (1537–47), *RSTC* 14109.7; *Impatient Poverty* (1560), *RSTC* 14112.5; (?William Stevenson), *Gammer*

Gurton's Needle (pre-1575), *RSTC* 23263 ('Played on stage, not longe ago in Christ's Colledge in Cambridge'); *Godly Queene Hester* (1561), *RSTC* 13251; *Gorboduc* (*c.* 1565), *RSTC* 18684 ('Set forthe as the same was shewed before the Quenes most excellent majestie, in her highnes Court of Whitehall'); Lewis Wager, *The Life and Repentance of Mary Magdalene* (?1566), *RSTC* 24932; G. Gascoigne, *Supposes* (1566), in *RSTC* 11635 ('A Comedie written in the Italian Tongue . . . Englished by George Gascoigne, of Grayes Inn, Esquire, And there presented'); *Liberality and Prodigality* (?1567), *RSTC* 5593 ('As it was played before her majestie'); *Gismond of Salerne* (?1567) *RSTC* 25764 (printed 1591, but described as a revised text of a play by the Gentlemen of the Inner Temple, 'most pithely framed, and no lesse curiously acted in view of her majesty' some '24 yeres' previously); Thomas Garter, *The Most Virtuous and Godly Susanna* (*c.* 1578), *RSTC* 11632.5; Richard Edwardes, *Damon and Pithias* (1571), *RSTC* 7514 ('Newly imprinted as the same was shewed before the Queenes Majestie, by the Children of her Graces chappell'); G. Gascoigne and Francis Kinwelmershe, *Jocasta* (?1573), in *RSTC* 11635 (a Grey's Inn play); and Thomas Lupton, *All For Money* (1578), *RSTC* 16949. The other texts containing references suggestive of a great hall performance are: Henry Medwall, *Fulgens and Lucrece* (*c.* 1512–16), *RSTC* 17778 ('devyded in two partes to be played at ii tymes', suggesting a performance during a banquet, probably at the residence of Medwall's employer, Cardinal Morton, perhaps in 1497); *Hick Scorner* (?1512–16), *RSTC* 14039.5 (probably a product of the household of Charles Brandon, Duke of Suffolk); *Mundus et Infans / The World and the Child* (1522), *RSTC* 25982; (?Heywood/Rastell), *Gentleness and Nobility* (*c.* 1529), *RSTC* 20723; John Skelton, *Magnyfycence* (?1530), *RSTC* 22607 (probably performed in a London merchants' hall); *Youth* (?1530–5), *RSTC* 14111 (probably a product of the household of Henry Algernon Percy, Fifth Duke of Northumberland); John Heywood, *Johan Johan* (1533), *RSTC* 13298 (probably the product of Heywood's period as a court musician and Sewer of the Chamber); Heywood, *The Pardoner and The Friar* (1533), *RSTC* 13299 (as above); Heywood, *The Play of The Weather* (1533), *RSTC* 13305 (as above); Heywood, *A Play of Love* (1534), *RSTC* 13303 (either a court play or designed for a lawyers' hall); Heywood, *The Four PP* (1544, but possibly following a lost 1534 edition), *RSTC* 13300, (see *Johan Johan*, above); *Wealth and Health* (1557–65), *RSTC* 14110 (contains direct reference to the queen as patron: possibly a children's play?); *Nice Wanton* (?1560), *RSTC* 25016 (the concentration upon education and the upbringing of children, added to the address in the epilogue to 'ye children', suggests a school play); *Jack Juggler* (?1562), *RSTC* 14837 ('A New Enterlued for chyldren to playe', with reference to an evening performance at New Year), *Thersites* (1561–3), *RSTC* 23949 (the references to Oxford and the Proctor and his men suggest a college play); R. Wever, *Lusty Juventus* (*c.* 1565), *RSTC* 25149; *King Darius* (?1565), *RSTC* 6277; Nicholas Udall, *Roister Doister* (?1566), *RSTC* 24508 (probably a Marian court play); *The Interlude of Vice* (*Horestes*) (1567), *RSTC* 19917 (references to London, the Lord Mayor and 'this noble citye' suggest auspices in the capital – probably the 'Orestes' played at court in 1567/8); William Wager, *Enough is as Good as a Feast* (1565–70), *RSTC* 24933; Ulpian Fulwell, *Like Will to Like Quod the Devil to the Collier* (?1568), *RSTC* 11473 (references to men and boys 'standing by' and the use of a gittern suggest an indoor, hall, audience); *Jacob and Esau* (1568), *RSTC* 14327 (the use of songs and large cast suggest a children's play); *The Marriage of Wit and Science* (?1569), *RSTC* 17466 (probably the 'Witt and Will' performed before Queen Elizabeth at Whitehall in 1567/8. The play calls for a consort of viols, and its use of music and songs suggests a children's play); Thomas Preston, *Cambises* (?1569), *RSTC* 20287 (the use of gittern music, and conspicuous use of the 'make room!' topos suggest an indoor, hall performance. The play between the vice, Ambidexter, and his brother Cutpurse – assumed to be among the audience – might, however, suggest an outdoor performance); William Wager, *The Longer Thou Livest the More Fool Thou Art* (?1569), *RSTC* 24935 (the songs and stress upon education as a virtue suggest a school or college play. The frequent use of the 'make room!' topos suggests a hall performance); Thomas Engelend, *The Disobedient Child* (?1569), *RSTC* 14085 (the use of music and the obsessive interest in schooling and punishment suggest a school play); 'R. B.', *Appius and Virginia* (1575), *RSTC* 1059 (the modesty of the prologue, suggesting a first attempt at playing, the songs for all the cast, and the reference to a 'worshipful' audience, suggest a children's play before a civic or courtly audience); George Wapull, *The Tyde Tarrieth for No Man* (1576), *RSTC* 25018 (references to London and the stress on the wealthy citizenry as the receptacles of godliness suggest a merchants' hall); *The Trial of Treasure* (1566), *RSTC* 14112 (reference to filling all the pots in the house suggest a hall or inn setting, the frequent classical allusions point towards a school or college play); George Whetstone's *Promos and Cassandra* (1578), *RSTC* 25347 (requires at least two 'houses', one representing a prison and 'some stage erected from the ground' in which five or six singers can be housed. The allusions to metropolitan mayoral ceremonials and the dedication of the text to William Fleetwood, Recorder of London, suggest civic auspices in the capital); and George Gascoigne, *The Glasse of Government* (1575), *RSTC* 11643 (academic drama, possibly merely closet).

Index

237